Praise for *The Witch's Guide to Animal Familiars*

"Madame Pamita's new book, The Witch's Guide to Animal Familiars, *feels like sitting down with a trusted mentor who knows how to bring magick into everyday life. With her signature warmth and down-to-earth style, she helps you connect with the power of animals in a way that feels both natural and inspiring. Whether you're just getting started or have been practicing for years, Madame Pamita makes working with animal allies feel accessible and meaningful, offering guidance that comes from a place of deep knowledge and care."*

— **Mat Auryn**, best-selling author of *Psychic Witch, Mastering Magick,* and *The Psychic Art of Tarot*

"Madame Pamita has given us an in-depth look on how to benefit and learn from our animal familiars. From a historical viewpoint all the way to our current disconnect with animals, she gently teaches us what is, and what is not, a familiar, as well as how to find and commune with your own. Included are spells and recipes for many different needs, sections on how to use animal offerings, and guidance on how to exchange energy with your familiar. I highly recommend The Witch's Guide to Animal Familiars *to anyone who wishes to experience the joy and challenges of working with a familiar, whether wild or domesticated. I truly believe this book will take your magickal practice to the next level."*

— **Christine Cunningham Ashworth**, author of *Scott Cunningham: The Path Taken*

"Madame Pamita offers readers the gift of better acquainting ourselves with the other-than-human beings with whom we share the planet. This love letter to the animal and insect realms offers so much to everyone*— not only those building a magical practice. You'll find animal history, behavior, and lore; traditional healing ways, regional superstitions, and folk beliefs; and fairy tales and mythology, not to mention many creative magical rituals. For anyone longing for a loving bond with nature, here you will find a path to that sacred place, strewn with beauty, to inspire a truly enchanting connection with the natural world."*

— **Deatra Cohen**, herbalist and co-author of *Ashkenazi Herbalism*

"Madame Pamita invites you to talk with the animals, walk with the animals, and commune with them. Animal familiars are a blessing, and Pamita addresses them as such. She'll teach you how to curate relationships with your familiars and even how to call on them for assistance. She offers warm advice and skillful spells to help your bond with your familiar become as easy as breathing."

— **Melissa Cynova**, author of *Kitchen Table Tarot* and co-host of *Cardslingers Coast to Coast* podcast

"Madame Pamita's The Witch's Guide to Animal Familiars *explores a wide range of the possible kinds of relationships, partnerships, encounters, friendships, and more that are possible when working with animals and animal spirits on this plane and others. She also gives excellent guidance on how to attract, approach, and commune with these wonderful beings. The book offers useful directions for working with insects, amphibians, reptiles, and fish, which are often underrepresented in this work. Most important,* The Witch's Guide to Animal Familiars *has a consistently deep-hearted and respectful perspective on the beauty of collaboration with our animal kin."*

— **Ivo Dominguez Jr.**, author of *The Four Elements of the Wise*

"Bravo, Madame Pamita! Few, if any, books have deep-dived into the subject of the acquisition, role, living power, and integrative magical practices of the time-honored role of the familiar in the witch's craft the way you have. This is no mere book of animal symbology. No, this is an apprenticeship-style grimoire of a rarely detailed component of the witch's way."

— **Orion Foxwood**, author of *Mountain Conjure and Southern Root Work* and *The Tree of Enchantment*

"Just like us humans, animals have souls. And because we have a special connection with our furry loved ones, why not learn how to energetically communicate and even partner with them? In Madame Pamita's newest book, The Witch's Guide to Animal Familiars, *she'll teach you how to connect deeply with your pets, farm animals, and even the wild creatures around you in profoundly meaningful ways. You'll find practical recipes and step-by-step guidance to deepen and enhance your spiritual relationship with the beautiful living creatures who give so much to us all. If you're an animal lover of any kind, this book is for you."*

— **Ainslie MacLeod**, author of *The Old Soul's Guidebook* and *The Instruction*

"Madame Pamita's The Witch's Guide to Animal Familiars *is brimming with wisdom, guidance, and heart, delving into the rich and fascinating relationship between human and animal, witch and familiar. A must-read not only for every witch but also anyone wishing to deepen their spiritual relationships with the animal kingdom."*

— **Tara Rae Moss**, shamanic practitioner, seidkona, runeworker, and international best-selling author of *The Ghosts of Paris*

"The Witch's Guide to Animal Familiars *has it all: history, hands-on spells and rituals, and lots of practical insight! You'll learn what familiars are and how to work with them, exploring a wide array of animals and their messages along the way. Each page is filled with magic, and I expect this to be a treasured reference for generations to come."*

— **Nicholas Pearson**, author of *Crystal Basics* and *Flower Essences from the Witch's Garden*

"The Witch's Guide to Animal Familiars *by Madame Pamita is an enchanting journey into the mystical bond between witches and their animal allies. With wisdom and warmth, Madame Pamita unveils the secrets of connecting to, communicating with, and divining through familiars—be they wild creatures, birds, fish, or even insects. As a cat lover, my personal favorite is the chapter on feline friends. I've had cat familiars for much of my life, and the spells in this book, I believe, will not just help but surely foster deeper connections with my furry, purry buddies. Whether looking to divine the future with critters or trying to find the right one for magical endeavors, this book is the perfect companion for any witch who believes in the power of animals."*

— **Theresa Reed**, author of *The Cards You're Dealt*

"Once again, Madame Pamita has provided a delightful, heartfelt, and wise tome for the modern witch. Kind, funny, and smart, The Witch's Guide to Animal Familiars *is the resource that magickally minded animal lovers will treasure and return to again and again. If you love working with animals, magick, or animals and magick, or simply love stories about either, this is the book for you."*

— **Courtney Weber**, author of *Hekate: Goddess of Witches* and *Sacred Tears: A Witch's Guide to Grief*

"In her new and uniquely themed book, Madame Pamita takes us on an adventure that is both vitally important and otherwise unobtainable. It is an essential guide for lovers of creatures, ritual, and magic. We human animals emerge from its pages profoundly changed in our understanding and our relationships with the other animals who help us bless and deeply influence our homes, our lives, and our world."

— **Amy Zerner and Monte Farber**, creators of *The Enchanted Tarot* and *The Intuition Oracle*

"In this wonderful book, Madame Pamita explores the magic of animal allies, guides, and familiars, and how they are relevant and enriching for a witch's magical practice. Drawing from history, folklore, and her own life experiences, Pamita weaves a tapestry of animal companions and demonstrates simple techniques and rites for incorporating their energies into your work. If you are interested in learning more about animal familiars or want to deepen your relationship to one you already have, definitely get this book."

— **Storm Faerywolf**, author of *Forbidden Mysteries of Faery Witchcraft* and *The Witch's Name*

"This book not only helps you deepen your connection to your animal companion but also teaches you how to continue that development long past the final page. With heartfelt anecdotes and her trademark sense of humor, Madame Pamita delivers exactly what you need to know in order to empower your relationship with your animal familiar!"

— **Devin Hunter**, author of *Modern Witch: Spells, Recipes, and Workings*

The Witch's Guide TO Animal Familiars

ALSO BY MADAME PAMITA

Baba Yaga's Book of Witchcraft: Slavic Magic from the Witch of the Woods

The Book of Candle Magic: Candle Spell Secrets to Change Your Life

Magical Tarot: Your Essential Guide to Reading the Cards

Please visit:

Hay House USA: www.hayhouse.com®
Hay House Australia: www.hayhouse.com.au
Hay House UK: www.hayhouse.co.uk
Hay House India: www.hayhouse.co.in

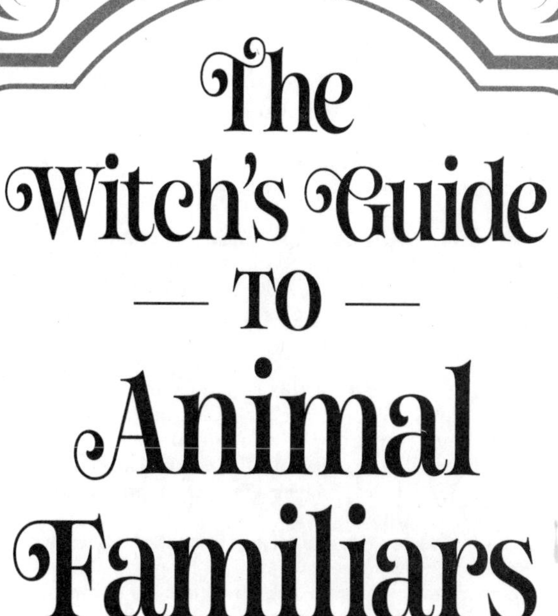

The Witch's Guide TO Animal Familiars

SPELLS, RITUALS & RECIPES FOR MAKING MAGIC WITH ANIMAL ALLIES

Madame Pamita

HAY HOUSE LLC
Carlsbad, California • New York City
London • Sydney • New Delhi

Published in the United States by: Hay House LLC: www.hayhouse.com® • ***Published in Australia by:*** Hay House Australia Publishing Pty Ltd: www.hayhouse.com.au • ***Published in the United Kingdom by:*** Hay House UK Ltd: www.hayhouse.co.uk • ***Published in India by:*** Hay House Publishers (India) Pvt Ltd: www.hayhouse.co.in

Cover design and interior design: Lisa Vega • *Interior illustrations:* Lea Androić (except page 142, illustration of a witch's ladder from "A Witches' Ladder" by Dr. Abraham Colles in *The Folk-Lore Journal*, vol 5, 1888, public domain; and page 163 and all framing devices, courtesy of Shutterstock.com) • *Author photo:* Chris Strother

Cataloging-in-Publication Data
is on file with the Library of Congress

Tradepaper ISBN: 978-1-4019-7881-5
E-book ISBN: 978-1-4019-7882-2
Audiobook ISBN: 978-1-4019-7883-9

10 9 8 7 6 5 4 3 2 1
1st edition, January 2025

Printed in the United States of America

This product uses responsibly sourced papers and/or recycled materials. For more information, see www.hayhouse.com.

Dedicated with so much love to
two beloved friends who truly
demonstrate what it means to live in the
magic of the familiar relationship:
Buchanan Moncure and her familiar,
Simone, and Gwendolyn Pogrowski
and her familiar, Roxy,
(and also to my own magical cats,
Glinda and Ozma).

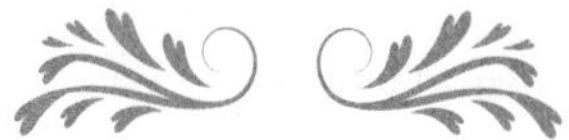

CONTENTS

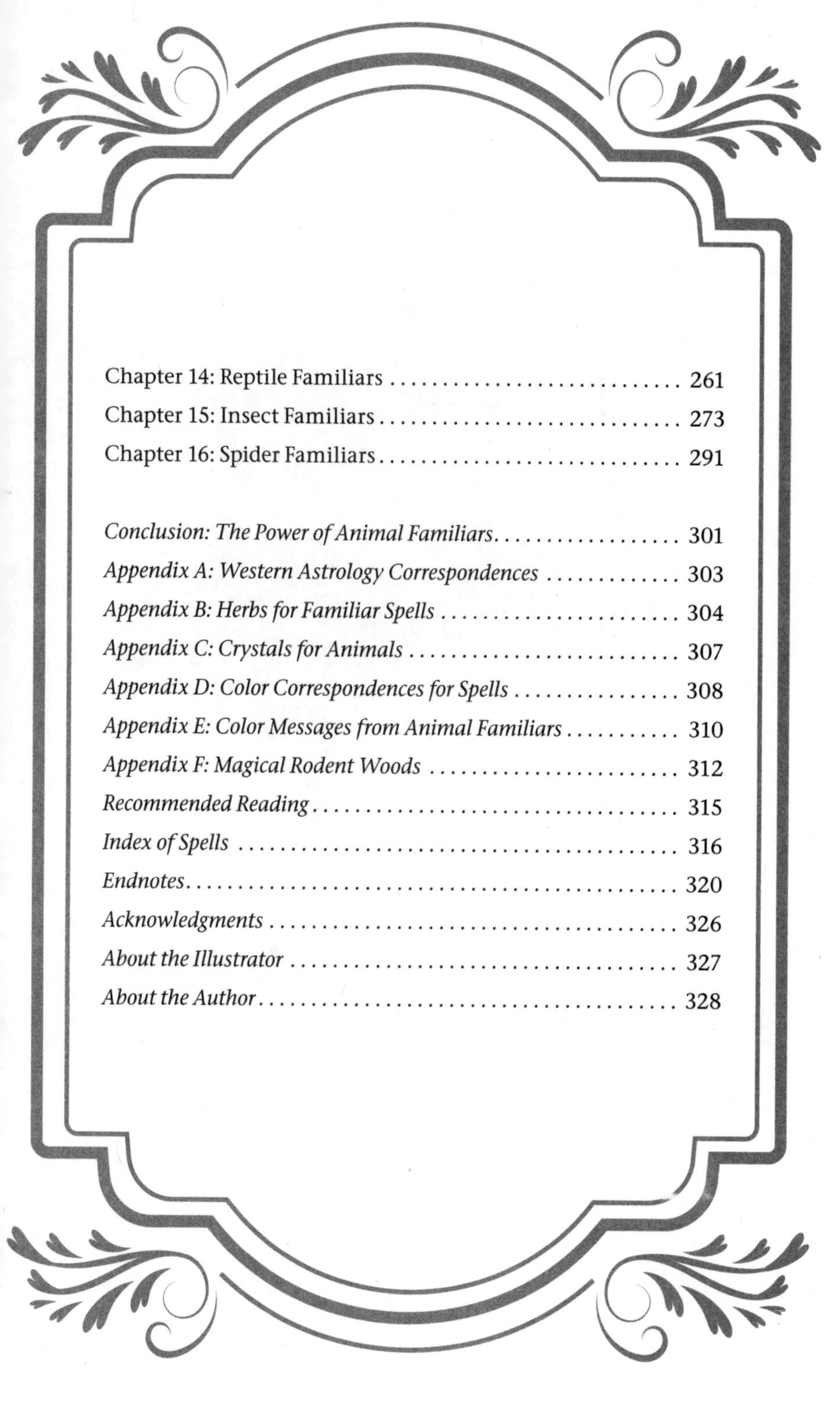

FOREWORD

The first time I met Madame Pamita was on a well-loved vintage couch in an eclectic bar in Portland. I am *very* energy sensitive, and when she sat down next to me, it was like a grounding rod had entered the space. In a room full of like-minded, magical folks, her presence was impossible to miss. It wasn't her bright purple hair or her warm smile. It wasn't her beautiful cloak or her bright eyes. It was something else altogether. It was as though she was able to shift the energy of the space by simply paying attention to you, and I recognized the sensation immediately. Madame Pamita was drenched in positive magic—and in love.

Even though we hadn't met in person before, I had known of her for many years. In the early days of social media, the online witchy and tarot communities were much smaller than they are now. Madame Pamita was there from the beginning, sharing videos of her cards, candles, and incantations long before I was brave enough to do so.

We were brought together by the 2022 Northwest Tarot Symposium, where I'd been invited to speak as a deck creator and the author of *The Light Seer's Tarot*. NWTS is a wonderful event that always brings together different characters from the tarot community for a weekend full of cards and magic. And after the first day of presentations, there was an author meet and greet at a little cocktail bar connected to the event venue, which I had fully planned on skipping.

After five hours of teaching and "being on" for so long, I would normally say no to evening soirées. I'm more likely to be found retreating to my bed early, hoping the hotel is free from wandering spirits as I prepare to enjoy my sleep. But I'm so glad I changed my mind at the last minute because it gave me the chance to meet the wonderful woman who is the author of this book.

When I walked into the lounge, I went straight for the most comfortable-looking thing in the room: a beautifully upholstered vintage couch. As more people arrived, a lively little group began to form around the couch and chairs; and by the time Madame Pamita joined us we all had to scooch over to welcome her into the conversation. I felt an instant connection with her.

We began to chat, and I immediately sensed her incredible depth. She was open, vibrant, rooted in peace, and most of all, completely authentic. We talked about the state of the world, the magic of tarot, spells, and Baba Yaga. Then we had the most delightful conversation about the magic of trees, bonding over their wisdom and power, and musing about mycelium and how we are all connected. I was studying Chinese medicine at the time, so the conversation meandered from mycelium to Cordyceps and back again. It was one of those unexpected, hypnotic interactions where two people are being totally authentic and at ease, and where superficial conversations are replaced by a deeply energetic and soul-satisfying exchange. *You know the kind of conversations I mean, right?* The ones where you go *very deep*, very quickly, and the room around you seems to slow down as if time itself has paused.

Madame Pamita not only saved my introverted heart from a night of potentially draining small talk but, as we chatted, I knew that she and I were going to become good friends. There are different types of friends one can have. Some are the laughter-and-dancing kind, some are lifelong besties, and some are the magical and spiritual kind. Spiritual friends are those we feel deeply connected to in ways we can't quite explain—people who share our rare perspectives on life. That night, Madame Pamita became one of my very special spiritual friends. She's the kind of friend who, when we see each other at events, we delight in stealing away for a few moments to catch up. And in the span of an hour, we often dive deeper into the heart of things than I might with someone else in a month. Her ancient soul fills my heart with so much peace, and our connection always feels effortless.

I feel very blessed to have crossed paths with Madame Pamita and her incredible magic, and I know that you are going to love her wisdom and her lessons as much as I do. She makes things simple but never surface level. She is a magnificent teacher who explains the "why" without boxing us into any one specific way. I've already started using the guidance from this very book with my own little pup, and I bet your future familiar will be so happy that you've started this journey with such a lovely and authentic guide! *She is the real deal,* and I think you're going to have so much fun connecting with her magic—and with the animals—in a whole new way.

With bright blessings and so much love . . .
XO,
Chris-Anne

INTRODUCTION

My Witch's Familiar Story

When you step onto the path of the witch, you'll soon discover that it is more like the mystical spiral of a ram's horn or the sideways slither of a snake than a straightforward interstate highway. You'll come to crossroads, discover hidden gardens, and, the next thing you know, you'll get gloriously lost following fae folk—and that is as it should be.

I have been practicing witchcraft for my entire life, and the road of discovery has been filled with more twists and turns than an overgrown trail in a dusky mountain forest. As I was growing up, I practiced the Ukrainian Catholic magic of my mother and grandmother. I began learning tarot and astrology in the 1980s, then formally studied Wicca in the 1990s. I started incorporating Spiritualism and New Thought into my practice and studied African American Hoodoo and Conjure in the 2000s. I finally began blending in a heaping helping of Hedgewitchery and Slavic Shamanism and brought back the Ukrainian Folk Magic of my childhood to my ever-evolving practice.

If you are a witch and don't know where to begin, start with wherever you are and go wherever you want. The path will surely lead you to all the most interesting places, including, if you're picking up this book, the magic of the animal kingdom. Throughout time and history, witches have been animal lovers. If you see the depth of the Universe in an animal's eye, become transfixed by a majestic bird circling in the sky, or feel the true healing that you get from holding your pet in your arms, you *know* the magic of animals.

In my life, I have had the pleasure of enjoying close friendships with so many animals. It all started with a cocker spaniel named Mr. Chips Worthington and extended through a delightful parade of parakeets, fish, hermit crabs, tortoises, snakes, and many, many cats. Currently, I have two darling felines who live with me, Glinda and Ozma, named after the witch and the princess in the Oz books. I have been honored to have each of these animals at my side to comfort me, amuse me, and provide true friendship.

Like most people, I grew up thinking that animals were there for my pleasure—that I was the boss, that I owned them, and they were "mine." But, as my own witchcraft path developed, I began seeing animals as individuals who had their own spirits. I began paying attention to their unique consciousness and learning valuable spiritual lessons from them. Rather than force them into my human world, I began to dip into their world and discovered what witches and shamanic practitioners have known for thousands of years—that animals can be some of our most powerful allies.

It is my greatest wish that this book sparks new inspiration for you on how to get even closer to the magical animals around you and leads you to new fascinating lands for you to explore on your twisty, winding spiritual journey.

Your Witch's Familiar Story

In this book, you will uncover the secrets of connecting with the animal kingdom to expand your magical and spiritual practice in phenomenal ways. You'll learn to tell the difference between an animal who is a friend and one who is a true familiar. You'll master psychically linking up with the animals around you to communicate with them and understand them on a deeper level. You'll discover ways to invite your familiar to participate in your magic, to teach you, to help you, and to empower your rituals. And you'll learn special spells to bless and protect your animal familiar in return.

As you dive in, you'll find chapters that have spells that apply to all animals and others that offer a closer look at specific animal families. While it might be tempting to just look at the chapter about your own special animal companion, I encourage you to peruse the chapters that are about animals other than your chosen familiar. With minor adjustments and adaptations, many of the spells, rituals, and recipes can be done with a variety of animal familiars, not just the ones specified. Get creative with your magic. There is no "one way" to do witchcraft, and throughout history people have been sharing, adapting, and building on spells from their elders and teachers. I hope you do this too.

Whether you want to learn from animals in the wild or build strong bonds with the animals in your care, with this book, you are about to embark on the journey of a lifetime—one that will empower you, expand your magical skills, and transform your life in enlightening and uplifting ways. I welcome you, intrepid explorer. It is my deep pleasure to meet you at the crossroads, and I look forward to traveling at your side as you read this book. May we meet again and again, throughout this lifetime and all the lifetimes to come.

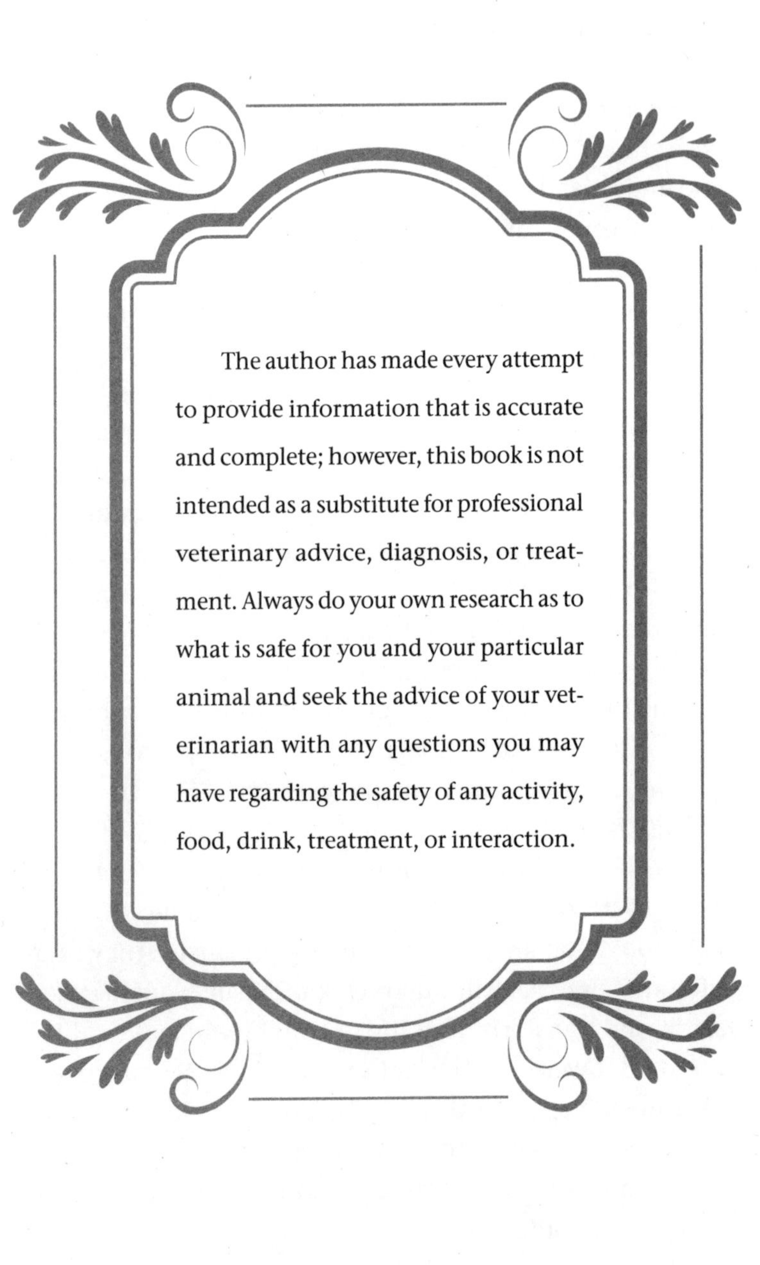

The author has made every attempt to provide information that is accurate and complete; however, this book is not intended as a substitute for professional veterinary advice, diagnosis, or treatment. Always do your own research as to what is safe for you and your particular animal and seek the advice of your veterinarian with any questions you may have regarding the safety of any activity, food, drink, treatment, or interaction.

Part One

The Magic of the Animal Familiar

—— CHAPTER 1 ——

Defining the Witch's Familiar

When autumn is in the air, all over North America and other parts of the world, we step into spooky season. The leaves of the trees transform to radiant gold, blazing orange, and fiery red. Fat pumpkins and nubby gourds appear in the market overnight as if sprouted by magic seeds. And as the temperature and the decor start to invoke chills, you will have a hard time missing one of the most emblematic symbols of the Halloween season: a witch with a pointed hat, a broom, and her black cat companion, the witch's familiar.

If you watch a show or a movie featuring a witch, there's a good chance you'll see a familiar slink their way into a co-star role. From Salem Saberhagen in *Sabrina the Teenage Witch*, Thackery Binx in *Hocus Pocus*, Jiji in *Kiki's Delivery Service*, to

Pyewacket in *Bell, Book and Candle,* familiars in media cajole, advise, assist, and banter with their witchy allies and delight and amuse us in the process. While this otherworldly relationship between human and animal may seem like a fantasy to most people, familiars are real—but not every animal you work with is a familiar. To define the familiar, we must first look at all the myriad magical ways that we can partner with animals in our spiritual practice.

Magical Animal Relationships

Can you imagine having hundreds of best friends? The idea is preposterous. Developing a friendship to the point of that special bond requires time and emotional intimacy. Even for the most sociable of us, it just isn't possible to maintain a deep connection to more than a handful of people. You might have a wide circle of people you know, a smaller group whom you would consider acquaintances, an even smaller group of close friends, and a select one or two whom you would call your besties.

You can think of your magical relationships with animals in the same way. Just as your social relationships with other people serve different purposes, the various levels of connection you can have with animals bring a variety of gifts to your life experience. The idea of levels might conjure up ideas that intimate relationships are more desirable and that casual ones are less so, but I invite you to set aside the idea of hierarchy when it comes to your connection to animals. Have you ever had the experience of a stranger showing up with exactly what you needed in the moment? They are not a friend, and you might never see them again, but they generously give you the perfect assistance. Encounters like these clearly show that all types and levels of connections to others can bring amazing gifts into our lives.

Think of animal relationships being on a spectrum, with each bringing its own unique benefits to your spiritual life. In this book, we discuss animal friends (pets), kin, allies, messengers, guides, and familiars. Animals may move between places on this spectrum as well. For example, an animal may start out as a messenger and become a guide, or your animal friend may grow into the role of familiar. While the focus of this book is on the animal familiar relationship, many of the techniques and spells you will find throughout this book can be adapted to these other special animal relationships.

Animal Friends or Pets

Animal friends are animals you bond with who may have no other spiritual significance. Pets whom you care for can offer you love, companionship, amusement, and protection without any deeper meaning than that. That does not mean that animal friendships cannot be profound. Many people experience this love of the animals in their lives where their pet becomes part of the family. Just as you have human friends whom you love to hang around with, you can have animal friends who delight you and draw you into their world, but their role may not be about lending their energy to your magical practice.

For example, my cat Ozma is definitely a lovable little cuddle bug. I adore her and consider her a member of the family. The casual observer might see my close bond with her as a sign that she is my familiar; however, like any good cat and witch relationship, she is the princess, and I am her humble servant. The love and affection she gives me fill up my heart, but she is decidedly disinterested in the magic that I do. That is not to say that she could not grow to take on another role in time, but for the past four years, giving me the healing power of her purr is as far as her interest goes.

Animal Kin

Animal kin are animals who groups of people connect to. This concept is found in many different cultures, in varied forms and names, such as *clan animal*. This is a special symbolic animal who embodies the characteristics of the community.

Animal kin can also be bestowed upon someone after an initiation, if the group is not a family group but a group of another kind that you join, such as a coven. Animal kin are not new animals who come into your life; they are there with you from the time that you are part of the community until the time that you leave. Your animal kin can show up in formal ways with the elders of the group sharing that information with you. Likewise, they can show up in more subtle ways, such as belonging to a long line of "horse people," for example.

Animal kin create a special connection between you and the others of your group, but found families can also form around animal kin. Close-knit groups of friends can form from being fans of a certain species of animal. Think of people who go to dog parks, pet shows, or who volunteer at wild animal rescues, for example. People who have a passion for these animals and connect to others who share that passion will form groups around their animal kin and will have a deep and special relationship with the others who gravitate to this kin animal.

Animal Allies

Animal allies are like those friendly strangers who help you out at just the right moment. An animal ally might show up for you unexpectedly when you need them, or you can consciously invite them to share their magic with you. Usually, they come in for a specific purpose and for a limited amount of time. You do not necessarily need to build a deeper relationship with them, although in some cases an animal ally relationship can grow into something deeper.

You can call on an animal ally to ask them to lend their energy to you in a particular situation. To discover which animal would like to lend its energy, you can use a divination spell, such as one of those in Chapter 2, with details adjusted for this purpose. You can also consciously reflect on the characteristics of the animal you would like to help you and invite them. For example, if you are facing a sticky situation and want to embody resourcefulness and intelligence to get out of it, you might call on the crow to lend you problem-solving skills or the fox to bring you the ability to get out of tricky circumstances.

To access the energy of the crow, you can pay attention to the crows who cross your path, observe them, listen to them, and do some research to make an offering to them that they would like. You can also access your ally on a spiritual level, invoking the spirit from a distance. You might find an image of a fox and put it on your altar, or light a fox candle for a spell, for example. Both these direct and indirect methods for connecting to animal allies are equally effective and using one or the other just depends on your access to the animals.

When you invite an ally into your magic, be sure that the exchange is equitable. An offering of food, shelter, or some other appropriate comfort to the animal family will be received with love. Do your research and see what supports that animal in the wild. If you are working with an animal virtually, you can make donations to organizations that protect and care for that animal to show your commitment.

Animal Messengers

Animal messengers appear to give us specific messages from the Divine. Animal messengers are never consciously invoked; they always appear in unexpected ways. Just like animal allies, messengers can appear physically or virtually. In whatever way they show up for you, the hallmark of animal messengers is the remarkable way that they appear. You might have an out-of-the-ordinary encounter or keep seeing images of the animal repeatedly until you get the message. Usually, you can interpret that message by the characteristics of the animal and clarify their symbolism in light of what is happening in your life at the moment.

I remember that when my adult son was going through a life-or-death health crisis, the image of the bear kept appearing for me. When my son got his diagnosis, an artist who is a client of mine (and who knew nothing about what I was going through) gave me an imposing six-foot-tall painting of a growling she-bear standing protectively on her hind legs. From that point on, bear images kept appearing everywhere.

People gave me bear figurines; I saw bears on bumper stickers, billboards, and street signs that I had never seen before. I read and heard the word *bear*, met people and animals named Bear, and stumbled across bear deities. It became an almost daily experience, one that I reflected on. *What qualities of the bear did I need right now? What message was she sending?* I meditated on bears and saw the protective power of the mother bear and felt her lending me energy to protect and advocate for my son. I saw that bears hibernate in the winter without excuses, so I pulled back from social and work obligations while I focused on his well-being without feeling guilty. I also saw that she was not afraid to confront frightening situations, which this most certainly was for both of us.

When my son pulled through and got well, the bear messages tapered off. Was it merely coincidence? Was I just noticing what had always been right in front of me? It is possible, but the timing and frequency—appearing in a torrent and then tapering off to a normal trickle after the health crisis was over—told me that this was the work of an animal messenger.

When you get a dispatch from an animal messenger, you can research the qualities of that animal or visit them in a vision journey, as I will describe in Chapter 2, to learn what message they have for you. If you get stuck trying to decipher the meaning, there are many books and decks out there that will share the spiritual significance of the animal who is coming forward with special energy and information for you. See what they have to say and use the interpretations that are relevant to your current situation.

Animal Guides

Animal guides are special animals that you connect to over longer periods of time. Just like what some people and cultures refer to as *spirit animals*, these are animals who are there to assist you and lend you their energy over years, decades, and sometimes an entire lifetime. Like an animal ally or an animal messenger, they can appear physically or virtually, but rather than appearing in response to a situation, they appear consistently.

When you connect to an animal guide, you are connecting to a collective animal rather than an individual. You may feel an attraction to a certain species of animal and when that connection opens, it will feel deep and intimate from the beginning. You don't necessarily need to contact these animals physically to feel the connection. Simply seeing images, watching videos, or reading and learning about the animal can deepen the connection.

The relationship may start out with a bang, with a rush of synchronistic messages for you that draw you closer in your curiosity, or your connection may grow slowly and more subtly over time. An animal guide will teach you about their different strengths and gifts that enlighten you on your spiritual path.

Animal Familiars

Animal familiars are relationships in which you collaborate spiritually and magically with an individual animal—almost always one who is in physical form. There are animal spirits who can also be familiars, but these would most likely be animals who were your familiars when they were alive whose spirits continue to collaborate with you.

The idea of collaboration is important. Your familiar is not there as your servant, but as an equal partner in your magic. They may teach you, lend you their energy, or hold space for you to work in the ethereal realm. They are active participants in your magic, sitting close by or quietly observing from a distance but always adding their energy to your work just the same. A familiar can also be a teacher, providing insights into your magical practice from their intuitive animal perspective.

An animal familiar will show up consistently. Your magical practice, and the relationship between you and your familiar, will become richer over time. Unlike a messenger animal, they won't come for a while and then disappear. You won't actively call a particular familiar in to help you with a single situation, as we do with an animal ally. Likewise, a familiar won't be handed down to you from your family as animal kin are. Your connection to your familiar will be individual to you and that animal, and your relationship will grow as you work together.

Just as you can have more than one teacher or partner in your life, you can have more than one familiar. As one familiar leaves your life, another one might appear. It is also possible to have more than one familiar at the same time, just as you may have more than one person in your circle of best friends. Even if they are the same type of animal, each of your familiars will help you in individual and unique ways.

A Very Brief History of Animal-Human Relationships

The phrase *witch's familiar* originated hundreds of years ago, so to begin to untangle the concept of the familiar, we need to time travel back to Western Europe at the dawn of the Middle Ages. In those times, when the Catholic Church was defending its consolidation of power, a peasant might be Christian in name or even devout in their beliefs but simultaneously taking part in older pagan rituals and rites. They made potions and brews for healing physical as well as spiritual maladies. They performed divinations and practiced folk magic for luck, protection, healing, and love. They participated in festivals centered around the ancient agricultural year. They knew that this older magic and the Otherworld of spirits was real and accessible. But by the 11th century, folk magic practices that had formerly coexisted peacefully within Catholicism began being associated with heresy, devil worship, and witchcraft. In 1486, Heinrich Krämer published the *Malleus Maleficarum,* "The Hammer of Witches," a judicial casebook for the detection and prosecution of witches.[1] Thus began the witch hunts that killed tens of thousands of innocent people, the vast majority of whom were women.

The *Malleus Maleficarum* is one of the first major documents to bring up the concept of the familiar, asserting that "familiar spirits" were minions who would serve a witch by performing malevolent deeds at her will, such as stealing her neighbors' milk, harming their crops, or even causing disease and death.

The sex, violence, and supernatural shenanigans of the *Malleus Maleficarum* turned it into a sensation. For more than 200 years, it was second in sales only to the Bible itself.

However, it was a work of misogynist fiction posing as fact written by a former inquisitor monk who was fired from his job for being obsessed with the sexual habits of the women he accused. The devil worship, perversity, and spectacular powers of the witch that filled the book did not come from hard evidence, but solely from his twisted and debased imagination.

While early writings of familiars described humanoid demons such as imps, incubi, and succubi, there were mentions of witches being aided by familiars in the form of animals. By the time the witch hunt frenzy was hitting its peak in the 1600s, descriptions of interactions between witches and animal familiars had become a commonplace accusation in English witch trials and were featured in the sensationalist pamphlets sold to the public. In England, the Witchcraft Act of 1604 made it a felony to "consult, covenant with, entertain, employ, feed, or reward any evil and wicked spirit to or for any intent or purpose"; this spirit, of course, could be disguised as an animal.[2]

Nearly every animal that a human interacted with could potentially be accused of being a familiar. Cats, dogs, ferrets, frogs, birds, and even bees aroused suspicion. While the forced confessions of accused witches were made under torture or coercion, there is no doubt that the accused were found guilty and killed on evidence as skimpy as having a loving friendship with a pet. As witch-hunt fever reached a crescendo, even the animals themselves were accused, put on trial, and executed.

Does all this mean that the concept of the witch's familiar was created from the perverse imagination of misogynists in power? Did animal familiars ever really exist?

The True Witch's Familiar

Tens of thousands of years ago, people coexisted and interacted with wild animals, hunting them for food, of course, but also observing them for information and learning about the world around them. When people began domesticating the wild animals around them, they created a new dynamic in their relationships. Mastery over domesticated animals and the move to agricultural societies coincided with people moving from animism, the belief in the sacred spirit in all things, to theism, the belief in deities. As monotheistic religions superseded the other belief systems of the time, people began to view animals as slaves to be worked or food to be eaten.

During the Middle Ages, the relationship between humans and animals degraded. Animals kept as pets were seen as frivolous—something exclusively for wealthy nobility—and most literature mentioning pets criticized people for the selfishness of keeping companion animals when they could be using their resources to help the poor.[3] Animals that weren't "useless pets" suffered horribly from the Middle Ages through the Industrial Era. With animal abuse such as cock fighting and bear baiting being the norm and companion animals being considered an over-the-top indulgence of the very rich, the stage was set for kindness and connection to animals to be seen as highly questionable. Suspicious folk could root out anything even slightly odd as a sign of witchcraft. Therefore, deep friendship with a companion animal became just another out-of-the-ordinary behavior that could be used in a court to convict a witch.

In a time when nonconformity might mean death and old traditional folkways were being brutally wiped out in favor of Christian authoritarianism, carrying on the ancient animistic belief that all beings have a spirit, and that connection to nature can be a way to share life force, would be seen as outrageously rebellious.

We now have the opportunity to redefine and rectify the definition of the familiar. If you go back to the original and most authentic view of the familiar relationship, it *is* a kinship with a spirit. Not a disembodied demon but the spirit of a living being. The witch's familiar is a friendship between a witch and a vital sentient being, an animal they can work together with in the magical realm. A loving alliance where both the human and the animal lend each other energy, learn from each other, and become a true cooperative partnership.

—— CHAPTER 2 ——

Discovering Your Animal Familiar

Are you ready to go on a treasure hunt? The prize you are about to discover will be furry, feathery, or scaly and much more valuable than some dusty old doubloons. The process of finding an animal familiar is a truly magical adventure.

If you don't already have a familiar or would like to invite an additional one, there are many techniques to discover who your familiar is and the role that they will play in your magical practice. Remember that the familiar relationship is one that both you and the animal enter willingly. Forcing an animal to be your familiar is as unethical as forcing someone to work for you, and an enslaved animal will not willingly lend their energy to you.

Often, a familiar will appear at a certain stage in your spiritual practice. Like the oft-repeated quote, "When the student is ready, the teacher appears," your perfect familiar will arrive at just the right time.

Inviting Your Familiar

If you would like to bring a familiar into your life, you can do a ritual to invite a new familiar. Whatever method you use, be the most open-minded you can be about the animal who comes to you. In magic, the more trusting you can be, the faster you can see results. It does not mean that you can't ask the Universe for a dog familiar, for example, if you really want to work with the energy of a dog. Even within that category, see if you can be open to the breed and gender.

Ritual to Invite an Animal Familiar

Use this small ritual to invite your animal familiar in.

What you will need:

- Juniper incense or dried juniper (*Juniperus communis*), sweetgrass (*Hierochloe oderata*), or thyme (*Thymus vulgaris*) herb bundle (smudge stick)
- Cauldron, tray, or incense holder
- Attraction oil (See the note in the recipe that follows.)
- Purple taper candle
- Taper candle holder
- Matches

1. Prepare a sacred space to perform this ritual indoors by first getting in touch with the spirit of the space. If possible, crouch down and touch the floor, close your eyes, and thank

the building and the land on which it stands for lending their energy to your work.

2. Light the incense or herb bundle and waft the smoke around the room, walking in a counterclockwise direction to clear any unwanted energies and set the space apart from ordinary reality.
3. Set the incense or herb bundle aside in the cauldron, tray, or holder.
4. Apply a few drops of attraction oil to your hands and arms.
5. Pour a few more drops of oil into your palm and apply it to the purple candle in an upward direction, from the base of the candle toward the wick. Then place your candle in the candle holder.
6. Light your candle as you speak your intentions of attracting a familiar. You can use the words in your heart or say this incantation:

Come to me, O animal friend,
That your magic you may lend.
Beak, paw, snout, and scales,
Together we will cast strong spells.
Fins, hooves, feathers, claws,
I invite you to join my magical cause.
Bring me a sign, radiant and clear,
To show that you are drawing near.
Come to my side, familiar of mine,
And we will ride the currents divine.
In trust, companionship, and love,
Creating below that which is above.

7. If possible, step outside or open a window. Light the incense or herb bundle again, if needed, and wave it in a beckoning manner toward yourself as if you are calling your familiar from out in the world toward you.
8. Allow the candle to continue burning while you are awake and at home. If you leave the house or go to sleep and the candle has not finished burning, snuff it out (don't blow it out), and then relight it when you return or awaken.
9. On the day or days that the candle is burning, you can reinforce your spell by repeating affirmations. (Affirmations are positive incantations that you can use to quickly cast a spell.) If you have a favorite method of repeating affirmations, you can use that or you can simply repeat the affirmation out loud three times as you light the candle. Choose the type of affirmation to bring the results that you would like, such as:

"My animal familiar comes to me."
(Most open with the fastest results)
"My perfect wild animal familiar comes to me."
(Still open and fast)
"My snake familiar comes to me."
(More focused but possibly slower)
"My female king snake familiar comes to me."
(Most focused but slowest)

10. Once the candle has completely burned, the spell is cast. Look for signs, such as seeing the animal or images of the animal more frequently, until your actual familiar contacts you.

Safety Notes: When working with incense or candles, it's important to light them only when you're at home and awake and able to monitor them. Place them on flat, stable, fireproof surfaces where no draft can send stray, flammable cloth, paper, or other objects into the flame. If you have a pet, familiar, small child, or anyone else at home who loves to explore and get involved in your magic, you may want to invest in a decorative metal birdcage that you can put burning incense or candle spells in and keep them at a safe distance. If the instructions say to let a candle burn out, a small candle may burn out within a few minutes, but a large candle may take hours or days. With longer burning candles, you should put them on pause when you cannot attend to them by snuffing them out—do not blow them out. Then relight them when you can keep an eye on them.

Attraction Oil Recipe

An attraction oil is used in spells to draw good things, people, opportunities, or even familiars to you. If you wish to purchase one rather than make one, look for an oil that uses real herbs and essential oils to harness the magical power of botanicals. You can use the herbs listed here or browse Appendix B for other herbs you can use.

What you will need:

- Small glass bottle with dropper to hold your oil
- One pinch of herbs of your choice: dried catnip (*Nepeta cataria*), cedar bark (*Cedrus*), and/or coriander seed (*Coriandrum sativum*)
- 7 drops of juniper (*Juniperus communis*) essential oil
- 1 to 2 drops of vitamin E oil (as a preservative)
- Sweet almond oil (to fill bottle)

1. Add the herbs, essential oil, and vitamin E oil to your bottle.
2. Add sweet almond oil to fill the bottle.
3. Shake while you focus on the intention of attracting good things into your life.

Discovering Your Animal Familiar Through Synchronicities

Animal familiars will often come into your life in a surprising and unusual way. Once they do appear, they will stick around. Unlike an animal messenger who shows up just to deliver a message, a familiar will move in or continue to visit you regularly, most likely for their entire lifetime. Everything in the Universe lines up to bring you and your familiar together so that the two of you can create magic. This can mean that you find a lost puppy or rescue an injured bird, or that someone gifts you with an animal unexpectedly that you later discover is your familiar. You might take the same route on a weekly nature walk and find the same little squirrel trying to get your attention every time you pass by.

One encounter, particularly with a wild animal, is not enough to consider that animal a familiar. Instead, you must look for regular multiple encounters or events that are out of the ordinary. Those encounters can be in the physical realm, but when you really get the sign that an animal is your familiar, they will show up again and again, through different modalities such as dreams and divination as well as in the physical. For additional ways to connect to your familiar in dreams, see Chapter 3.

Familiar Divination

Divination is the art of discovering deeper spiritual wisdom, often using tools and methods that can be interpreted. You can use divination techniques to discover your animal familiar, confirm whether an animal you connect to is your familiar, and explore what animals are willing to have a familiar relationship with you. In this chapter, I recommend several methods that are fairly accessible and don't require expert knowledge to get started right away.

Pendulum Ritual to Divine Your Familiar

Since antiquity, pendulums have been used as a method of divination. A pendulum is any weight suspended by a string or chain. You can purchase a beautiful pendulum made of gemstone, metal, or other materials; you can create your own from a pendant necklace; or you can even make a simple one by tying a piece of thread to a ring.

You can use a pendulum for all kinds of divination. Once you have a relationship with your familiar, you can use your pendulum to communicate with them, as I will outline in Chapter 3.

For this divination, you will be invoking your spirit guides for answers. Your spirit guides are a council of positive, high-vibration entities who protect, assist, and guide you with advice from an enlightened perspective. Each of us has a unique team of guides who can include beloved ancestors, deities, angelic beings, saints, ascended masters, elemental spirits, and, of course, animal spirits. You don't need to know who each of your guides is before you begin working with them. They often speak collectively, as they are all tapping into the same information. So, you can call on your spirit guides as a group and get truly helpful enlightened guidance.

1. First, rest the elbow of your dominant hand on a table or other surface while gently holding the top of the string or chain, allowing the weight to swing freely.
2. Steady your hand and the pendulum until it is absolutely still.
3. Invoke your spirit guides. You can use the following invocation that I use or create your own:

   I invite my spirit guides,
   spirits of the highest vibration,
   to give me clear, helpful, and
   accurate answers to my questions.

4. The first time you work with a pendulum, it's a good idea to confirm how the answers will be received. Ask your spirit guides, deities, or the

pendulum itself to show you how it will indicate a yes answer.

5. Holding your hand as steady as possible, observe how the pendulum begins to swing. It may swing in a clockwise circle, toward you and away, side to side, or some other movement.
6. Stop the pendulum from swinging. Ask your guides to show you a no answer.
7. Observe the direction the pendulum swings, such as a counterclockwise circle, from left to right, or some other movement.
8. Once you have determined your yes/no, which only needs to be done the first time you work with a pendulum, you can begin asking questions about your animal familiar. Holding your hand and the pendulum steady, ask a yes/no question and then observe the pendulum to see if the guides say yes or no.
9. Choose questions that resonate for you, but likewise feel free to come up with your own as they pertain to your personal familiar journey. Here are some examples:
    - Is there a familiar who wishes to work with me?
    - Is this familiar a pet/wild animal/domestic animal/etc.?
    - Is this familiar a cat/dog/bird/horse/etc.?
    - Will I encounter this familiar sometime this year/month/week?

- Should I go to this animal rescue/hike in this area/etc. to find my familiar?
- Is (name of pet/animal) my friend/kin/ally/messenger/guide/familiar?

10. Once you are finished asking for information, thank your guides and put your pendulum away.

Here are some helpful hints for using the pendulum:

- Take your time to allow the pendulum to swing in a definite direction.
- If you are questioning whether you are consciously influencing the answer, ask your question and then close your eyes for about a minute. Then, open your eyes to see the direction the pendulum is swinging.
- Do not ask the pendulum frivolous or snarky questions.
- Do not ask the same question of the pendulum repeatedly. Instead, if you would like confirmation about an answer you received, use a different form of divination to verify the answer.

Card Ritual to Divine Your Familiar

Another method to get guidance as to who your next familiar may be is to use oracle or tarot cards. It is easiest and in the best spiritual alignment if you use a deck with animal images to determine who your familiar is. I've created the perfect deck specifically for communicating with and accessing information about your familiar called *The Familiar Magic Pocket Oracle,* which will be released by Hay House in 2025. Here are some other decks you might also want to explore that can help you discover who your familiar is:

- *Animal Guides Tarot* by Radleigh Valentine
- *Power Animal Oracle Cards* by Steven D. Farmer, Ph.D.
- *The Spirit Animal Oracle* by Collette Baron-Reid
- *The Witch's Familiar Runic Oracle* by Athene Noctua
- *Everyday Witch's Familiars Oracle* by Deborah Blake and Elisabeth Alba
- *The Druid Animal Oracle Deck* by Philip and Stephanie Carr-Gomm
- *The Animal Elders Oracle* by Asha Frost

1. Just as with working with a pendulum, you will invoke your spirit guides before doing a reading. You can use the same invocation described in the pendulum directions above.
2. Focus on the question, "What animal is willing to be my familiar?" as you shuffle the cards.
3. When you get an intuitive sense that the cards are shuffled (which is really no different than the feeling you get when playing cards are shuffled for a mundane game), stop. Cut the deck into three stacks, and then restack in any order back into a single stack.
4. Turn over the top card to see what animal is willing to be your familiar.

5. When you receive this information, reflect on it, and then thank your guides for their help in seeing what familiar is interested in working with you.

Professional Reading to Divine Your Familiar

If you don't feel confident doing divination for yourself or would like objective information not influenced by your rational mind, consider getting a reading from a trusted intuitive. Before you make an appointment, ask them if they do readings to discover animal familiars. I offer consultations of this type, for example, but not every reader does.

Readings can be done with oracle cards, animal-centric tarot cards, through a spirit guide session, or via a shamanic journey session. During the session, a talented intuitive may be able to divine what familiar is willing to work with you as well as how you can connect with them and what assistance they will bring to you.

Dreamwork to Discover Your Animal Familiar

Another path that familiars might use to guide you to them is through your dreams. Before you go to sleep at night, ask for your future familiar to visit you as you sleep. Pay attention to the animals who appear in your dreams. If the same one shows up repeatedly, they are indicating that they would like to work with you. If you practice lucid dreaming (when you are aware that you are dreaming and can direct the action in your dream), ask the animal if it is your familiar. For additional ways to connect to your familiar in dreams, see Chapter 3.

If you are not able to remember your dreams in the morning but would like to, try recording or writing down your dreams when you awaken. Even if all you can note is just a fragment or an impression, the more you do this, the more you will train your brain to remember details. Within a few weeks of doing this practice daily, you should be remembering dreams well enough to recall any animal encounters you have. (Also refer to the familiar dream potion in Chapter 3.)

Vision Journey to Discover Your Animal Familiar

You can also try the technique of visualization to discover your familiar. Put on some meditative music, close your eyes, and imagine yourself out in your favorite natural surroundings. Ask an animal who would like to be your familiar to meet you there and see who appears. If no one appears right away, you can try exploring the terrain and see if you discover an animal.

If many animals appear, continue to explore. If you find that the same animal appears three times, they are letting you know that they would like to form a bond. If you are interested in joining forces with this animal, you can ask them questions such as:

- Are you my friend, kin, ally, messenger, guide, familiar, or other?
- Where can I find you in the physical realm?
- What magic can we make together?

Intuition to Discover Your Animal Familiar

If you have attuned your intuition, you may be able to sense who your animal familiar is before you meet them. Maybe you suddenly have a passion for a certain species of animal that you have never had an interest in before. If the call is persistent, ask for some signs or synchronicities to confirm that this animal would like to develop a familiar relationship with you. In addition, you can get confirmation by doing one of the divination techniques outlined earlier in this chapter.

Astrology to Discover Your Familiar

You can also use astrology to determine what type of animal will be a compatible familiar. Look at the charts in Appendix A to spark some ideas on animals to keep an eye out for. You can look at your sun sign in Western astrology for clues. If you know your moon sign and rising sign, those can also be helpful to discover more options.

Numerology to Discover Your Familiar

The method of numerology believes that each of us has a life path number that is determined by the date that we were born. This life path number can be calculated by writing out the numbers for the day, month, and year of your birthdate, then adding the digits together. For example, a person born on the 26th of February in 2000 would have the digits 2+6+2+2+0+0+0. Adding these together equals 12. This number can be further reduced by adding 1+2 to produce a life path number of 3.

Once you have determined your life path number, look at the chart below and see if any of the animals listed have shown up in your path or light a spark in your heart. If so, this animal familiar will be a great companion on your journey in this lifetime.

1. Animals with qualities of independence, leadership, and solitude: armadillo, hamster, mole, moose, roadrunner, skunk, tortoise, woodpecker
2. Animals with qualities of partnership, cooperation, and balance: angelfish, duck, goose, lovebird, peacock, swan, wolf
3. Animals with qualities of creativity, expression, and playfulness: cat, coyote, cricket, dog, guinea pig, hare, otter, parrot, rabbit, seal
4. Animals with qualities of practicality, enterprise, and diligence: ant, beaver, bee, gerbil, raccoon, snail, spider
5. Animals with qualities of adventurousness, spontaneity, and bravery: bear, cardinal, cougar, hawk, horse, hummingbird, scorpion
6. Animals with qualities of empathy, support, and community: chicken, chinchilla, deer, dove, tetras and other schooling fish, frog, seahorse, sheep
7. Animals with qualities of rationality, exploration, and intelligence: crow, dolphin, fox, ladybug, octopus, pheasant, rat, raven

8. Animals with qualities of abundance, success, and ambition: bat, bull, cow, goat, grasshopper, pig, squirrel
9. Animals with qualities of wisdom, altruism, and mysticism: butterfly, dragonfly, lizard, owl, salamander, snake

Receiving a Familiar You Are Not Interested In

When you use one of these methods, remember that the familiar-witch connection is a joyful and inspiring one for both of you. You are using these divination methods to discover which animals are willing to work with you as a familiar. Reflect on the information that you receive. If you get a message for connecting with an animal who you are not interested in working with, there is no harm in you declining that connection and looking for another. However, don't hastily skip over the information that is provided to you. If you are offered an animal familiar who is scary, difficult, or simply unwanted, spend some time learning about that animal by observing it in its natural habitat or watching documentaries about the species before you dismiss it out of hand. You may discover that a new and exciting familiar relationship blossoms for you by keeping your mind open.

Nevertheless, if you truly have no desire to work with a particular animal even after spending some time considering the possibility, you can politely decline the connection just as you would turn down a date with a nice person in whom you had no interest. Thank the animal or the spirit of the animal for offering to work with you and wish them well in finding their perfect magical partner.

Finding the Perfect Familiar Match

While you might be eager to get started making magic with a special animal, don't rush the process of discovering your familiar. Just like meeting "the one," finding your perfect familiar might take some time. Instead of rushing to the finish line, savor the journey. Find joy in the exploration of all the possible animal familiars that the natural world has to offer. Get curious about the animal kingdom and get to know some animals you've never connected with before. You can discover them in the world around you and research them in documentaries, articles, and books.

Your process of discovery can begin right here in this book, where we will look at making magic with many different types of animals. While you might want to jump ahead to Part II and the specific chapters about the animals who live with you or who you often come in contact with, I encourage you to explore all the chapters. You will find spells, recipes, and rituals that can be adapted to your familiar, and along the way you might discover an amazing new friend who is waiting to make magic with you.

CHAPTER 3

Communing with Your Animal Familiar

The most magical part of having an animal familiar might be building a relationship with them. Like any good friend, developing that relationship means talking, sharing, and getting to know one another. Communing means communicating, but it also means something more. You can communicate with your dog by giving them commands to roll over, and they can bark to communicate that the delivery person is dropping off a package, but that isn't *communing*.

Communing is something more immersive. It is a heart connection, a dance that you have when you fall in love. Communing is found not just in romantic love but also the feeling between a parent and a child, seeing your best friend after a long absence, or discovering a beloved teacher or mentor. Communing is communication plus heart connection. It is building a community of two.

The goal of this chapter is to help you develop this true fellowship with your familiar.

Listening to Your Familiar

If your familiar is a domestic animal, then they have already trained you to understand them to some degree: "This noise means I'm hungry," "The way I am looking at you means I want to go outside," and so on. You have already started the process of deepening communion with your familiar by getting inside their head. Animals think in some ways that are different than ours and in other ways that are not so different. Our familiars have the same basic needs for food and safety that we all do. However, like people, they have differing needs for companionship and connection, depending on their species and their individual personality.

Pay attention to the cycles that your familiar moves through and honor them. When are they most active? When do they need some alone time? Meeting their needs and creating routines can help both you and your familiar to find a special rhythm. If you feed them at the same time every day, for example, it can give your familiar a sense of security and connection to you.

If you are paying attention, you may also learn to read some more subtle messages. Rather than automatically assuming that a growl is aggression, see if there is something else going on. Was your familiar startled? Are they in pain? Are they annoyed? Rather than interpret the communication at face value, double-check to get a more refined interpretation.

Heart Connection Spell with Your Familiar

You and your familiar will develop an affectionate connection that begins at the heart. Familiar animals have feelings and can create alliances through these emotions just as you do. This spell is designed for strengthening a bond to a new familiar. If your familiar is a pet, you may already have this heart connection activated, but doing this spell can nurture that love even more.

1. Sit or stand in a place where you can see your familiar.
2. Close your eyes and place your hands over your heart.
3. In your mind's eye, see, sense, or feel your familiar.
4. Focus on the profound feelings of genuine loving emotions that you feel in your heart.
5. Take your hands off your chest and rub them together in front of your heart for about a minute to build energy.
6. Position your hands as if you were holding a radiant ball of light and energy in front of your heart.
7. Feel the energy radiating between your palms and imagine the love in your heart filling up the ball with even more energy. If it's helpful, you can infuse that ball with a color, sound, scent, or

flavor that expresses your love. (Refer to Appendix D for color references.)

8. When you have filled the ball with all the love in your heart, face your hands outward toward your familiar. You may have to take a peek to see where they are, but once you do, close your eyes again and refocus on the ball.
9. Imagine the ball of love and light floating toward your familiar and them receiving this gift of unconditional love from you and letting it infuse their entire being.
10. Now visualize a ball of love, light, and energy forming in front of your familiar.
11. Imagine them gently pushing this ball of light toward your heart.
12. With your hands still facing outward, receive this ball of light and love and hold it in your hands.
13. Place your hands back over your chest as you gently push this energy into your heart. Feel it grow and spread throughout your body and into your aura.
14. If you like, you can repeat this spell a few times in succession, playing a loving game of ball with your familiar, "tossing" it back and forth and amplifying the love and connection each time.

Talking to Your Familiar

To move closer in communion with your familiar, you can begin to speak their language. Just as you can learn "How much does this cost?" and "Where is the toilet?" if you travel to another country, you can learn to speak the basic language of your familiar. You might never get fluent in rat squeals, dog howls, or chicken clucks, but if you meet them at least halfway you will be well on your way to developing a closer connection.

Animals communicate with body language, vocalizations, touch, and scent. If you are cultivating a familiar relationship with an animal who is new to you, start by learning the way that they communicate. Even if you have a longstanding relationship with your familiar, reading books and articles and watching documentaries about your chosen species will open your eyes to new discoveries about how they talk.

Once you have an idea on how they converse, then, if possible, talk to them in their language. For example, I learned that cats "smile" by slowly blinking their eyes. When my cats, Glinda and Ozma, do the slow blink while looking at me, I slow blink right back at them. I like to think of this as our secret way of saying, "I love you." Each species has their own system of sounds and body language that you can use to let them know that they are safe and loved by you.

Open Clear Communication Spell

When you are ready to enhance communication with your familiar, you can do a ritual to facilitate this. For this spell, you will need to prepare some valerian tea. Valerian is an herb used in spells for animal communication. It is also a sedative herb with a strong aroma and taste. It may be best to do this spell before bedtime or when you are able to relax with your familiar. While valerian is considered safe to drink, as with any ingestible herb, please research to make sure it is safe for your particular health conditions. If you have concerns, you may skip the tea and do the rest of the steps.

What you will need:

- 1 teaspoon (2 to 3 g) dried valerian root (*Valeriana officinalis*)
- Mug or teacup
- Tea strainer
- *Optional:* sweetener, lemon, milk, or milk substitute

1. Pour a cup of boiling water over the dried valerian root in your mug or teacup.
2. Hold your hands over the infusion as it is brewing, focus your intention, and recite the following incantation:

Creature of land, of sea, of sky,
Open the mouth, the ear, the eye.
By claw, by paw, by beak, by fin,
Communication now begin.
No matter where they roam or dwell,
Let my familiar hear and tell.
Share your gift of words divine,
And let me understand in kind.

3. Steep for 5 to 10 minutes, and then strain out the root pieces.
4. Valerian root has a strong flavor, so feel free to add sweetener, lemon, milk, or a milk substitute of your choice.
5. Bring a cup of your potion with you as you sit in the presence of your familiar in a calm and peaceful place. This link requires concentration on both your parts, so if your familiar is focused on getting fed, getting outside, or there are other distractions, then take care of these needs first.
6. You don't have to be in physical contact with your familiar, but position yourself so you can see each other. If your familiar is a pet, you might find that they come to sit close to you during this ritual.
7. Drink the potion in their presence without looking directly at them. Direct eye contact is threatening to most animals, and you want them to feel safe with you.
8. Once you have consumed the potion, close your eyes, place your hands in prayer pose over your heart, and feel the energy of the presence of your familiar.
9. In your mind, visualize yourself and your familiar communicating through gentle, loving sound, gesture, and touch.
10. Hold this vision for one to three minutes, and then gently open your eyes.

11. Observe your familiar. If they are looking at you, you have created a successful link. They know that they can send and receive communication from you. If they are looking elsewhere or have left during the ritual, they are indicating that they don't have the focus to do this work at this time. Don't get discouraged. You can try again another day. For some animals it takes several requests before they can find their own communication link to you.

Psychic Communication

Many people who develop animal relationships discover, sometimes by chance, that they are also able to communicate with their familiar through psychic channels. If you have not had a spontaneous psychic connection with your familiar, don't drop into disbelief and say, "Oh, that's for pet psychics. I could never do that." The truth is that we all have the ability to communicate with animals if we are willing to turn that gift on. If you have never received psychic communication from your familiar or have found your connection to be spotty and inconsistent, try these techniques for activating the channel between the two of you.

Calming the Rational Mind

The rational mind is amazing. It helps us solve problems, create masterpieces, and communicate our ideas to other humans. The rational mind is less helpful when it comes to tapping into intuition and receiving subtle psychic messages.

I like to think of intuition as a soft, gentle whisperer and the rational mind as a big, blustering bellower. If your rational mind is engaged with its loud, shouty voice, it is impossible to hear the gentle whisper of your psychic self.

To begin to tap into your intuition, you first need to learn how to dial down the volume of the rational mind. One way of doing this is to practice meditation. By learning the skill of refocusing your thought onto your breath, you'll create that quiet space that will allow your psychic hits to come through even when you are not actively in meditation. If you have not yet practiced meditation, starting with a simple guided breath meditation will be the training wheels to help you learn this skill of quieting the mind.

Pendulum Ritual for Communication

If you don't have experience using your psychic senses, I recommend building those muscles by working with a pendulum. Use the technique described in "Pendulum Ritual to Divine Your Familiar" in Chapter 2; however, instead of asking your spirit guides for information, ask your familiar to communicate through this method. Before asking questions, say, "I invite my [species of animal] familiar, [name of familiar, if they have one], to communicate with me through this pendulum and give me clear, helpful, and accurate answers to my questions."

It is ideal if you can sit close to your familiar or sit in the environment that your familiar lives in as you work with your pendulum; however, if that is not possible, close your eyes and see, sense, or feel the presence of your familiar before you begin.

Ask your familiar to show you a yes and then ask it to show you a no, and note the different ways the pendulum swings for the two answers. Once you have established this, you can ask your familiar questions. As you build your psychic awareness through other modalities, you can also use the pendulum to confirm answers that you are unsure of or to bring clarity to fuzzy messages.

Meet "the Clairs"

The next step to developing an extrasensory connection to your familiar is to learn your psychic modality. When I was a young witchling back in the pre-Internet days, the only psychic modality that anyone talked about was clairvoyance. Clairvoyance is the ability to see psychic information in your mind's eye. Back then, although I had difficulty seeing images in my mind, I sure as heck had an inner knowing when something was off or right on the money. I would get goosebumps when I got a hunch about something, and I could even get verbal messages in what I called "my mind's ear." It wasn't until years later that I learned that these were also ways that one could get psychic information. Now we have names for what people commonly call "the clairs":

- **clairvoyance:** seeing images in the mind's eye
- **clairaudience:** hearing in the mind's ear
- **clairsentience:** receiving physical sensations in response to psychic phenomena
- **claircognizance:** inner knowing

- **clairalience:** receiving psychic information through phantom smells
- **clairgustance:** receiving information through phantom tastes
- **clairempathy:** the ability to pick up psychic emotional information
- **clairtangency:** receiving information through the sense of touch

With this wide buffet of psychic possibilities, you probably have a sense of which one you already know how to do. If you're not quite sure, ask yourself, "When I have a hunch about something, how do I know?" The answer is right there.

Receiving Psychic Communication Ritual

Once you have discovered your clair, then you know the easiest way to receive messages from your familiar. Most animals are strong clairvoyants, clairsentients, and clairempaths. Look to your familiar's natural physical strengths to guide you as to what their other clairs might be. A dog with a powerful sense of smell is likely to have the gift of clairalience. Your super touch-attuned tarantula is undoubtedly a clairtangent. The magic of psychic communication is that it can automatically be translated. So, while your familiar probably doesn't speak human language (unless they are a parrot), their messages can get translated into any of the clairs, including clairaudience. While you are learning to receive psychic communication, it's important to quiet the rational mind and let your psychic senses take the floor.

1. Set the intention of receiving messages from your familiar.
2. Close your eyes and place your hands over your heart or in prayer pose, palm to palm, in front of your heart.
3. In your mind or out loud, say the following or put it into your own words: "My mind, heart, and body are open to receive clear and helpful messages from my familiar."
4. When you are ready, open your eyes and begin the process of connecting. If you are clairtangent, and it's safe to touch your familiar, you may make physical contact with them.
5. If you can observe the rhythm of your familiar's breathing pattern, work to match your breathing to theirs. If they are panting or breathing quickly, you can breathe in half time, inhaling for one (or more) of their inhale-exhale cycles and exhaling for the second round. Focus on breathing in rhythm and just being present with your familiar. If you can't observe your familiar's breath pattern, then just bring your breath to a slow and rhythmic pattern of your own.
6. When your mind feels calm and focused, ask your familiar a question aloud and then bring your attention back to the breath.
7. Avoid forcing thoughts or trying to elicit communication from them. Hold this space for several minutes.

8. If your familiar has something to communicate to you, you'll get a sudden ping—a vision or words in your head, goosebumps or shivers, a flood of emotion, or an interesting phantom smell or taste. If you don't get a message after several minutes, it doesn't mean that you are doing it wrong. Your familiar may not have an answer at the moment. You can try again at a later time.

When you get a message, you may need to interpret it. Sometimes psychic messages are direct and at other times they can be symbolic. You might see a classical musician dressed in green playing a violin in your mind's eye, but your chicken may be telling you, "I'm hungry for some grasshoppers." If you are unsure what the message means, I recommend writing it down in an animal communication journal. Never disregard a message, even if it seems confusing in the moment. Writing it down will help you remember the message, and you may have an aha moment hours or even days later when your familiar's psychic communication suddenly makes sense.

Sending Psychic Communication Ritual

Once you are able to receive psychic transmissions, you are ready to start sending your familiar messages. Some of the easiest messages to send are messages about treats. If your familiar has a favorite food or activity, use your own strongest clair to convey that message to them. Visualize holding out some food treats for them or imagine the smell of the grass where they like to play, for example. Hold this psychic message for a minute or two, if possible, and observe your familiar's response. If you can practice this when your familiar is out of sight, you'll probably find that they come around. Be sure to reinforce the psychic message by giving them the treat that you promised.

When you talk to your familiar with normal human speech, you are also sending psychic messages to them. You can supercharge your verbal messages by adding your clair as you speak. When you get ready to give your familiar a treat but before you show the treat to them, say something such as, "I've got something for you that you are going to love," without showing them or indicating what it is. Then see, sense, or feel the joy of giving and your familiar receiving for about a minute before you give it to them. Keep doing this before you give them a treat, and your familiar will learn that this psychic message means a treat is coming and they will respond simply to the thought.

As you get more adept at sending messages, you can call a pet familiar home if they go wandering, or call a wild familiar to you when you are out in nature.

Tarot or Oracle Communication

If you are struggling to understand what your familiar is trying to communicate to you, you may want to use oracle or tarot cards to get a clearer picture. For the clearest messages, choose a deck that centers around animals or highlights the species of your familiar. For some suggestions, check out "Card Ritual to Divine Your Familiar" in Chapter 2.

If your familiar is a wild animal, bring the cards to their habitat to do this reading. If your familiar is a pet, do this reading when they can be nearby.

Shuffle, cut, and lay out four cards in front of you. The cards will relay the following messages:

- **Card 1:** what your familiar is trying to tell you
- **Card 2:** what your familiar is feeling or desires most
- **Card 3:** what your familiar needs most from you at this time
- **Card 4:** what you can do to help your familiar

Dream Communication

Your familiar can also communicate with you through dreams. When you are sleeping, the resistance that your rational mind can put up is lowered. You are wide open to receive messages from your familiar in detailed ways that might not be available to you in waking life. Pay attention to any dreams in which your familiar appears and make note of the circumstances.

- Did they say anything psychically or verbally?
- In what location did the dream take place?
- Was the mood happy or anxious?

All these small clues can be messages that your familiar is trying to send to you. You may have to interpret the symbols in your dreams just as you do the other psychic messages that your familiar sends to you.

Familiar Dream Potion

If you have trouble remembering your dreams when you wake up, try this dreamwork spell right before you go to sleep. For this spell you will need to prepare some mugwort tea. Mugwort is a bitter herb used in spells to open psychic ability and invite vivid dreams. While mugwort is considered safe to drink, as with any ingestible herb, please research to make sure it is safe for your particular health conditions.

What you will need:

- 1 teaspoon (2 to 3 g) of dried mugwort (*Artemesia vulgaris*) leaves
- Mug or teacup
- Tea strainer
- *Optional:* sweetener, lemon, milk, or milk substitute
- Dream journal or recording device

1. Pour a cup of boiling water over the mugwort in your mug or teacup.
2. Hold your hands over the infusion as it is brewing. Focus your intention and recite the following incantation:

   Nighttime sky and bright moonbeam,
   Open up my mind to dreams.
   What I do and what I say
   Can be recalled at break of day.

3. Steep for 5 to 10 minutes, then strain out the leaves. Leaving the potion to steep longer will

give it a stronger flavor but will not change the power of the potion.

4. Mugwort has a bitter flavor, so feel free to add sweetener, lemon, milk, or a milk substitute of your choice.
5. Drink the tea and set your dream journal or recording device next to your bed so that you can record what you remember when you awaken.

Don't worry if you don't have a dream featuring your familiar the first time. It may take your familiar a while to connect to you in the dream realm and send a message. Keep trying and you will link up.

Animals Who Are in Spirit Form

Once you have touched on communicating with animal familiars in physical form, you can begin to communicate with familiars in spirit form. A spirit familiar can be an animal who you connected to in life that has since passed to the spirit realm, a guardian spirit that you have only had a connection to in the ethereal realm, or an animal mother spirit that you can connect with to protect your familiar. Each of these spirit-form animals has their own unique vibration and special ways to communicate and connect.

Communication Rituals for Animals Who Have Passed

When a familiar, pet, or animal companion leaves their physical form and moves on to the spiritual realm, the love for them doesn't end. You can still connect to the spirit of your animal, which is still vibrant and alive and in a state of pure positive energy. If they had emotional, mental, or physical ailments, they are completely free from those mundane concerns. An animal spirit is their pure essence and their personality without any of their problems, no matter how debilitating. It doesn't matter how long they have been on the other side, even if it has been decades, your animal friend desires the connection and would love to hear from you.

If your animal has recently passed and you are feeling deep grief, you might long with all your heart to receive messages from them. However, these stirred-up emotions can actually be a hindrance to connecting clearly. If this is the case, you might want to consult with a medium or pet psychic who can be a clear and calm channel for your animal spirit or wait until your own emotions have settled a bit. Do the Help Your Familiar Transition Spell in Chapter 5 to connect with them and help heal your own grief.

There are ways that you can know that your animal in spirit form wants to connect to you. You may hear their distinctive vocalizations even though there is no animal of that kind around. Likewise, you might hear their footsteps, wing flaps, or other movement that are distinctly theirs. You might see a flash of them out of the corner of your eye or smell their scent. And, just like living familiars, they may visit you in your dreams. You can use any of the techniques above to receive and send messages to your animal who has passed or try automatic writing or automatic drawing from Chapter 5 as another option for receiving messages from them.

Animal Guides

It is indeed possible to have a close connection to an animal who is totally spirit and has never been a part of your life in physical form. Animal guides can be animals who exist only in the ethereal realm, but you can still call on them to protect, guide, teach, and share energy with you. They are remarkably similar to what are referred to as *power animals* in core shamanism; however, you don't need to be a shamanic practitioner to connect to your animal guide.

You may already be aware of your animal guide. They may have appeared to you in meditations, dreams, or visions. They may be a common animal from your locale, an exotic animal who comes from a land far from where you live, an animal who has sadly become extinct on earth, or even a mythological creature that has never existed on the earthly plane.

If you have not yet met your animal guide but would like to, you can do so by having a session with a shamanic practitioner who performs power animal retrieval or do it yourself by going on a vision journey.

Animal Guide Vision Journey

Approach this journey without any preconceived notion as to which animal will come forward for you. All the most enlightening and special magic leaves space open for the best possibilities. Trust that you will be matched with the perfect animal to teach, guide, and guard you.

1. Create a safe and comfortable place and time for your vision journey. Make sure that you can be seated or lie down comfortably and that you

won't be disturbed. If it helps you to turn inward and go deeper, put on some instrumental meditation music.

2. Set the intention for meeting your animal guide.
3. See, sense, or feel yourself in front of a door leading to the outside world.
4. Open the door and envision yourself stepping into a natural space, such as a garden, desert, jungle, swamp, forest, seashore, mountains, or park.
5. Walk through the area, exploring the landscape around you. The landscape may change as you go on your walk, for example, from forest to desert or garden to seashore.
6. You will start to meet animals on your journey. You may interact with them and get to know them or just watch them as you are passing by.
7. When you have encountered the same animal three times, ask them if they are your animal guide.
8. If they say no, then keep walking and observing the animals that appear until you see another one appear three times. Then ask that one the same question.
9. Once an animal says yes, invite them to climb up into your arms or move beside you. Make your way back through the landscape and through the door.
10. Open your eyes and record your vision journey in a journal or grimoire.

Your guardian animal can meet with you any time you want to do a vision journey. Simply step through the door and meet your guardian animal in their habitat. They can teach you about magic and the animal kingdom and even be an intermediary between you and the animals you encounter in the mundane world.

Communicating with Familiar Mother Spirits

Familiar mother spirits are the nurturing, caretaking quintessence of any animal who lives on earth. In some traditions, this ethereal spirit is called an *oversoul*. For humans, we might call this oversoul *creator, great spirit, goddess,* or *god.* However, each creature on earth has an oversoul that guides and protects the animals of that species. So, for example, all sparrows share the same sparrow mother spirit who guides and nurtures them.

One of the reasons you might want to connect to the mother spirit is to protect an animal who is in danger or distress. If you spot a wild animal who is in trouble, such as a coyote running along a freeway, you can call on the coyote mother spirit to guide that coyote to safety. Likewise, if you know an exterminator is coming to remove a nest of wasps, you can ask the wasp mother spirit to get them to move to a safer, less-populated location before the exterminator comes. The mother spirit will direct them, but each animal has their own free will and may or may not want to follow those directions. However, the mother spirit can intervene when it is not safe for you to do so, and she can do so more effectively.

Your animal familiar in the physical world also has a mother spirit, and you can call on her to bless and protect them. If your animal is lost, you can call on the mother spirit to guide them home. When your animal is going to the vet, you can call on her to calm and assist in healing them. If your animal is unsupervised or unprotected at any time, you can call on the mother spirit to keep them out of trouble.

Communing with an Animal Spirit

With an animal familiar in the physical world, you can spend time with them to build your relationship. The same is true of animal spirits. You might not be able to pet them or give them treats, but these relationships still need attention and reciprocity to thrive. If you want to deepen your connection to any animal spirit, whether an animal guide, mother spirit, or an animal who has passed on, there are many ways to nurture that relationship.

- Research your animal spirit. Read books and news articles, watch documentaries, and learn about their exceptional gifts. Even if your animal spirit is of a species that you have been around your entire life, there are new discoveries made every day about your animal and you can always learn more.
- Create an altar to your animal spirit and decorate it with photos, artwork, and figurines of your animal. (See "Familiar Altars," page 60, for more detail.) If the animal was formerly a pet or you had contact with them in real life, you can place items on it that hold their essence, such as a collar, toy, tuft of fur, feather, or even their cremated ashes. These can help you link up to your animal's spirit.

- When you wake up in the morning and before you go to bed at night, honor your animal spirit and invite them to walk, slither, swim, or fly beside you. Simple phrases such as, "Good morning, hedgehog. Thank you for walking beside me throughout my day," in the morning and "Thank you for walking beside me during the day and joining me in my dreams," at night will activate more contact with your animal spirit.
- If your animal spirit has a real-world counterpart, perform acts of reciprocity. Donate to an animal rescue of that species, work to preserve the environment where they live, or leave offerings of healthy food, flowers, or other safe biodegradable items in their natural habitat.

The Magic of Communion

When you are working on developing a close relationship with another human, you spend time with them to empathize and understand each other. Building that connection with your familiar or an animal spirit is no different except that you must use means beyond human speech. While it may seem daunting at first, if you are willing to persist and have patience, you will discover that you can blur the lines of where you end and your animal begins. You will reach the mystical state called *communion.*

CHAPTER 4

Making Magic with Your Animal Familiar

One of the most exciting ways that you can work with your familiar is to invite them to make magic with you. Inviting your familiar to be by your side, literally or figuratively, as you do your magic can exponentially increase the power of your spells. It can also lend you energies and strengths that can compensate for areas that you have not yet developed and bring the two of you even closer together in friendship.

The keyword here is *inviting*. You are not commanding your familiar to work with you if they don't want to. This applies not only to asking them to be your familiar, but also to individual rituals and spells. Don't assume that a familiar is going to want to be a part of every single magical thing that you do. They may have the good judgment to know that they are not the right ally for every type of magic or just may be uninterested in the work that you are doing. Even an animal familiar that is eager to make magic with you in general might not want to be a part of every single spell and ritual that you do. Always ask and invite every time you would like your familiar's help and companionship, but, likewise, always give them grace if they decline, and don't take it personally if they do.

Working with Altars

When you see the term *altar* in this book, it is usually used to denote what is known as a *general* altar. This is a sacred focal point for your intentions, often decorated with symbolic and meaningful magical objects.

Another type of altar is the working altar, which is a sacred worktable used for putting together spells, often set up only temporarily. A working altar doesn't have to be an area dedicated for doing magic only. Even a kitchen table can become a working altar if you clear it off and put down a pretty tablecloth or some other sign to mark this space as special to you for the duration of the spell. The point is that you set up a space and time to focus on your spell. (In this book, you'll set up a working altar in Help Your Familiar Transition Spell and Otter Crystal Cleansing Spell.)

Familiar Altars

Making a general altar dedicated to your familiar is one way that you can honor them. To create an altar doesn't require elaborate or expensive equipment. You probably have most of what you need on hand and the rest can be easily sourced.

1. Start by finding a place for your altar—a small end table, a shelf, or even a windowsill can serve as an altar space. Wherever and however you set up your altar, make sure that it is a space solely dedicated to your familiar and not the table by the front door where you drop your keys and mail.

2. Place a tablecloth, scarf, or shawl over the altar. If you can find one in colors that match your familiar or has a print featuring your animal, all the better.

3. Place an image of your familiar on the altar. It can be a statuette, a candle shaped like your familiar, a drawing, or a photo of them in a frame.

4. Place offerings on your altar. Candles, crystals, and water are all appropriate offerings. You can add a plant, flowers, or dried herbs that are liked by your familiar and safe for them. (*Safety Note:* Please do your research. Some common plants that are safe for humans are dangerous for animals. Unless your animal has absolutely no chance of coming in contact with the plant, always err on the side of caution. The next section delves more deeply into animal familiar offerings.)

5. Spend time in meditation near your altar anytime you are going to work magically with your familiar. Take care of your altar by keeping greenery and water fresh.

Safety Notes: If you are using a candle or incense, light it only when you're at home and awake. If you leave or go to sleep, put the candle on pause by snuffing it out rather than blowing it out; you can relight it when you return or awaken. If you have a familiar at home who loves to get very involved in your magic, you may want to invest in a decorative metal birdcage that you can put burning incense or candle spells in and keep your familiar at a safe distance.

Animal Familiar Offerings

Magic practitioners in the most ancient times, and in some cultures more recently, had quite an interdependent relationship with animals. Hunter-gatherers relied on animals to inform them about the weather, counted on them to help find food, and, of course, depended on them to be a source of food themselves. Hunting was a laborious and intensive process and so all parts of the animal were respectfully used in both magical and mundane ways. Sacred rituals were performed that connected the spirit of the animal to the hunter, and seers would divine where the hunted animals could be found.

As some societies became agricultural, people relied less on hunting and gathering and more on raising animals and crops for their food and materials. Up until the Industrial Era, animal parts were still treated as valuable, even if the animals themselves became increasingly mistreated. Now, in our modern technological age, we are so disconnected from the process of death of all kinds that animal parts are a commodity that people rarely think about. Not everyone with a familiar works with animal offerings in their magic, but if you do, it can be a meaningful and respectful way to connect to the ancestral spirit of your familiar.

Wild and domestic creatures can offer gifts to you. In the case of corvids like crows and ravens, they may bring you objects that they find in the hopes that you will feed them. If you do develop a familiar relationship with an animal who brings you gifts, you can look at the symbolism of the objects that they bring you and interpret them as omens. But these aren't the only type of offerings that wild animals can leave. Antlers, fur, feathers, and skin sheds, for example, can be a way that an animal expresses its interest in working with you. Even coming across the remains of an animal who has died can be the way that another animal from that species is sending you a sign.

When you find these artifacts, you can notice them and leave them be or, if it is safe and legal where you are, you can collect them and add them to your familiar spells. Please note that some places require special permits for collecting things as seemingly harmless as a dropped feather. (Of special note is the Migratory Bird Treaty Act, which prohibits the possession of feathers and other parts of more than 1,000 species of birds without a permit.) These rules are in place to protect both you and the animals, so it's worthwhile to research the laws where you live.

If the remains are gathered ethically by you and cause no harm to you or a living animal, they can be considered a gift and can be used in your magic. Purchasing animal parts is not a gift and will do little to connect you to that species.

It goes without saying that killing an animal to use their body parts in magic is cruel and unnecessary. A spell ingredient from an animal should always be a gift from them. No spell is worth taking the life of another being. Furthermore, it sets up a very unbalanced relationship between you and that species, which is detrimental to building a familiar bond. Does that mean you can't wear snakeskin boots if your animal familiar is a snake? That is for you and your snake familiar to decide. Personally, unless the snake died of natural causes and you made the boots yourself, I believe it has an air of disrespect.

The Symbolism of Different Offerings

Whenever you work with animal offerings, first honor the animal who delivered the gift to you. A simple heartfelt "thank you" as you hold the item is all that is necessary, but you may feel inspired to continue to hold the item and meditate on the essence of the animal. What are their qualities? Is it a tuft of fur from an agile mountain goat who can scamper up sheer cliffs, or an antler from a courageous buck who is willing to stand up for what he wants? Reflect on how the animal can lend you their unique qualities.

You can also think about the part of the animal and what purpose it serves and apply that symbolism to your work with that offering as well.

- **Antlers/Horns:** represent masculine energy in some species, defense, fertility, growth, competition, status, and higher consciousness
- **Bones:** represent the element of earth as well as longevity, structure, support, and ancestry. Individual bones can also represent the purpose

of that body part, such as skulls symbolizing thoughts and the mind, and toe bones meaning mobility and agility

- **Claws:** represent defense, hunting, grooming, grasping, and digging
- **Fur:** represents warmth, expression, camouflage, protection, and insulation
- **Feathers:** represent the element of air, flight, travel, adornment, communication, and freedom
- **Sheds:** represent transformation, growth, change, rebirth, evolution, and healing
- **Shells:** represent the element of water (if from water animals), home, shielding, armor, fertility, safe passage, emotions, and memories
- **Teeth:** represent bravery, nourishment, defense, industriousness, and creativity
- **Whiskers:** represent psychic senses, information gathering, and enlightened awareness

Animal Offering Magic

Once you have attuned to the essence of your animal offerings, you can get creative and use them in your spells and rituals. There are many ways that you can bring these into your spiritual practice and strengthen your familiar tie or borrow the energy of your familiar animal.

Altar Items from Animal Offerings

Animal offerings can be displayed on an altar, either on your general altar or your familiar altar. If you have many offerings, you can even create familiar offering grids, arranging bones, horns, antlers, feathers, shells, teeth, and claws in a meaningful pattern. Beautiful arrangements of grids can be created for a particular manifestation, such as healing, protection, or a deeper connection with your familiar. (View the illustration here for inspiration, or look up the mandala-like patterns used in crystal grids.)

Mixing crystals and animal offerings can make beautiful altar focal points for meditation or manifestation. Each item can amplify the power of the others, creating a customized visual spell that can be infused with your wishes and intentions. See Appendix C for crystals to consider incorporating into your practice.

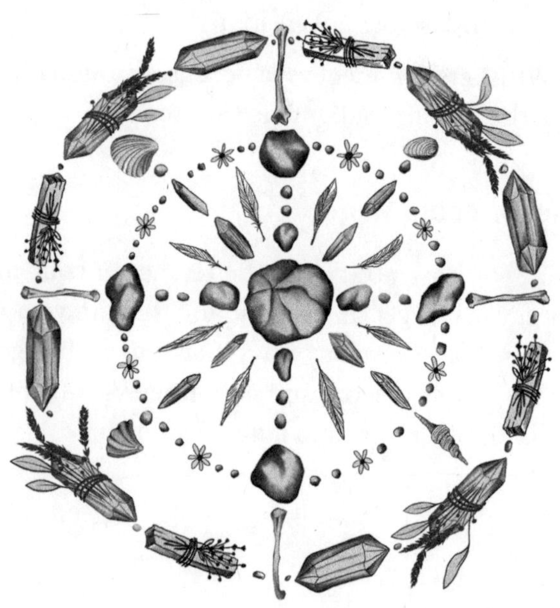

Ritual Adornments from Animal Offerings

Feathers, bones, claws, shells, and teeth can be made into ritual adornments. Claws, teeth, and small bones can be drilled or wrapped in jewelry wire and turned into necklaces, bracelets, and earrings that can be worn in rituals to connect to your animal familiar. Feathers can be turned into earrings, ear cuffs, or hair ornaments. Antlers, horns, and fur pelts can be turned into hats or capes for shapeshifting or Otherworld walking. Wool, fur, or hair can be felted or spun and woven, knitted, crocheted, or crafted into clothing to connect you deeply to your familiar.

Ritual Tools from Animal Offerings

Antlers, horns, and larger bones can be turned into magical tools such as wands, knife handles, or candle holders. Antlers and horns can be crafted as hooks for hanging ritual clothing or, if you have many antlers, a wreath that can imbue your space with protection, success, and fertility. Skulls and shells can be used as bowls for offerings or burning incense. Feathers can be used singly or made into a fan to spiritually cleanse the auric field or for fanning incense or herb smoke. Larger feathers can easily be turned into quills for writing petitions or crafting sigils.

Ritual Instruments from Animal Offerings

It is believed that the earliest recorded musical instruments were created so that humans could imitate the sounds of birds and other animals. Ancient people also made these first instruments from animal parts, so working with animal offerings to make music not only connects us to our animal familiar but also to our most ancient ancestors. Hollow bird bones can be made into flutes, pipes, and whistles. Horns and large shells, like conch shells, can be fashioned into musical horns. Animal skins can be stretched over frames and turned into drums. Larger bones and antlers can be made into drum beaters or hit together like claves. Jawbones with loose teeth, rattlesnake rattles, shells, horns, toenails, and hooves can be turned into rattles and noisemakers.[1]

Divination Sets from Animal Offerings

Smaller hard artifacts, such as bones, shells, teeth, and claws, can be gathered and turned into a bone reading set. Bone reading requires casting a random handful of these items onto a cloth and divining by seeing which items were chosen, the position in which they land, and which items are touching one another. Each artifact has a symbolic meaning, based on the essence of the animal it comes from and what the artifact is. For example, a bear claw would carry the essence of the bear (protectiveness, attunement to seasonal cycles, courage) and the symbolism of the claw (defense, hunting, and digging). If a bear claw showed up in a bone reading, it could mean, for example, defending your right to hibernate for a while.

Bones, horns, and antlers can be cut and carved to make rune sets—either Norse runes, ogham, witches' runes, or any other cleromancy system.

Charm Bags from Animal Offerings

Bones, claws, teeth, and shells can be added to charm bags that are carried in a pocket or purse when working with your familiar or calling on their energy.

Spell Ingredients from Animal Offerings

Scraps of hair, fur, and other small artifacts can be kept in jars or vials and used in spells to invite the energy of your familiar. They can be burned along with incense, sprinkled around a spell candle, added to a charm bag, or simply displayed in the jar to share their energy.

Inviting Your Animal Familiar to Ritual

Whether you are casting a circle, lighting a candle for a spell, or taking out your tarot cards for a reading, you can invite your animal familiar to join you and lend their energy to your magic. For many witches, they find that their familiars just show up whenever they are doing these activities, but if you'd like to make the partnership a little more focused, you can invite them to your ritual.

Before you begin your ritual, communicate what you are working on to your animal. I like to speak out loud to my cat familiar, Glinda, and tell her what I will be working on, but you can also send and receive psychic messages in any of the ways described in Chapter 3. I recommend telling them the type of magic that you will be working on, the magical goal, why you think they might be helpful, and then inviting them. For example, I might say, "I am going to be doing a candle spell to protect our house from negative energy. I know you are really great at protecting yourself with your claws and you have a great psychic ability to sense energies, so I'd like to invite you to do this work alongside me and lend your energy to a spell we do together."

After making your request, look for a sign of agreement. This is where understanding how your animal communicates can come in handy. In the case of my cat, she will look at me and do a slow blink and hang around while I prepare the spell to let me know that she would like to be involved. If she walks away from me or something else catches her attention, then I know that she is not going to work with me on this.

If your familiar is disengaged, you can either proceed with the spell by yourself or wait till later and ask them again. It's okay to be less formal and use less detail when asking for the second time. If the spell is not urgent, I will often wait a day or two, then say something like, "Hey, Glinda. Would you like to do that house protection spell with me now?" and look for her answer. I may go as far as to ask three times, but if she says no every time, I gracefully accept the fact that this is a spell that I need to do on my own.

When doing a spell with a pet familiar, you can perform your rituals in the home that the two of you share. If you're working with a farm animal, you can do your magic out where they live, but you might have to get creative and use common sense to adapt certain steps to the situation. It's easy to do a candle spell at home, but I wouldn't recommend it in a barn full of flammable hay. If I wanted to do a candle spell with a horse familiar, for example, I might bring the unlit candle to the stable, ask my familiar to lend their energy, and then take the candle back inside for the rest of the ritual. Some curious indoor familiars may want to get too close to a burning candle, so make sure to keep it at a safe distance from them or put it in a decorative birdcage to keep them both safe.

When working with a wild animal familiar, you will have to get even more inventive. You might not see them every time you venture into their habitat. If you are going to ask your fox familiar to lend their magic to your tarot reading, take your deck into the woods every time you go out. When you spot the fox, be prepared to ask them to bless your cards and see what they have to say. In most cases, if they run away, they are not interested in helping. If they stop and look at you, even for a moment, they are sharing their energy with you.

Whenever you receive the help of your familiar, always have the good manners to thank them. You can simply touch your heart and say, "thank you," or send them a psychic message of gratitude. If you want to thank them in a bigger way, you can give them a treat of some kind. Make sure it is healthy for your animal familiar and something that is special. Of course, most animals appreciate a delicious tidbit but, depending on your familiar, it may be something else, such as taking them for an extra-long walk or some playtime together. Giving them this treat will strengthen the bond between you two, but it will also create a positive association with making magic with you and may make your familiar more eager to help you again in the future.

Exchanging Energy with Your Familiar

Don't just ask your familiar to lend their energy to your spells and rituals; you can exchange magical energy on a regular basis. An energy exchange is a meaningful way to build your bond and connect more profoundly. They can activate and accelerate the discovery of your spiritual gifts, enlighten you as to what you were meant to accomplish in this lifetime, impart wisdom, and help give you insights into spiritual truths. They can allow you to tap into the Anima Mundi, the world soul and the connection between all living things. They can bring you to a higher vibration and move you closer to alignment with your highest and deepest selves. Best of all, energy exchanges can activate blessings of all kinds for you and your animal familiars.

Before doing your first energy exchange, make sure your mood is positive and you feel invigorated and ready to share. Check in with yourself to make sure you're not hungry, tired, ill, or feeling emotionally, physically, or spiritually depleted. After you have made many energy exchanges with your familiar, you can turn to them when you need cheering up or a second wind from time to time, but it's a good idea to have a balanced energy exchange in most sessions. (And balanced energy is an absolute must when you are just starting this practice.)

Make sure that you set aside expectations about your sessions. Approach each one with openness, allowing it to unfold in its own way.

Physical Energy Exchange with Your Familiar

If you have a familiar that enjoys physical touch, then this is one of the easiest methods of creating an energy exchange.

In fact, if you have an animal who you pet, scratch, or gently tickle, then you are already doing a rudimentary energy exchange. You can magically amp up your cuddle time by adding the following elements:

1. Before beginning a physical energy exchange session, turn off all distractions, such as your phone, computer, or television, so that you can be totally focused on your familiar.
2. Get clear about what you would like to receive. For example, "I would like to develop my creative gifts."
3. Position yourself near your familiar and invite them to come as close as they would like.
4. Discover what your familiar would like to receive. Most often it is something simple such as unconditional love, protection, or a closer connection with you. You can ask and receive the message using some of the techniques discussed in Chapter 3.
5. Communicate with your familiar, letting them know what energy you are going to offer and what energy you would like to receive.
6. Stroke and pet them, paying attention to the signals they give you that tell you what they like.
7. Remember the maxim: "Energy flows where attention goes." Keep your attention on your familiar, always bringing your focus back to what energy you are giving them. If you find your mind wandering, gently tell your familiar what you are giving them to help you maintain focus.

8. When your familiar falls asleep or gets up, the session is done. Some familiars will take all the loving touch that you offer, so if you are getting tired, you can also wrap things up.
9. Thank your familiar for the energy that you received and for your wonderful relationship.
10. *Optional:* If you know animal massage or reiki, these can easily be added to enhance this practice. See the Dog Familiar Blessing Massage in Chapter 8 for guidance that can be adapted to your familiar.

Spiritual Energy Exchange with Your Familiar

If you are not able to physically touch your familiar, then doing a spiritual energy exchange is the perfect way to deepen your connection. This method can be done when your familiar animal is far away, you can't be close to them, or they don't want to be touched.

1. Just as with a physical energy exchange, create a quiet, distraction-free environment. Focus on what you would like to receive, and determine what your familiar would like to receive.
2. Using psychic communication techniques, let your familiar know what energy you are going to offer to them and what energy you would like to receive from them.
3. If it is possible to sit close to them, doing so can help with your focus. For example, you can't hold a fish familiar, but you can sit close to their tank.

4. Close your eyes and in your mind's eye, see, sense, or feel your animal familiar. Visualize their heart radiating a golden light.
5. Visualize your own heart filling up with a bright golden light that radiates toward your familiar heart.
6. As these light beams between your two hearts meet, visualize a pulse going from you to your familiar, then a pulse going back from your familiar to you.
7. Keep moving this pulse back and forth for as long as you like.
8. When you are finished, open your eyes and thank your familiar for the energy that you received and for your wonderful relationship.

Familiars and the Spirit Realm

One of the things that familiars excel at is sensing the spirit realms. Many animals have finely attuned senses that surpass our basic human ones. These supersenses can also help them to notice the spirits that live around us, even when we can't sense them.

Learning to understand your familiar's language will be helpful in interpreting the spirits around you. Are they staring off into space? Playing with an imaginary friend? Barking at nothing? Fearful to go into a room? You can look at these clues as messages from your familiar about the spirits that are nearby. If you understand their communication style, you can interpret whether spirits around you are friendly or tricky.

Just as search-and-rescue teams offer their tracking animals positive reinforcement when they find clues, you can reward your familiar every time they alert you to something. This treat can be food, attention, play, or whatever motivates them. Rewards will let them know that you are interested in having them tell you about the spirit activity they detect.

If you find your familiar focusing their attention on what appears to be empty space, take a photo of the area that they are looking at. Often, these photos will show orbs, shadows, mist, and other spirit phenomena. If you are a ghost hunter, you can also set up recording devices or any other equipment to confirm what your familiar is sensing.

Exorcising an Unwanted Spirit

Once your familiar alerts you to the presence of a spirit, you can decide what to do about it. There are good spirits who you may want to have around, such as an ancestor, a guardian spirit, or a house spirit. There are other spirits who are neutral, for example, a spirit who inhabited the house but is like a gentle invisible roommate. And there are other spirits who may be disruptive or problematic. If you come across any spirit who is unwanted, you and your familiar can work together to get them to move along.

What you will need:

- 1 teaspoon (2 to 3 g) dried angelica root (*Angelica archangelica)*
- Wide-mouthed jar
- Fresh branch of juniper, sage, blackberry, fern, or pine
- Hand bell

1. Pour a cup of boiling water over the dried angelica root in a wide-mouthed jar. (*Safety note:* Be sure to use *Angelica archangelica*, which is safe for humans and animals. *Aralia spinosa* is toxic to cats, dogs, and horses.)
2. Allow to steep at least 10 minutes. When cool, bring your infusion, branch, and bell to the area where you suspect the spirit is hanging out.
3. When your familiar alerts you to the location of the unwanted spirit, dip the branch in the infusion and flick the water in the direction of the spirit, saying the following incantation:

Begone, O spirit, from this plane.
There is nothing here for you to gain.
In the world of the living, you must not stay.
I send you with light upon your way.
Out the door and through the glass,
To the other side you must pass.
Good-bye, farewell, the time is at hand,
And be you well in the Summerland.

4. Once you have sprinkled the area, ring the bell three times to seal the spell, and say the following incantation:

Our home is safe, our doors are locked.
All unwanted spirits blocked.
Never again to enter here,
And disturb the folk who we hold dear.

5. Ritually dispose of any remaining angelica root and infusion by pouring it back into the earth with gratitude.

Divination with Your Familiar

Animals and divination go hand in hand. Animal behaviors have been interpreted as omens by people since the dawn of humanity. Throughout this book, you can find specific divination methods for a variety of animals. However, you can also invite your familiar to join you in your divination practice. If you read tarot, oracle cards, runes, or any other divination system, you can also invite your familiar to lend their energy. If you find that your familiar pricks up their ears or comes around whenever you take out your tools, you probably have a familiar who wants to help. Of course, they can assist simply by being nearby, but there are some other ways that you can involve your familiar in your divination practice.

Pajaritos de la Suerte

One of the most delightful animal divinations I have ever seen was one that I experienced for the first time many years ago in Mexico. The *pajaritos de la suerte*, or little birds of luck, are tiny canaries who are trained to tell your fortune. When you approach a street vendor with these birds in a cage and pay a small fee, the canaries will perform some charming tricks and then pull a slip of paper from a box. The paper is printed with a fortune just like the Zoltar fortune-telling machine in an arcade, but having it chosen by a bird is just so much more magical.

This fortune-telling system is not unique to Mexico. Similar fortune-telling birds can be found in Iran, India, Singapore, Japan, Brazil, South Korea, and elsewhere. If you have a pet bird familiar who is easily trained, you may be able to teach them to do some divination too. Simply write some fortunes on slips of paper and teach the bird to pull out one at a time. This is a delightful way to work with your familiar and let them guide you with some sage advice or impress your friends with your magical bird.

Of course, this divination system is not limited to birds. Depending on your familiar and how they can touch an object, you can train them to select tarot or oracle cards. A cat or dog can be taught to touch a card with a paw; a farm animal can touch an object with their nose, snout, or hoof; and a bird can peck at a card with their beak, for example. Shuffle and cut an inexpensive deck that you don't mind if your familiar pecks, chews, or slobbers on. Place the first three, five, or seven cards in front of your familiar, let them tap one, and turn it over to receive your message. Of course, no matter what card they pick, give them a treat of some kind as a "gratuity" for their reading.

Familiar Magic

Making magic with your familiar is one of the most gratifying ways to connect with them. It really is the essence of the familiar relationship. Once you have established your connection, casting spells and doing divination will seem like the natural next step. Invite them to join you and you will learn some wonderful wisdom that only an animal familiar can share.

— CHAPTER 5 —

Spells for Your Animal Familiar

If you're a witch, it's a given that you are going to want to do spells with your familiar, but there is no doubt that you'll also want to do spells *for* your familiar. Throughout this book you will find spells for particular animals. Be sure to look at the spells that are for animals other than your familiar species. With a little ingenuity, many of these spells can be adapted to your familiar. In this chapter, however, you'll find general spells and rituals that can be used for a variety of animals to protect them, heal them, bless them, and more.

Familiar Naming Spell

Naming your familiar can be a delightful way to express your creativity and capture the essence of your familiar. Some witches have two names, one they use in their mundane life and one they use in magical circles. There is no reason you can't do this with your familiar too. If your familiar is a pet and you'd like to give them a new secret magical name that only the two of you share, you can do a familiar-naming ritual. If you have a new familiar that you haven't named, you can also do this spell to give them their first name.

What you will need:

- Letter tiles from a game such as Bananagrams or Scrabble
- Small cloth bag
- Rosemary (*Rosmarinus officinalis*) incense or a rosemary censing bundle (smudge stick)
- Small blue chime candle or birthday candle
- Tiny candle holder or small saucer or dish
- Matches
- Paper and a pen

1. Place the letter tiles in the bag. (If the tiles came from a board game with a small carrying bag, it's fine to use that.)
2. Waft the rosemary smoke around the bag to cleanse and bless the tiles for your ritual.

3. Place the candle in a candle holder or affix it to a small saucer or dish by melting the bottom of the candle with a match and pressing the base of the candle into the dish for several seconds until it stands on its own.
4. If you are able to and it is safe for your familiar, touch the bag to a part of their body or have them touch the bag. If your animal is a wild familiar, then bring the bag to their habitat and sit for several minutes, then return home with the bag.
5. Light the blue birthday candle with the intention that you will pick the perfect name for your familiar.
6. Pull out 13 letters at random from the bag, and place them next to the candle.
7. Start reordering the tiles to create a name from only the chosen letters. *Notes:* You don't have to use all the letters you selected. If there is a letter that you chose that you would like to repeat in the name, feel free to do so.
8. As you come up with names, write them down on the paper. They don't have to be traditional names; they can be names that you invent.
9. Once the candle has burned completely (which can take from 5 to 15 minutes), it is time to stop writing.
10. Bring the list to your familiar, and ask them to choose the name they like.

11. Slowly read the names on the list to them one by one, and look and listen for their reaction. If you have established psychic or mundane communication with them, you'll see a positive sign when you come to the name that they prefer.

Protect Your Animal Familiar Spell

If your animal familiar is in the wild or you have an animal who goes outdoors, you may want to cast a charm to protect them. A candle spell can work to protect your familiar whether they are near or far. For extra empowerment, you can begin this candle on the night of the new moon and repeat every new moon, or whenever you feel your familiar needs an extra dose of spiritual safety.

This spell asks for a candle that resembles your familiar. This is easy to find for a cat, dog, or horse, but may be more challenging if your familiar is a guinea pig, salamander, or cricket. As an alternative, you can buy a wide, plain pillar candle and carve a simple drawing of your familiar into the wax, or you can purchase a glass-encased candle and affix a photo or drawing to the glass. If you can, you may want to choose a black candle for protection or another color to bring the blessings that you want to bestow. See the color correspondence chart in Appendix D for suggestions.

What you will need:

- An inscribing tool, nail, or knife
- A candle that resembles your familiar
- Protection oil (See the note in the recipe that follows.)

- *Optional:* an artifact related to your familiar such as a feather, a tuft of fur, or a collar

1. Use an inscribing tool, nail, or knife to carve your familiar's name and a pentacle for protection on the surface of the candle.
2. Dress the candle with protection oil, then light it while speaking this incantation:

[Name of familiar], whom I love so dear,
May you be safe, whether far or near.
May the great [familiar's species] mother be at your side,
To guard, protect, and be your guide.

3. Place the candle on your familiar altar, along with any artifacts, if you have any.
4. Let the candle burn for about one hour and then snuff it out.
5. Relight the candle each day for one hour until the candle burns completely.

Protection Oil Recipe

A protection oil is traditionally used in spells for spiritual protection and can be applied to your skin or a candle, as described in the previous ritual. If you wish to purchase protection oil instead, look for one made with herbs and essential oils to access the magic of these botanicals. You can use the herbs listed here or browse Appendix B for other herbs you can use.

What you will need:

- Small glass bottle with dropper to hold your oil
- One pinch of herbs of your choice: dried basil (*Ocimum basilicum*), rue (*Ruta graveolens*), and/or blessed thistle (*Cnicus benedictus*)
- 7 drops of black pepper (*Piper nigrum*) essential oil
- 1 to 2 drops of vitamin E oil (as a preservative)
- Sweet almond oil (to fill bottle)

1. Add the herbs, essential oil, and vitamin E oil to your bottle.
2. Add sweet almond oil to fill the bottle.
3. Shake while focusing on your intention of protection.

Bless Your Animal Familiar Spell

Whenever you would like to bless your animal familiar, you can use a wand of fresh rosemary (*Salvia rosmarinus*) to add some extra potency. Rosemary is nontoxic to cats, dogs, and horses if accidentally eaten, but double-check to make sure it is safe for your familiar's species, and, if not, substitute a safer herb or use a traditional wood or metal wand.

1. Cut or purchase a wand of fresh rosemary. If cutting, ask permission from the rosemary plant and thank them for their gift.
2. When your familiar is resting or sitting still, take the wand and wave it in two slow arcs over your familiar, as if you are drawing a small rainbow

from left to right and front to back. If your playful animal tries to catch or bite the wand, it's okay. It just means that they want to take part in the magic too.

3. As you move the wand, focus on the intention of your blessing (health, happiness, safety, peace, etc.) and visualize your familiar in this state.
4. Repeat the two arcs three times, and close by saying, "It is so!"

Healing Spell for Your Familiar

The body is in the material world, and so both magic and physical action need to be accessed when doing a healing spell. If your familiar gets sick, your first line of defense is to get them to a vet, but you can do this spell to help you find the right diagnosis, the best healthcare providers, the most accurate information, and the perfect treatments to get them to their optimal health. All the herbs below are powerful ones for healing magic and are generally safe for cats, dogs, and horses if accidentally eaten, but check to confirm that they are safe for your particular familiar species and leave out any that are not.

What you will need:

- A drawing of your familiar, a copy of a photo of them, or their name written on a slip of paper
- Pinch of althea (*Althaea officinalis*)
- Pinch of goldenseal (*Hydrastis canadensis*)
- Pinch of self-heal (*Prunella vulgaris*)

- A small piece of blue cloth
- A piece of red or white string or yarn
- Myrrh incense (*Commiphora myrrha*)
- Matches

1. Lay the image or name of your familiar on a flat surface and place the herbs over it.
2. Say the following incantation:

   If the Fates your health foretell,
   All conspires to make you well.
   You are healthy, you are fine,
   Strength and wellness will be thine.

3. Fold the image or name around the herbs to make a packet.
4. Place the packet on the piece of blue cloth and gather the ends together to make a bag.
5. Tie the bag together with the string.
6. Light the incense and place it in a holder. Bless and empower the bag by waving it through the smoke as you repeat the incantation above three times.
7. Place the bag in a safe place near where your familiar rests to support their healing. If your familiar is a wild animal, you can prepare the charm at home and then place the bag in their usual environment, as it is not recommended to get close to an injured wild animal.

Call a Wandering Familiar Home Spell

If your familiar has gone for a wander, either out of their cage or out of the house entirely, use this simple spell to help them find their way back quickly and safely.

What you will need:

- Two magnets or naturally magnetic lodestones
- Two chime candles, birthday candles, or small tapers
- Two saucers or small dishes
- Matches
- Two small food treats that your familiar enjoys
- Some magnetic sand or iron filings

1. Hold the magnets or lodestones in your hands so that they are touching one another.
2. Recite the following incantation as you send a psychic message, envisioning your familiar back in their home:

   Little adventurer, wandering friend,
   The time for travel has come to an end.
   Your rambles will soon be in the past,
   And safe at home you will be at last.

3. Affix a candle to each saucer by melting the bottom of the candle slightly and pressing it onto the dish.
4. Place one magnet or lodestone and one treat on each saucer.

5. Place one prepared saucer near your familiar's home, bed, or food dish and one at your front door.
6. Recite the incantation above as you light each candle.
7. If needed, you can repeat this spell once a day until your familiar returns.
8. When your familiar reappears, give them the treats and "feed" your magnets or lodestones with a pinch of magnetic sand to thank them for helping bring your familiar back safely.
9. Keep the magnets or lodestones, and reuse them in this spell any time you need to call your familiar back to the nest.

Find a Lost Familiar Spell

If your familiar is lost and you have already developed a psychic connection with them, you should begin by using the Receiving Psychic Communication Ritual described in Chapter 3. If you have a psychic connection, your familiar can show you where they are and what state they are in from their perspective. Of course, if they are in a dark closet, they won't be able to show you much, so you can use a talking spirit board, popularly known as a Ouija board, to get more detailed information. You can work with the spirit board by yourself or with another person, if you wish.

What you will need:

- Seven small white chime candles, birthday candles, or tapers and a candle holder
- A talking spirit board
- An image (photo or drawing) of your familiar

1. Light one of the candles and place it in a safe holder.
2. Set the spirit board on a table with the image of your familiar next to it.
3. Say the following invocation:

I invite the Mother of [your familiar's species],
A goddess of the highest vibration,
To provide clear, helpful,
and accurate information,
And assist me in finding your child
[name of familiar].

4. Sit with your fingers lightly resting on the planchette and ask a question to help you find your familiar. Questions of any kind can be asked, but here are some helpful examples:

    - How far away is my familiar?
    - Is my familiar moving or staying in one place?
    - Are they safe and healthy?
    - Are they inside or outside?
    - Is there a landmark near my familiar?

5. After a few minutes, the ideomotor effect will cause the planchette to move, spelling out words for you. Most nonhuman spirits will not be able to tell you addresses and street names (animals can't read), but they will be able to count blocks; tell you directions of north, south, east, west; and point out identifiable landmarks, such as "near the yellow house with the big pine tree."
6. When you have received enough information to start looking, close the session by actively pushing the planchette toward "good-bye" and thanking the Mother Spirit for sharing the information.
7. Let the candle burn completely.
8. Use the answers as guides while also taking action in the material realm. Put up signs, call for your pet, and leave out things with their scent or yours to help them find their way back.
9. If you don't find your familiar right away, light one candle and let it burn completely each day for the following six days or until they are found.

Help Your Familiar Transition Spell

Unless your familiar is one of those that have lifespans longer than we do—a tortoise, a large bird, a koi fish, or a salamander—a familiar coming to the end of their life is something that most witches must face. Whether your familiar dies on their own or is ethically put to sleep to relieve their suffering, there are a whole range of emotions that you will inevitably go through.

When a familiar passes, it can feel like half of you is in the world of the living and half of you is in the world of spirit. This separation is really an illusion. The fact is that the spirit never dies, nor do the threads of connection between you two. While your relationship in physical form has come to an end, the truth is that you two will meet again. You might meet in the afterlife to create a soul agreement to come together again in an upcoming life. Your familiar might even be reborn in a new body during your current lifetime and find their way back to you. Either way, the separation is only temporary. This ritual is perfect to both assist your familiar in their transition to spirit form and help you to process your grief.

Many cultures share the belief that a being that passes takes about 40 days to fully transition to the spirit realm. In that interim time, they are moving back and forth between the world of spirit and the world of the living. During this period, you are more likely to see, sense, or feel your familiar around. You may have dreams about them. They may show up as a shadow out of the corner of your eye, you may get a whiff of their scent, or you may hear the sounds that they made in life. When you do, you can acknowledge them and tell them that you love them.

You can help with this transition by setting up a special altar for your familiar over these 40 days. This spell is equally effective whether it is started while they are transitioning or after they have passed. If you have old, unresolved grief, it can also be done, even if it has been years since your animal left the physical plane.

What you will need:

- A framed image of your familiar in their prime
- An artifact connected to your familiar, such as fur, feather, sheds, a toy, a collar, a pebble from their aquarium or terrarium, or, in the case of a wild familiar, something from their habitat
- A small offering bowl
- A tiny bit of their favorite food treat
- Three glass-encased vigil candles or other long-burning candles: one black, one gray, and one white
- Spirit guide oil (See the note in the recipe that follows.)

1. Set up the altar with the image, the artifact, and the offering bowl with the treat in it. If you like, you can add additional optional elements such as an altar cloth, crystals, or figurines.

2. Prepare the three candles with three drops of spirit guide oil on the top of each one and place all three on the altar.

3. If your familiar is at the end of their life but has not yet passed, you can leave this altar up to help them transition peacefully and painlessly, but wait until they have passed to do the following steps.

4. Light the black candle that represents the deep grief and illusion of separation that you are experiencing, as well as the mysteries of the spirit realm.

5. As you light the candle, say the following incantation:

[Name of familiar], familiar of mine,
As you enter into deep mystery,
Let the threads between us remain strong.
Let the memory of our connection always live long.
Let your spirit soar high, let your spirit soar free.
Let the suffering end and pain cease to be.
Let us meet again in the Summerland.
Let us frolic together [paw, wing, fin, leg, claw] in hand.
Let us merge our hearts in loving and giving,
To join once again in the world of the living.
Hail the traveler!
Hail the traveler!
Hail the traveler!

6. Let the black candle burn each day when you are at home and awake. When you leave the house or go to sleep, snuff the candle out (don't blow it out) and relight it when you return.
7. When the black candle has burned completely, light the gray candle and repeat the incantation.
8. When the gray candle has burned completely, light the white candle and repeat the incantation.
9. Let the candles burn over the 40 days. If 40 days have passed and your candles have not finished burning, continue to burn them until all three are done. If your white candle is completed before

40 days have passed, dress another white candle in spirit guide oil and burn it until 40 days have passed, then continue to burn it until it is done. Over the 40 days, you should feel a shift in the balance, with your heart feeling the love and connection between you two more and more, and the deep grief less and less.

Spirit Guide Oil Recipe

A spirit guide oil is used for spells to open the connection between you and your positive spirits, spirit guides, ancestors, and, of course, any animal companion or familiar who has passed beyond the veil. If you wish to purchase it instead of make it, look for an oil with real botanical ingredients, such as herbs and essential oils, that can add their power to your intention. You can use the herbs listed here or browse Appendix B for other herbs you can use.

What you will need:

- Small glass bottle with dropper to hold your oil
- One pinch of herbs of your choice: dried celery seed (*Apium graveolens*), wormwood (*Artemisia absinthium*), and/or sweetgrass (*Hierochloe odorata*)
- 7 drops of anise (*Pimpinella anisum*) essential oil
- 1 to 2 drops of vitamin E oil (as a preservative)
- Sweet almond oil (to fill bottle)

1. Add the herbs, essential oil, and vitamin E oil to your bottle.

2. Add sweet almond oil to fill the bottle.
3. Shake as you focus on the intention of connecting to your loving spirits.

Contact Your Familiar's Spirit Spell

Once your familiar has passed over, you have an amazing ally in the spirit realm. You may not be able to experience them as you once did—no head scratches or loving kisses—but they can do many things that were not available to the two of you in the physical realm. Your animal familiar spirit can protect you from unwanted energies, they can alert you to opportunities, they can even bring good fortune to you. If you formed a psychic link in life, that connection still continues, and they can show you what they are experiencing in the afterlife.

Automatic writing and automatic drawing are two methods of receiving clear messages from your familiar's spirit. Automatic writing is the process of writing and receiving messages from a being who is in spirit form. Like passing notes back and forth in school, automatic writing lets you communicate to your familiar and receive messages back from them.

Automatic drawing allows you to receive symbolic visual messages that you can then interpret. Both are beautiful ways that you can get communication from your familiar. Try them both and see which method resonates with you.

What you will need:

- An artifact that once belonged to your familiar such as a feather, a tuft of fur, or a collar
- Music that supports you going into a trance state
- A pleasant-sounding bell
- Two different-colored pens (for automatic writing)
- A notebook (for automatic writing)
- A timer (for automatic drawing)
- A sketchpad (for automatic drawing)
- A pencil (for automatic drawing)

Automatic Writing

1. Hold your familiar's artifact in your hands and listen to 5 to 10 minutes of trance-inducing music, allowing yourself to relax and enter into an altered state of deep connection with your familiar's spirit.
2. When you feel ready, set the intention by speaking the following invocation:

   I invite the spirit of my familiar
   [your familiar's name]
   To connect with clear, helpful,
   and loving communication.
   If there are any hungry spirits nearby,
   now is not your time.

3. Set the artifact nearby and ring the bell three times.

4. Choose a pen of one color for yourself and another color for your familiar.
5. Open the notebook and, with your pen, write down a greeting to your familiar and then ask them a question.
6. Pick up the other color pen and write the first thing that comes to mind. In fact, when you get adept at automatic writing, the mind will get out of the way and the words will simply flow through you.
7. When your familiar has finished answering, you can pick up your pen again and make a response or ask another question.
8. Keep going back and forth until you complete your conversation.
9. Ring the bell three times to close the session and thank your familiar's spirit for coming through and communicating with you.

Automatic Drawing

1. Complete steps 1 to 3 of the Automatic Writing spell above.
2. Set the timer for 2 minutes and pick up the pencil and sketchpad.
3. Psychically or out loud, greet your familiar and ask them a question.

4. Put the pencil to the paper, close your eyes, and start drawing a single line without looking at what you're drawing or lifting your pencil.
5. Let your hand move freely as if guided by your familiar's spirit. Remember that the goal is not to draw a representational picture, but just to fill the paper with abstract lines.
6. Keep drawing until the timer rings.
7. Put your pencil down, open your eyes, and look at the abstract image that you have created.
8. Look for hidden images in the scribbles, just as you would look for recognizable shapes in clouds in the sky.
9. Take note of any symbolic images that you see and interpret them accordingly. For example, if you saw the shape of an elephant, you could recall that an elephant has a great memory and then interpret this as a message from your familiar telling you that they haven't forgotten you.

The Magic of Familiar Spells

Casting spells to communicate with, name, bless, protect, and guide your familiar are all part of the pact that the two of you have made. If you love your familiar, it will feel natural to want to do spells for them. As their partner in magic, you receive innumerable blessings from them and doing spells for them can show them just how much you love and appreciate your magical collaboration.

Part Two

Your Animal Familiar

— CHAPTER 6 —

Wild Animal Familiars

Lessons from Your Wild Animal Familiar

When you remember that the oldest familiar connections were the ones that humans made with animals in their natural habitats, you awaken to the deep and ancient magic that wild animal familiars can bring to your practice. In cultivating this relationship, you are going back to *your* most ancient roots, to a time when humans were much wilder.

Wild animal familiars can unlock so much for you. They offer you the opportunity to connect to nature in her most authentic form, they can teach you so many marvelous things outside of your day-to-day life, and they invite you to step out of your civilized nature and re-wild yourself to meet them. The wild familiar relationship can open your eyes to profound spiritual awakenings. To develop this relationship, you will master some foundational aspects of witchcraft—patience, humility, and problem-solving—to work cooperatively and share energy with your wild familiar.

There is a delicate balance in cultivating this connection. More than any other familiar relationship, the goal is not to enforce your will on the animal. In the case of some wild animals, it can even threaten their lives as they get too comfortable around humans and put themselves or other people in harm's way. The wild animal familiar partnership requires you to be very respectful, using both research and common sense to assess the situation and re-wild *yourself* rather than "tame" the animal.

Connecting with Your Wild Animal Familiar

You can meet a wild familiar out in nature, which is what we will be focusing on in this chapter, but you can also connect with them in preserves, rescues, sanctuaries, rehabilitation facilities, zoos, or other places that allow closer contact. Get creative and adapt some of these spells and rituals when working with wild animals in institutions, but always defer to their rules for safety.

Another way that you can connect is through observation of them in the wild. If you are lucky enough to live near an area where animals are known to forage, you can set up a wildlife camera to capture the comings and goings of your special familiar. No matter where you live, however, you can also access online wildlife cams to observe these amazing creatures. Even if you never encounter your wild animal familiar in person, if you watch them on camera over time, you can develop a relationship with them. All animals have great psychic senses, so you can send love and appreciation and receive their blessing in return, even across many miles.

When you do have that special moment where you see them on camera, be fully awakened to their majestic presence and receive the energy that they share with you. Send your familiar respect, love, protection, and appreciation. You may only see your animal on camera occasionally, but that doesn't mean that they are not reachable. Do visualizations where you can encounter your animal's spirit up close. In these visualizations, you are totally safe with your wild familiar. They can talk to you and teach you, and you can even go on adventures together.

This chapter will discuss working with wild animals in general and then some particular magic for some popular familiar species. There are so many possible animals out there that can become a wild familiar. Adapt spells to work with your particular familiar, but also check out the chapters dedicated to individual animal families. For wild birds, horses, fish, amphibians, rodents, reptiles, rabbits, insects, and arachnids, please see the individual chapters dedicated to those animals. For wild animals that also have a domestic counterpart, such as goats, chickens, ducks, geese, sheep, and cattle, check out Chapter 7.

Developing Your Wild Animal Familiar Relationship

Developing a familiar relationship with a wild animal is a different path than cultivating a relationship with a domesticated one. The requirements of building this relationship and the habits that you need to cultivate, what I call *re-wilding*, not only help you connect to your familiar but also can be profoundly healing for you on spiritual, emotional, and physical levels. The process also must be truly cooperative and requires the following set of rules to keep the connection safe and happy for both of you.

- Get out in nature
- Be patient
- Look for interest coming from the animal
- Research
- Keep coming back

Get Out in Nature

If you spend time in nature, you are bound to come across wild animals. Even in the city, squirrels, crows, sparrows, rats, and pigeons are all around us. Spending time outside is bound to give you opportunities to meet wildlife, so if you are an outdoorsy witch, this will be natural. If you would like to cultivate a wild animal familiar, you will need to get outdoors or at least view it through a window or camera.

Be Patient

You don't generally walk up to strangers and tell them that they are your best friends; that would be weird. Both human friendships and animal familiar relationships take time and, well, familiarity. Just like popping into your favorite coffee shop where you see the same folks every morning, spending time on the same routes or in the same places can open opportunities to get to know one special animal until you become, as the fox said to the Little Prince in the eponymous book by Antoine de Saint-Exupéry, "unique in all the world" to each other.

You can develop a relationship with a wild creature if you "observe the proper rites," as the fox taught the Little Prince to do. "You must be very patient . . . First you will sit down at a little distance from me—like that—in the grass. I shall look at you out of the corner of my eye, and you will say nothing. Words are the source of misunderstandings. But you will sit a little closer to me, every day . . ."

Most wild animals you encounter will be prey rather than predators, so they may not be comfortable with you tramping around and making lots of noise. The process of getting to know a particular animal can blossom when you take the time to quietly sit still in their habitat. Always remind yourself that you are a guest in their home, not the other way around.

Most animals see eye contact as a threat. So, just find a comfortable place to sit in nature, rest, listen, and if you see an animal, just give it a loving sideways glance.

Look for Interest Coming from the Animal

No familiar relationship can be forced, but this maxim is the truest for our wild friends. Once you have observed a particular animal, try returning to the same place around the same time and see if you see them again. If you become known to them and show them that you are not a threat, they may decide to come closer and investigate you. As long as the animal can't harm you, this curiosity is a positive sign. Keep returning and see if the relationship grows and they become more comfortable with you.

Some animals will always prefer to keep a safe distance no matter how much time you spend in their habitat. Perhaps they would rather look at you through a window or connect to you through a wildlife cam. Honor their wishes and their desire for friendship at a distance.

Research

Once an animal starts showing interest in you, it is time to do your real homework. The first step is to positively identify the species. This is not just so you know what to call it. This is the first step to deepening your relationship or making a sharp U-turn. Some animals are aggressive, venomous, toxic, or even deadly. Some carry diseases or can be harmed by germs that humans transmit. Others might be endangered or have special needs.

Even a relationship with a safe and friendly animal can be enhanced by this research. You can discover what foods they prefer and which foods can harm them. You can provide shelters and other comforts that help them thrive. And you will definitely want to know what kind of damage their claws, teeth, beak, or tail can do.

Research online, read books, and watch documentaries so you can understand your new friend well. Discover how your special animal communicates happiness, curiosity, irritation, and aggression. Try to imitate the more positive messages and avoid accidentally sending negative messages. At first you might feel silly cawing back to a crow or bobbing your head at a pigeon, but when you show them that you understand them, they may become more curious and feel safe getting closer to you.

Animals are highly intuitive and can sense our emotional states as well, so when you imitate their body language or calls, make sure to feel calm and curious and radiate positivity. Think, but do not say aloud, what you would like to express, such as, *Hello, you friendly deer. I'm glad to get to know you.* (For more on communicating with your familiar, check out Chapter 3.)

You will also want to be able to read the signs if your animal feels threatened. Don't take it personally if they do. Most wild creatures frighten easily and so are more likely to attack in self-defense over a perceived threat, even if you mean them no harm.

An animal can also act aggressively if it is injured. Your instinct might be to help a wild animal who appears to be sick, injured, or in trouble, but your intervention might do more harm than good. The first thing to do is to leave the animal alone and contact a wildlife rehabilitation facility. They have the experience, equipment, and treatments to properly care for them.

Keep Coming Back

Developing a friendship with any animal requires a level of commitment and consistency. A wild familiar is almost always a permanent relationship, just as much as one with a pet. Like all relationships, it can grow the more time you spend around one another. Keep coming to the same location around the same time of day, and spend some time in the presence of your wild animal familiar.

A Sweetening Spell to Develop a Wild Animal Familiar Relationship

Along with following the guidelines above, you can enhance the development of your wild animal familiar relationship with a touch of magic. If you have been patiently waiting for your familiar to trust you but have not seen any progress, doing a sweetening spell can be an excellent way to connect more deeply with your familiar and make them warm up to you faster. While this spell is excellent for wild animals, it can also be used on shy pets or reluctant farm animals as well.

What you will need:

- A piece of your hair
- An artifact connected to your familiar such as a tuft of their fur, some hair, a whisker, a feather, or dirt lifted from a track that they made
- Jar of honey with metal lid
- Spoon
- Small taper, chime candle, or birthday candle in green, pink, or brown
- Image of you and your wild animal familiar (this can be a single photo or drawing of the two of you together or two separate images)
- Herbs for friendship, attraction, and connection (See Appendix B for suggestions.)
- A special plant food treat that your wild animal familiar would appreciate (e.g., nuts, grains, grasses, berries, plants)

1. Tie your hair around the tuft of fur, hair, whisker, or feather, if possible.
2. Open the jar of honey and dip in the spoon.
3. Eat a small amount of honey off the spoon as you say the following incantation:

   (Species of animal), who is so sweet to me,
   I call you forth, as familiar-to-be.
   Leave the safety of your lair,
   And find your way to trust and care.
   Make it clear through song and sign,
   That we can forge our path divine.
   No fear shall we have of one another.
   We will be spiritual sister and brother.
   My magic and yours is thus entwined,
   An alliance that's true, respectful, and kind.

4. Add the images, artifacts, and herbs to the jar.
5. Seal the jar and light the candle on top and allow it to burn completely. (When working with candles, be sure that your surface is stable and free of flammable objects. And be sure to use one of the smaller candles that can burn completely in a short amount of time, rather than a large taper candle that you might be tempted to leave unattended for hours.)
6. Light one small candle each day until you see a positive shift in trust with your animal familiar. (Keep lighting candles every day until you see the

shift. Magic is *work* sometimes—and so is developing a friendship with a wild animal.)

7. Once your familiar is showing trust, put the jar away and use it again in the same way anytime you want to increase the connection between you and your familiar.

Wild Animal Familiar Signs

Depending on the animal, you may see different signs that they are interested in becoming a familiar. Not all animals will send all these signals, but seeing more than one, experiencing them in remarkable ways, or seeing the same sign repeatedly is worth noting. You can confirm that the animal wants to be your familiar by using one of the techniques described in Chapter 2.

Physical Encounters

One of the surest ways a wild friend can let you know that they are interested in developing a familiar relationship with you is through the same individual appearing multiple times. Cultivate these meetings but don't force them. For example, looking into a bird's nest or crawling into a coyote den would not count as an animal encounter, as it is initiated by you. It would also be terribly stressful for the animal. They don't want you forcing your way into their safe haven any more than you would enjoy a giant stranger walking into your home uninvited. However, hanging around in their habitat can be a gentler way to encourage an encounter that respects the animal's free will.

Not all encounters carry the same weight. Multiple encounters with the same animal will show a stronger familiar bond than encounters with different individuals of the same species. Encounters with wild animals who have adapted to living with humans will be less impactful than animals who typically have little human contact. For example, seeing a pigeon one time is not as dramatic and meaningful as gazing into an owl's eyes for several seconds. When gauging these special invitations, take into consideration how unusual the encounter is and weigh it accordingly.

Spiritual Encounters

Pay attention to other ways that the animal can indicate their desire to work with you. Seeing meaningful images of the animal, especially if they are a species that you might not encounter in your day-to-day life, can be a sign that you are being called to work with them. Synchronicities, such as overhearing the name of the animal in passing conversations, can also be a way they show interest. Seeing or even meeting the animal in your dreams is a particularly powerful way to send you the message that they are ready to connect.

Working with Wild Familiars

There are over a million species of animals that can be found in the wild. While it would be impossible to list them all, we can take a brief look at some of the most popular, widespread, and beloved wild creatures. Remember to check out the chapters for birds, horses, fish, amphibians, rodents, reptiles, rabbits, insects, and arachnids if your wild familiar falls into one of those families or Chapter 7 if your animal has a domestic counterpart.

Bats

Bats are remarkable even if you are not someone who likes to hang out at goth clubs. Many people fear their bite, but out of the 1,400 species of bats, only 3 drink blood; the rest eat insects and drink nectar. (Some also help pollinate the agave plant that is used to make tequila. Cheers, bats!)

If you have a bat familiar, you have access to good luck and a great deal more. In many cultures, they are seen as quite lucky. The bat is a harbinger of good fortune and happiness in China. To see a bat means that good luck is dropping in as quickly and unexpectedly as that bat flying overhead.

You are probably aware that bats have the skill of echolocation, using sound to "see" in the dark. This finely tuned skill of vocalizing and hearing allows them to detect objects as fine as a human hair and hear the footsteps of a beetle walking on sand from six feet away.[1] Your bat familiar can lend you their energy to help find your way in life using alternate senses.

Bats are also the only mammals that have the gift of flight, so if you have a bat familiar, you are undoubtedly a unique soul who marches to a different drummer and can do things that others find impossible.

Bat House Spell

Bats are important to our ecosystem, but their populations are dwindling drastically. If you have a wild bat familiar or would like to invite one, you can create a habitat to support them. Look online for bat-friendly plants, such as night-blooming flowers or flowering trees, that grow easily in your zone.

When you are ready to be a good neighbor, find out the species of bat in your area and what home is appropriate for them. Likely, you can make or purchase a wooden house to provide them with a safe environment. You can decorate it with the symbols of air, fire, water, earth, and spirit to bring the magical blessings of those elements to both you and your bats. You can also do this spell on animal houses of any kind, including birdhouses, bee hives, dog houses, chicken coops, and so on.

1. Use a wood-burning tool, paint, or a paint pen to inscribe the blessings of the elements on the exterior of the bat house.

2. Use these five traditional alchemical symbols for the five elements or create your own.

Air: symbolizes blessings of thought, idea, and communication

Fire: symbolizes blessings of passion, energy, and action

Water: symbolizes blessings of emotions, intuition, and psychic ability

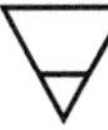

Earth: symbolizes blessings of health, wealth, and material concerns

Spirit: symbolizes blessings of spirituality, wisdom, and enlightenment

3. Depending on where you live, you may have bats inhabiting the house seasonally or all year round. Whenever you have occupants, note the time that they emerge from the cozy nest that you have created for them. It will usually be a couple hours after dusk.
4. Try to spend some time each night observing them when they leave their home to go on the hunt for their favorite foods.
5. As they fly in or out of their home, you can speak or visualize wishes for the blessings of the five elements.

Bears

Big, beautiful bears are a part of the legends and spiritual lore of every culture that they have contacted. For millennia, humans have admired and even worshipped them for their ferocity, strength, and speed. If you have a bear familiar, you are connected to a fearless apex predator who can lend their energy whenever you need a dose of courage and resilience. If you are facing challenges, your bear familiar can teach you to not back down, to defend what or who is important to you, and to "feel the fear and do it anyway."

Bears are also extremely intelligent with the largest and most complex brains of land mammals their size. They can not only remember abundant food foraging areas years after their last visit but also can thwart hunters with sneaky tricks such as covering their tracks. They are even toolmakers, using rocks to get at those troublesome itchy spots on their back.

Most bears are protected as vulnerable species. For your protection and theirs, the most respectful familiar relationship will be one that is experienced at a distance. Feeding a bear to get them to visit you can make them too comfortable around humans and civilization, putting both of you in danger. However, with all their radiant power, you need only to glimpse your bear familiar from a distance to receive a huge dose of their energy.

Bear Hibernation Spell

Bears are well known for their ability to hibernate throughout the winter, slowing down their metabolism so that they can spend months at a time resting without food when resources are scarce. You can bond with your bear familiar in a very witchy way by honoring the changing of the seasons along with them. If your normal mode is go-go-go, then when the weather gets colder, make a commitment to mindfully slow down.

While this spell is perfect for your bear familiar, it can also be done with any animal familiar that hibernates, such as frogs, hedgehogs, bats, turtles, wild snakes, bumblebees, and so on. Here are some suggested ways to get in hibernation mode:

- **Consciously perform tasks in slow motion:** Your bear familiar's metabolism slows to a crawl while hibernating. Slowing down the motions of your daily activities even by 25 percent can allow more awareness, mindfulness, and centeredness. If you find your mind wandering to your to-do list, bring your attention to your five senses and what is happening in the here and now.

- **Hang a "Do Not Disturb" sign:** Bothering a bear in hibernation causes them to ratchet up their metabolism and uses up valuable stores of energy that they need to get through the winter. Be mindful of your own energy, especially during the frantic end-of-year holiday season. If you're an overscheduler, don't be afraid to take a break from obligations, even for a short time. Like a bear, you can always come back to these things later.
- **Go on a media fast:** While you definitely don't have the bear's ability to fast all winter long, you can give up consuming electronic media. Silence your phone alerts, stop endlessly scrolling social media, and put your news subscriptions on pause. You can try doing this media fast for a few hours every day, for a whole week, or, if you truly want to be in alignment with your bear familiar, all winter long.

Coyotes

The coyote has long been seen as a powerful spirit by the Native peoples of the prairies and desert areas of Mexico and central North America. While each culture has its own unique take on coyotes, they almost universally view them as crafty, intelligent, and resourceful—traits which are defining characteristics of coyotes in real life. Coyotes have adapted to human civilization encroaching on their territory as far back as the times of the Mayan civilization and now inhabit urban areas as well as wild ones. Despite humans trying every method to eradicate them, their numbers have increased, rather than decreased. If you have a coyote familiar, you have a unique source of energy to help you overcome adversity, find clever solutions, and adapt to the changes that life throws at you.

Coyote Howling Magic

If you have a coyote familiar, you probably have heard the yipping and howling of coyotes when they get together. This noisy nighttime ruckus is the way that they communicate with each other for mating, to define territory, or simply to tell fellow family members, "Hey! I'm over here!" When it comes to howling, coyotes truly *are* tricksters. Due to the "Beau Geste" effect, an auditory illusion that coyotes create by varying their vocalizations, the howling of a couple of coyotes can sound like a dozen.

You can tap into your coyote familiar's energy by doing spells of any kind while coyotes howl in the background. You can vocalize along with them a little, but this may cause them to become curious and draw closer, so it's best to howl along once or twice and then just listen and allow their energy to empower your spiritual practice. You can also do this ritual with any animal that howls to communicate, such as wolves, foxes, and even your pet dogs.

Deer

Deer are part of the mythologies of many cultures, as they are found on every continent except Antarctica. In Celtic mythology, the god Cernunnos is closely aligned with the stag and is depicted with antlers on his head. In many traditions, the stag is a messenger between the worlds. Seeing a stag in a remarkable way was often viewed as a sign that one was about to embark on a heroic journey.

Deer may seem like a common animal to take on as a familiar, but they embody surprising contrast. They can be both shy and aggressive, hidden and strikingly visible, gentle and dangerous. These combinations make a deer a familiar with surprising depth. If you have a deer familiar, you have a magical partner who can help you make sense of co-existing with contradiction. They can help you to tap into your own internal dualities, your *anima* and *animus*, the classical feminine and masculine energies that make you a whole person.

Deer Familiar Exchange Spell

If you live in an area that has deer, you can support them by providing clean water for them to drink and planting seed blends specifically designed for feeding deer. (Make sure it is safe to do so. Don't attract deer to hunting grounds!)

Bucks shed their antlers every year and often do so in places where they go for food, so you may find the precious and deeply magical gift of an antler from your familiar that you can use in one of the ways described in Chapter 4.

Foxes

Like their cousin the coyote, the fox has a reputation for being a trickster. Savvy, tactical, and quick, they are great at outwitting predators and coming up with creative solutions to problems. These stealthy nighttime hunters have been revered in legends and mythology since classical antiquity for their shrewd sensibilities. For example, in Japanese folklore, *kitsune* are supernatural foxes that are "witch-animals" gifted with magical powers such as shapeshifting, invisibility, and the ability to create illusions. Having a fox familiar can enhance your magic in the more advanced arts of glamour magic and transfiguration. They can also lend their energy to help you retain information or do some creative problem-solving.

One of the little-known aspects of the fox's nature is their playfulness. Fox parents play with their kits, kits play with each other, adults play with each other, and they even play by themselves. Foxes have been known to retrieve golf balls from courses just so they can play with them. They even play with animals of other species such as deer, pestering them until the deer gives chase.[2] Your fox familiar can lend you their impish energy to bring more fun and laughter into your life.

Fox Familiar Eye Contact Spell

There is power in eye contact. Eye contact with your familiar can allow you to exchange energy and develop trust. This is a technique that can be done with any wild or domestic animal, but remember that sustained eye contact is often interpreted as "I'm going to eat you." So if you have a skittish or aggressive familiar, you may want to limit eye contact to a brief glance or avoid doing it altogether.

If you want to invite a closer bond with your fox familiar, go out for a walk at night. Move like a fox yourself—stealthy and quiet—and observe your surroundings carefully. You might just come across a fox out walking too. When you share a brief moment of eye contact, you can ask the fox to lend you their gifts. In return, you can do all that you can to help foxes thrive in safety.

Otters

From the rivers to the sea, otters are some of the cutest wild animals. If you have ever seen one in action, then you have witnessed the irresistible way they look and act like playful pups. Unlike dogs, though, an otter is not a pet, and it is best for them to be protected in the wild rather than tamed and brought indoors.

Of all their cute and playful behaviors, one of the most adorable is the fact that sometimes sea otters hold hands while they are sleeping. They don't just do this to be friendly, it keeps them from drifting apart as they bob along on top of the ocean. Otter mamas will keep their babies close for the six months it takes for them to reach independence, often carrying the pups on their tummies while they float on their back. If you have an otter familiar, then you can tap into their energy of close connection to family and friends. Your otter will bless you with optimism, playfulness, and fun with your loved ones and help you deepen those important relationships.

Otters are also clever toolmakers. Sea otters will use rocks as hammers or anvils to open tough shells and get the food inside. Scientists are starting to deduce that otters have a genetic gift for handling stones that makes this behavior easy for them.[3] Your otter familiar can lend their energy to empower your magic whenever you are working with crystals or other stones.

Otter Crystal Cleansing Spell

Crystals and stones belong to the element of earth and contain the qualities of stability and longevity. Crystals can be programmed to hold our magical intentions, but they can also pick up and hold the energy or intentions of others who have handled them. Whenever you get a new crystal or you feel like your crystals need a freshening up, you can do a simple crystal cleanse and invite your otter familiar to lend their magical stone handling energy. While you can do a crystal cleanse without inviting your animal familiar, bringing in any animal familiars who use stones as tools, such as sea otters, primates, and even some birds and fish, can add extra magic to your spell and deepen your connection.

What you will need:

- Image of your otter familiar (either a photo in a frame or a small statuette representing your otter familiar)
- Bowl of salt water
- Bowl of fresh water
- Crystals or stones

1. Meet with your otter familiar out in the wild and bring your crystals with you.
2. Observe your otter from a distance, and psychically ask them to lend you their energy in cleansing your crystals. If your otter doesn't run or swim away, then they are agreeing to assist you in your magic. If they do take off, try again another day.

3. Bring your crystals back inside and set up a working altar. (Remember: A working altar doesn't have to be an area dedicated for doing magic only. Even a kitchen table can become a working altar if you clear it off and put down a pretty tablecloth or some other sign to mark this space as special to you for now. The point is that you set up a space and time to focus on your spell.)
4. Place the image of your otter in front of you but leave workspace between the image and you.
5. Place the bowl of salt water on the left of the image and the bowl of fresh water on the right.
6. Lay out your crystals in front of the bowls.
7. As you pick up each crystal, dip it first in the salt water and say the following incantation:

   Salt water, womb water, home of all life,
   Wash away negativity, trouble, and strife.

8. Then dip the crystal in the fresh water and say the following incantation:

   Fresh water, clear water, life-bringing rain,
   Restore, renew, bring purity again.

9. Close your eyes and hold the crystal in both hands as you speak or envision the intention you would like to program or reprogram your crystal with.
10. When you are finished cleansing and charging all crystals, pour both waters down the drain. Now you can take apart your working altar setup.

Raccoons

Raccoons are nicknamed "trash pandas" with both affection and scorn, but the traits some disparage are this animal's greatest gifts: adaptability, intelligence, and dexterity. They are both carnivores and opportunistic scavengers. With their dexterous paws that look like slender human hands, they can loosen, break through, and figure out any lock that a toddler can unlatch, including those critter-proof locks you put on your trash cans. Your raccoon's dogged determination to get a meal can be an amazing energy that they can lend you whenever you want to give up or you can't figure out a way around an obstacle.

Raccoons are highly skilled at problem-solving and adaptability. Wherever humans have encroached on raccoon habitats, raccoons have adapted by living side by side with humans. A raccoon familiar can help you to discover abundance in the unlikeliest places, find opportunity in adversity, and see that one witch's trash is another one's quite valuable treasure.

Raccoon Altar Spell

To connect more deeply with the spirit of your raccoon familiar (or any resourceful animal familiar who is a scavenger), become a resourceful repurposer. If you have an artistic streak, go thrifting or scavenging to find materials to create a collage or assemblage. If you're a handy witch, fix broken tools and machines that others throw out. Pick up "trash" on your walks and decorate a familiar altar to honor your raccoon with beautiful creations you make from castoffs. If you're not sure where to begin, look to outsider art, folk art, and artists who work with found objects for some inspiration.

Wolves

Wolves are another animal that humanity has had mixed feelings about, both appreciating their nobility but simultaneously fearing them as dangerous. Wolves should be granted a very respectful distance, but remember that humanity poses a much bigger threat to wolves than they do to us.

Despite the cliche of the "lone wolf," wolves are most definitely pack animals, living, playing, and hunting together in families of 4 to 10 individuals. Pack structures include a dominant pair and offspring, but also other family relationships and sometimes unrelated individuals. Every member has a role, and all group members contribute to the care of the pups, providing food, teaching skills, and "pup-sitting."[4] A wolf familiar can provide magical assistance to help you develop close bonds with family, both birth and chosen family, and get help from others.

Wolves are also adept communicators, using scent, body language, touch, taste, and vocalizations to communicate with the pack. While there is a romantic notion that wolves howl at the moon, the truth is that they are using howls to communicate with each other over distances as far as 10 miles (16 km). The howls can communicate, "This is *our* pack's territory," "Hey, fam! I'm separated from you. Where are you guys?" or "We're over here!"

The legends of werewolves have existed since antiquity, but in the Middle Ages the belief of shapeshifting into a wolf became blended with witchcraft. Inquisitors accused witches of turning their enemies into werewolves or witches turning into wolves themselves.[5] A version of shapeshifting called *familiar merging* can be done to open your senses to not only your wolf familiar but also any animal familiar you are working with.

Wolf Familiar Merging Spell

Familiar merging is a form of astral projection where your spirit and your familiar's spirit come together in a single body. When you merge with your familiar, you retain your consciousness while seeing through their eyes and experiencing their senses. You don't replace the spirit of your familiar; instead, you go for a ride alongside their spirit and receive the gift of witnessing your familiar's experiences through their eyes, ears, and other senses.

This spell can be done with any type of animal familiar, not just the wolf or a wild animal specifically. Your familiar's spirit can also merge with you and enter your body, with your permission, but in this spell, you are going to focus on merging into your familiar's body.

1. Find a place where you can lie down and be undisturbed for an hour or so. Put on some meditation music or trance-inducing music if it is helpful to you.

2. Set the intention for your journey by saying:

   I safely merge with my wolf familiar,
   with their permission, to see, sense,
   and feel their experiences and return safely
   back to my own body when I am ready.

3. Close your eyes and begin by sensing the room where you are lying. Imagine walking around the room.
4. Picture yourself opening your front door and seeing the habitat where your wolf familiar lives.
5. Sense your wolf familiar come bounding up to you. (If you don't sense your wolf familiar, then they are not willing or able to merge at this time, and you can try again another day.)
6. Stand next to your familiar and feel your spirit step into and merge with their body.
7. At this point, you should be able to sense the world around you through your familiar's senses while still maintaining your own consciousness.
8. Observe the environment as your familiar trots along, sniffs, communicates with their pack mates, and shows you their world.
9. If you like, you can ask your familiar to show you certain places and experiences.
10. When you are ready to return to your own body, ask your familiar to take you back to your door.
11. Step out of the body of your familiar, and thank them for the awe-inspiring experience.
12. Walk through your front door, back into the room where you are lying, and merge with your own body again.

13. Wiggle your toes and fingers. Feel your body awaken as your awareness comes back to the room.
14. Open your eyes and write or record your experiences while they are fresh in your mind.

Befriending a Wild Animal Familiar

While a wild animal will never and should never become a pet, you can add so much to your magic by developing a familiar relationship with an animal that is truly free. Rather than bringing them into your world, you can meet them on the bridge between the wild and the domestic. The wild animal familiar relationship can teach you about your own wild nature, show you how to be your authentic self, and help you develop patience, trust, and deep self-acceptance.

CHAPTER 7

Farm Animal Familiars

Lessons from Your Farm Animal Familiar

Farm or ranch animals offer a unique connection to the animal kingdom. They are not quite pets, and they certainly are not wild, but they straddle a world in-between the two. A relationship with a working animal is a two-way street: the animal depends on you to provide food, shelter, and care, and you depend on the animal for labor, wool, eggs, milk, or other products.

Working with farm animal familiars brings us back to the lives of our ancestors. Going back even a few generations, you are bound to discover relatives who worked the land and co-existed with domestic animals. If you have a farm animal familiar, you also get the wonderful feeling, as they did, of building a relationship with one of these noble, hardworking creatures.

Farm animals like cattle, goats, sheep, and swine, and farm fowl such as chickens, ducks, and geese all bring their unique and amazing gifts when they become your familiars. Beyond these, there are two other farm animal familiars whom you will discover in later chapters: horses in Chapter 10 and bees in Chapter 15.

How Your Farm Animal Familiar Can Heal You

It's easy to see how farm animals help you on the material level by providing all that they do, but they can also help to heal you mentally, spiritually, and emotionally. Interacting with them can help calm you if you are anxious, improve your mood if you're feeling low, and give you a sense of purpose if your self-esteem is struggling. Mental health researchers are discovering that farm-based therapy can provide numerous positive benefits to individuals with mental health challenges.[1]

Connecting with Your Farm Animal Familiar

Our two and four-legged friends can provide so much affection and entertainment in addition to all the work that they do. If you are lucky enough to live alongside these special creatures, you can build this familiar relationship in your daily interactions, but you don't have to live on a farm to get to know them. Look for sanctuary farms and animal rescues in your area that save abused and neglected farm animals and give them a chance at a happier life. Most of them offer tours or opportunities to interact with the animals in a safe way.

Because the animals are cared for their entire natural lives, you can develop a magical relationship with a special animal there and make magic with them, adapting any spells to fit within the sanctuary's rules.

Making Magic with Your Farm Animal Familiar

On a magical level, one of the advantages to working with a farm animal familiar is the ease and frequency of contact. Each of these points of contact can be turned into a spell to bond the two of you. Think of the daily tasks that you perform for your familiar as a way to thank them for all the help and healing they provide and get creative in turning them into magic rituals. Here are a couple ideas to get you started:

Gratitude Blessing for Domestic Animals

Your domestic familiar works so hard to provide for you; thank them with a quick gratitude blessing every time you feed them. Before you give them their feed, hold your hands over your familiar and say words of gratitude for all that they give to you. Bless the food to nourish them and make them healthy and strong.

For example, you can say the following blessing:

Dear familiar, faithful and true,
For all that you give, I say thank you.
As you drink this water and eat this food,
May it bless you and all of your brood.

Grooming Spell to Spiritually Cleanse

When you comb, brush, shear, or trim your domestic animal familiar, you can easily turn it into a ritual for removing negative energy from them. Before your session, bless your grooming tools by waving them gently through incense or a smudge stick smoke. While any incense can be used as a medium for blessing an item, you can add extra support by choosing a botanical incense that is aligned with the particular energy that you would like to bless your animal with. (Refer to Appendix B for specific suggestions.) As you groom your domestic familiar, chant a short phrase such as "clear and clean, calm and serene" or visualize any unwanted energy dissolving into nothingness as you brush or trim.

Cattle

Cattle have a range of docility, from gentle milk cows to aggressive bulls. Depending on the breed you are bonding with, you may get to have a quite cuddly and affectionate relationship or you may have to treat them more like a wild animal. Cattle from gentler breeds that are hand-raised and get a lot of human touch from the start are likely to act almost like pets, with a lot of trust in you. They will crave getting a touch from you after sniffing and licking your hand to say hello. Having a warm and loving bond like this is the hallmark of a familiar relationship, but even a relationship from a respectful distance still offers magical benefits.

Spiritually, cattle are sturdy sentinels and generous givers. In both ancient and modern religions, cattle are seen as divine, the original "sacred cows." They represent abundance, selflessness, and the benevolent Mother Earth. In magic, they can lend energy to spells of increase, fertility, virility, and humility. There is a dual nature to cattle. Think of the cow and how she expresses motherly nurturing by giving milk to her young and to humanity. Then, focus on the bull with his strength, will, vitality, and raw sexuality. Lean into the energy of your bovine familiar to lend fortitude, determination, and abundance to your magic.

Cattle Kulning Spell

Cattle can be trained to follow your voice and come when you call, which is a stress-free way to get them to the barn, move them to another pasture, or make magic together. There is a beautiful ancient Scandinavian tradition of herd calling called *kulning* or *lokk*. The high-pitched singing almost sounds like a slow, wordless yodel and, like yodeling, the sound can carry for distances of up to three miles (five km) away. Cattle that are allowed to graze in open pastures can be heard at a distance because of the loud cowbells they wear and the moos that they make, and thus the herder can tell which direction to call. This back-and-forth between the lowing and bells of the cattle and the mournful sounds of the *kulokks* creates a haunting chorus that echoes off the hills and valleys like an ancient and ancestral melody. Learn to sing with your cattle to enrich your familiar bonds.

Goats

Goats are highly intelligent, inquisitive, and social. They can be trained to do tricks, follow commands, and recognize their names when called. Like sheep and cows, they can provide milk and some of the most sought-after fibers for spinning, knitting, and weaving: mohair and cashmere. They are foragers who can clear brush and be trained to work as a pack animal or pull a cart. They climb cliffs, trees, rocks, and mountains as easily as a walk up a staircase. Also, is there anything cuter than a frolicking kid?

Goats are incredibly intuitive and connected to humans. They can recognize and respond to human emotions and body language. Most goats will avoid people with angry expressions but will willingly nuzzle a smiling, friendly person. Goat intelligence means that they are problem-solvers, but they will also rely on their trusted humans for help. In a research study, a group of goats were trained to remove the lid from a box and receive a reward. For the last session, they were given a similar box with a lid that could not be removed. When confronted with this problem, the goats gazed at the humans in the room, looking them in the eye as if they were asking for help.[2] This trait for connection can make it quite easy to bond with your goat familiar and make magic with them.

Goats have a long history of being seen as divine. From the wild, lusty satyr to the sea-goat Capricorn, the simple goat is a powerful figure in Greek mythology. The she-goat goddess Amalthea who nursed the infant Zeus is the source of our concept of the cornucopia, or horn of plenty. Zeus broke off one of his foster mother's horns and it produced an endless supply of food for him, which is why the horn became a symbol of prosperity, wealth, and abundance. That connection between goats and abundance is also seen in the mythological Norse goat Heiðrún, who lives in Valhalla, grazes off the magical tree Læraðr, and produces mead for heroes instead of milk.

Your goat familiar can lend their energy of abundance and prosperity to your magic. They can also help in spells where you need to solve a problem or come up with a clever solution. Goats have a long association with virility and lust, so your goat can lend their energy to spells of a sexual nature. Goats are not afraid of heights, so if you are doing magic to reach higher levels of success or elevating your spiritual practice, your goat familiar can help show you the way. The goat's horns represent higher consciousness and psychic awareness, so your goat familiar can also lend you energy to develop your intuitive abilities.

Sheep

Sheep are curious, affectionate, and entertaining. They are intelligent, capable of problem-solving, can remember up to 50 faces—human or other animals—and are able to retain those memories for years. Like natural herbalists, they can discern which plants or other substances they can eat to cure their own illnesses and teach their lambs to do the same. If you are an herb witch who forages, makes healing potions from herbs, or is fascinated with the plant kingdom, your sheep familiar can be a special ally, lending you the energy to learn to discern the magical and medicinal properties of the plants you work with.

Sheep are also highly social and prefer to be in a flock. They are naturally friendly and will wag their tails just as dogs do. They create close bonds between mother and child but also create friendship connections with other sheep, goats, and people, as well. Young lambs that are hand-reared will easily bond to you too, just like they do with their mother. Developing a close, loving relationship with your sheep familiar can help you build or find nurturing communities and supportive relationships.

Sheep have an interesting dual energy. Young lambs and female sheep, or ewes, exude gentleness, cooperation, and kindness, while adult male rams can exhibit competitiveness, determination, virility, and the ability to break through the toughest barriers. Where your animal familiar shows up on this spectrum will give you some hint as to the kind of magic that they can help with. A gentle sheep can lend you energy of tolerance, patience, and peace, while a more aggressive ram can give you the power of persistence, resilience, and vigor.

Because of their rectangular pupils, sheep have up to a 320-degree field of vision that allows them to see nearly everything around them without turning their head. This characteristic gives them almost a sixth sense and means that your sheep familiar can help you with visioning, second sight, and clairvoyance. The spiral shape of their horns is an ancient goddess symbol of change, evolution, rebirth, life cycles, and intuition; and so they can lend you energy in spells of transformation or whenever you are moving through major changes in your life.

Spinning Magic Talisman

For eons, humans have had to create their own clothing. Up until the Industrial Revolution, creating cloth was one of the chores in every household. Spinning wasn't just practical, it was integral to magic. Goddesses and female saints from centuries ago are often depicted as spinners—the three Greek Fates who spin, measure, and cut the thread of each of our lives, the Slavic spinning and weaving mother goddess Mokosh, the Navajo/Diné Spider Woman who taught her people the skill of weaving.

If you have an animal familiar who makes fibers that can be spun into yarn, you have a wonderful opportunity to make some magic that will bond the two of you together. Take the yarn that you spin and make a sweater, scarf, cap, or other piece of clothing that you can wear during magical rituals and any time you want to connect to your familiar.

Spinning Divination

When you become proficient at spinning, you can also perform a divination as you spin these precious fibers from your familiar. Pay attention to the fibers as they wind out; they tell you how your immediate future will play out.

- **Smooth thread with no knots:** smooth, peaceful, and uneventful times
- **Tangled and knotted thread:** eventful times and experience gained
- **Even thread:** riches and good health
- **Uneven thread:** care should be taken to improve finances and health

Swine

Perhaps there is no other animal so misunderstood as the "lazy, dirty, greedy" pig. Contrary to how pigs are depicted in the media, they are curious, adventurous, enthusiastic, and radical optimistic enjoyers of life and all the fun it has to offer. They are friendly, playful, sensitive, and have exceptional memories, especially when it comes to locations where food is stored. They can even learn to play video games by using a joystick. They also love the finer things in life, like listening to music and getting massages. If the aim of your magic is to live life to the fullest, a pig familiar can teach you to get there.

Pigs have long been regarded as animals of good luck and prosperity. Just like a piggy bank, pigs represent abundance, luxury, and material wealth. Measured against human standards, pigs are consistently listed among the most intelligent animals on the planet. If you are close to one, you realize this supersmart magical companion can be so helpful in spells to communicate your needs, get those needs met, and just bring more optimism and joy into all aspects of your life. If you feel misunderstood, your pig can help you to connect to a group of like-minded souls and not care so much what people think of you. Your pig can also lend you energy of true self-love and authenticity.

Crafting a Pig Familiar Wand

Pigs have excellent communication skills. They can learn the names of objects and fetch the correct one by name. If you want your familiar to be an active participant in your magical practice, you can train a pig to fetch any spell casting tools that are safe for them to handle in their mouth.

Even better, pigs respond well to stick training, that is, using a stick as a pointer to teach them the behavior you want them to learn. Craft a special "magic wand" that you can use both for training and casting spells together. A simple wand can be made from a found branch.

1. Trim off any extra branches, and cut it to the length from your middle fingertip to your elbow.
2. Scrape off any bark, if you like, and sand it down smooth.
3. If you want a more finished look, you can polish it with a mixture of 1 part beeswax, melted, with 3 parts coconut oil. Mix the polish ingredients together, allow to cool, then apply to your wand with a soft cloth.

Making Magic with Your Farm Fowl Familiar

Working with chickens, ducks, geese, and other feathery fowl can offer you the material benefits of eggs but also the magical benefits of feathers and more. If you want farm life but don't live out in the country, you might be able to keep a few chickens in a coop in your yard. Fowl can delight and entertain you, are more social than you might think, and make excellent farm animal familiars.

Farm Fowl Witch's Ladder

A witch's ladder is a special knotted charm made with feathers that is hung in the home to amplify the wishes of the maker. You can make a witch's ladder with any feathers that can be legally collected, being mindful of the Migratory Bird Treaty Act. Domestic fowl are not part of the Act, so you can feel free to use any of the feathers your barnyard feathered friends gift you.

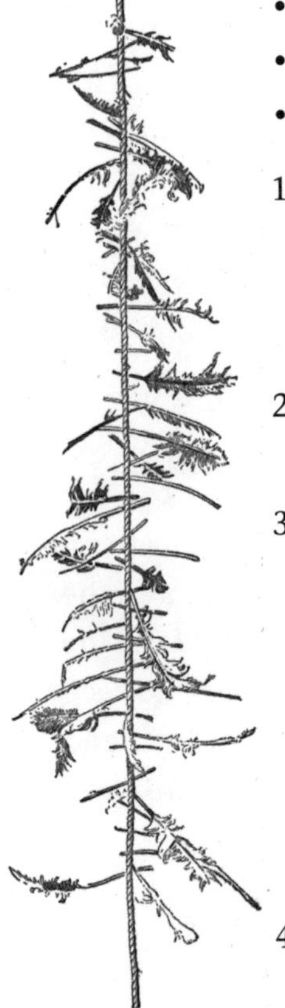

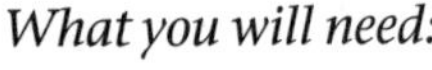

What you will need:

- 13 feathers from your farm fowl
- Yarn
- A metal charm or pendant

1. Focus on 13 wishes you would like this charm to bring to your home, such as health, wealth, happiness, laughter, peace, and so on.
2. Cut your yarn into three 1-yard (1m) pieces.
3. Gather the pieces together, fold the bunch in half, and knot about 1 inch (2.5cm) from the fold to make a loop for hanging the witch's ladder. Hook this loop over something stable, such as a drawer handle that will allow you to slightly pull the strands as you braid.
4. Separate the strands into three pairs and begin braiding them as you chant:

Knot and feather,
Come together.
Word and braid,
Come to my aid.

5. Every few inches, pick up a feather and stick it horizontally between the braided strands. As you do, say the wish that you would like to bring.
6. When you come close to the end, make a knot in the bottom of the braid and then tie the charm or pendant to weigh down the end.
7. Hang the witch's ladder in your home to bring in all your wishes.

Chickens

Beautiful, feathery chickens are another underestimated magical animal. Chickens have a surprising intelligence. Like Superman's alter ego, Clark Kent, chickens keep their superpowers on the down-low, so they can assist you when you need to blend in and hide your magical abilities in plain sight.

Chickens enjoy activities where they have to work for the reward, a behavior called *contrafreeloading*. They enjoy things like puzzle feeders, which expand on their natural instinct to scratch the ground to get food. If you are facing problems that require multistep processes to resolve, a chicken familiar can lend you their joy in accomplishment so that you too can feel satisfaction in solving the puzzles that life throws your way.

Chickens are aware of their special social hierarchy, called "the pecking order." These social rules even show up in what you could interpret as manners and respect. A rooster will take the ladies out to lunch by doing a "tidbitting" dance, where he picks up and drops food while making a gentle *tut tut tut* sound to let the hens know he has found something tasty. When they come around, the rooster will watch as the hens eat their fill before joining in himself. If you are doing magic to bring more cooperation and kindness into your relationships, a chicken familiar can help you attract generous and courteous friends.

Chicken Soothsaying (Alectryomancy)

Alectryomancy is an ancient form of divination in which a person performs a ritual and observes the behavior of a sacred chicken to prognosticate the future. There are many variations of this practice. In ancient Rome, members of the senate, generals, and other leaders would consult with a priest/diviner/chicken caretaker called a *pullularius* before making major decisions. He, in turn, would pour out grain and release a sacred rooster from a basket to observe what his reaction was. If he ate the grain avidly while stamping his feet and scattering it about, the prospects for the event were good. If the rooster refused to eat, the outlook was bad.[3]

In Ukraine, Poland, and other Slavic lands, variations on this rooster divination were done to predict the outlook for the year ahead. Twelve grains were placed on the floor on New Year's Eve. Then a rooster, preferably a black one, would be placed in front of the grains. If the rooster ate all 12 grains, the 12 months of the year ahead would be happy ones. Less than 12, you would have a year with a number of unlucky months equal to the number of grains remaining.

A slightly different version of this divination can be done any time of year whenever you would like to know if a wish will come true. Place a handful of grains on the floor in front of your chicken familiar. Let them peck as you count to 12, and then separate them from the grains. Count the remaining number of grains. If their number is even, then the wish will come true; if the number is odd, then the wish will be deferred.[4]

Feather Divination

Feathers naturally have many uses in magic. In Chapter 4 and Chapter 12, you'll learn some ways that feathers in general can be used. However, there is a Ukrainian divination using chicken feathers that can help determine the answer to any yes/no question. Feel free to adapt this spell to any feathered familiar.

1. Place a chicken feather just inside the threshold of the front door at midnight.
2. As it is placed, say the following incantation aloud:

   There is an oak tree with twelve nests on it.
   There are four eggs in each nest.
   And seven chicks in each egg.
   One of them appear and show me what will happen in the future.

3. The next morning, as the door is opened, look at which direction the feather flies. If it flies out the door, the answer is a yes; if it flies inside, the answer is not now.[5]

Ducks

If you find yourself connecting to a duck, you have a unique familiar that embodies a triplicity of elements. Ducks move effortlessly from shore to sky to lake and are equally at home in any of these environments. If you partner with these magical animals, you can move along with them through the element of air, which stands for rational thought and communication. You can ground yourself walking the earth, as they do on the lakeshore, and connect to the physical and material realm. You can also dive deep or gently bob along on the top of the water, the element associated with emotions and psychic ability.

Many are familiar with the concept of *imprinting*, the trait of young birds to bond and identify with the first being bigger than them who cares for them like a mother. In the wild, ducklings will bond with their natural mother or another duck, but domestic birds without a mother can imprint on other animals around the farm, such as a dog, cat, or even you. This imprinting instinct is strongest between 12 and 36 hours after they are born but can last up to two weeks.

If you are raising pet ducklings without a mother, imprinting gives you an opportunity to bond with them and form a strong familiar relationship. Please be aware that imprinting shouldn't be taken lightly and should never be done with wild ducks. Caring for a duck as a surrogate parent requires time, patience, and deep commitment. Ducklings will treat you as their parent for their first year, and then as family for the rest of their lives. If you have only one duck, they will stay bonded to you for life, which can be as long as 20 years. However, if you're raising a duck that you would like to develop that special familiar relationship with, it can be a completely magical experience.[6]

Duckling Familiar Imprinting Spell

For the strongest imprinting, a duck needs to see you and primarily just you for the first two weeks of their life. They can imprint on other ducks or pets, so make sure you are up front and center. Do this incantation once a day for the first two weeks of their life, and you will form a strong friendship and familiar bond.

1. Bless a little duckling food before doing this spell by holding your hands over the food and visualizing your duck growing healthy, strong, and lovingly attached to you. Set the food aside.
2. Gently pick up your duckling and recite the following incantation:

   Magical duckling, duck to be,
   May you trust and follow me.
   I will care for you like a mother
   And you will love me like no other.
   In sun, in rain, in any weather,
   May we make our magic together.

3. Set your duckling down and offer the blessed food to reinforce your bond.

Geese

Geese have great significance as magical animals. For thousands of years, their migration was a sign of the changing seasons, and their behavior was thought to foretell upcoming storms. While most of us are familiar with Mother Goose, geese are featured players in many fairy tales and folklore. Frau Holle is a Germanic crone goddess who shapeshifts between her human and goose forms and shakes her goose feather quilt over the world to make white flakes of snow. You might be familiar with the Grimm's fairy tales "The Goose Girl" or "The Golden Goose." However, the most famous tale of all is one of Aesop's Fables, "The Goose that Laid the Golden Eggs."

Golden Goose Egg Talisman

Your goose familiar can assist with some fairy tale magic by giving you an egg that you can turn into a talisman to bring you wealth and golden opportunities. Gold is a metal used in magic to attract wealth, and eggs are symbols of new beginnings, so you can make this talisman to attract new income streams with the help of your familiar. You might think working with real gold would be expensive, but gold leaf is flattened into extremely thin sheets, making it a relatively inexpensive material. You can adapt this spell to use any egg, especially if you have a hen, duck, or other egg-laying bird familiar.

What you will need:

- Egg from your familiar
- Large needle
- Bowl
- ½" to 1" (1 to 2.5cm) wide paint brush
- Water-based gilding adhesive or gilding size
- Egg carton
- 24k gold leaf sheets in a booklet
- Soft cotton cloth, such as a piece of a T-shirt
- Spray varnish

1. Empty your goose egg of the liquid by poking a small hole in the top and bottom of the egg with the needle and blowing out the yolk and white into a bowl. Be sure to pierce the yolk so that it can pass through the hole.
2. Wash the outside of your egg with water and dish soap, rinse the inside, and allow to dry.
3. Using the paint brush, apply the gilding adhesive to the entire egg. Allow the egg to rest on an egg carton for 15 to 30 minutes (or per the adhesive instructions) to allow the glue to get tacky.
4. Gently pick up the egg and roll it over the gold leaf or lift the gold leaf with its accompanying tissue paper and apply it to the surface of the egg.
5. If you want a more distressed-looking golden egg, you can leave some areas without gold and let the shell show through, but if you would like a

completely gold egg, you can apply an overlapping piece of gold leaf to cover the blank spots.

6. If there are any spots that did not take the gold leaf, you can apply another coat of glue, let it get tacky, and then apply gold leaf to that area.
7. Using the soft cotton cloth, gently rub the gold leaf on the eggs to smooth down any bumps and remove any extra leaf.
8. Let the gold leaf glue cure completely for about three days, and then spray your egg with clear varnish and let it dry on the egg carton.
9. Display your egg on your altar or thread a ribbon though the holes and hang in your home or any place you'd like to invite prosperity.

The Magic of the Egg

Eggs don't have to be gold to be magical. In cultures throughout time and all over the world, the egg was seen as a divine object. Eggs represent all potential: the circle of birth-life-death-rebirth, and a symbol of life to come. The Cosmic Egg, or World Egg, is a mystical icon that appears in the lore of many different cultures, telling the story of the beginning of Earth or sometimes the birth of the Universe. Eons before the physics of the Big Bang were discovered, ancient people understood the egg as a condensed form of power and expressed it in these creation myths.

Egg Charm Spell

An egg from your familiar can be used as a unique and special charm. Draw, paint, or dye them with magical symbols or words representing the wishes you have for something new in your life. It can be new love, a new job, a new home, or anything that is not present now but that you would like to manifest. Place the egg on your familiar altar to let it do its magic.

Like the golden goose egg talisman in the previous ritual, you can remove the white and yolk of the egg by poking a small hole in either end and blowing out the liquid inside. However, this isn't a necessary step as long as you don't seal off the eggshell entirely with paint or varnish. Eggs have a naturally slightly permeable shell, so the liquid inside will slowly dry out and, after a year or two, you'll end up with a hollow egg with a small pea-sized dried yolk rattling inside. Note that this only works as long as there are no cracks in the shell; you have used dyes, colored pencil, watercolor paints, or another material that allows the shell to breathe; and you leave your egg in a place out of direct sunlight and away from excessive heat.

Eggshell Home Protection Spell

Even the broken eggshells of an egg from your familiar that you have eaten or that has hatched have power in them. Rinse them in cool water to remove the gooey albumin membrane, and dry the shells on a cookie sheet in a low oven (200°F/93°C) for about 20 minutes. Once they've cooled, grind them with a mortar and pestle until you make a fine powder. This powder can be used in spells for protection and purification. Bless the powder and sprinkle it around your home, inside or out, to create a boundary of protection from negativity.

Eggshell powder is a healthy source of calcium and is good for strengthening bones in many animals—dogs, cats, and even humans can benefit—and for strengthening the shells of eggs in animals that lay them. It can be blessed with an intention of strength before mixing a small amount in the food of your familiar. Eggshell powder is also good for many of the plants in your garden and can be added to the soil as a fertilizer.

Eggshell pieces in bigger chunks can be left outside in early spring as an offering for wild birds that are nesting to help them lay eggs with strong shells. While offering eggshell powder or pieces is healthful for many animals, use common sense and research if it is safe for your particular animal familiar.

Befriending a Farm Animal Familiar

When you befriend a farm animal familiar, you create a bond like no other. Farm animal familiars start out with a reciprocal relationship, giving us as much or more than we give them. These smart, magical creatures can enhance your spiritual practice and give you more than just the magical milk, eggs, fibers, and feathers that can be used in your spells. With their unique abilities and personalities, they can delight, entertain, and teach you about the magical gifts both you and they share.

CHAPTER 8

Dog Familiars

Lessons from Your Dog Familiar

Loyal, protective, affectionate, and optimistic, dogs seem to embody every admirable characteristic we look for in a magical partner. Any dog-loving witch will testify that there is nothing like the unconditional love and tried-and-true companionship that a dog familiar gives so generously. When we think of a witch's familiar, cats might come to mind first, but the scientific name for dogs, *Canis familiaris*, actually includes the word *familiar* and there are plenty of legends and myths that teach us about our deep and ancient partnership with these magical canine companions.

In every culture, there are tales of heroic dogs and their connection to the divine. Some dog legends may be familiar, such as the Greek goddess Hekate and her black hounds that guard the Underworld; the jackal-headed Egyptian god of the afterlife, Anubis; the Greek goddess Artemis and her pack of hunting hounds; or the legendary Irish warrior Fionn mac Cumhaill and his giant, multicolored twin dogs, Bran and Sceólang, who stand as tall as Fionn's shoulder.

It's no wonder there are so many stories of deities and heroes that include dogs. Dogs are believed to be the first animal that ancient humans domesticated more than 30,000 years ago.[1] This long history has created a symbiotic relationship between people and dogs that blurs the lines of self and other.

Dogs can teach us so much about how to be a better person. Their infectious enthusiasm can remind you to take a moment to savor life's little pleasures. If you want to develop a mindfulness practice, dogs show you how to genuinely appreciate what is right in front of you. Think about how a dog will exude pure joy when you even *say* the word *walk* or *treat*. You never have to worry about a dog saying, "been there, done that."

Dogs also use their physical senses in ways that you can tap into. Our canine friends have better peripheral vision than we do, which allows them to see more of the world and can teach you to keep an eye out for opportunities that may not be directly in front of you. They also have exceptional senses of hearing and smell, so they can show you how to pick up on small clues that others miss and use them to bring more success into your life.

Dogs can also teach you how to truly express unconditional love. A dog doesn't care what you look like, how much money you make, or whether you are famous or not. They see the authentic, loving *you* and give back the love that you give them a hundredfold. And anyone that has tried to take away a dog's favorite toy can tell you that they are tenacious, holding on to the things that they value at any cost. When you work closely with a dog familiar, you can look to them to teach you these admirable qualities to become the witch your dog thinks you are.

How Your Dog Familiar Can Help You

Dogs are natural helpers. In the U.S. alone, there are about half a million service dogs helping people with daily tasks. While you might not have a highly trained service dog, this natural affinity to help can be part of your magical relationship. Depending on your dog familiar and their temperament, you can train a dog to sit patiently beside you and lend you their energy as you perform spells or guard a magical circle that you cast in your rituals. You can also involve your dog familiar in your spiritual practice in more playful ways, such as having them perform tricks based on how you wave a wand. Ask them to pick a tarot or oracle card with their mouth or tap it with their paw—just make sure it's a deck you don't mind getting slobbery or bent! (See "Tarot or Oracle Communication" in Chapter 3 and "Divination with Your Familiar" in Chapter 4.) Do you know what a witch calls a dog that can cast spells? A labracadabrador, of course.

How Your Dog Familiar Can Heal You

There are remarkable stories of dogs sniffing out cancer and alerting the person affected about it, but you don't have to have a serious disease to benefit from the healing your dog familiars can offer you. There are so many ways that your dog familiar can share their energy and help heal you emotionally, mentally, and physically.

First, just by having a dog in your life, you're doing wonderful things for your health. Getting outside to take your pup for a walk or play a game of fetch in the backyard has enormous benefits for your body and mind. For people who are socially isolated or have other trouble forming connections, dogs can provide that friendship bond that boosts mental health. For those who are struggling with depression and have a tough time performing routine tasks, taking care of a beloved pet can also remind them to do some self-care too.[2]

Making Magic with Your Dog Familiar

You can add a dose of magic to important mundane tasks such as grooming and dog walking. Let's start by giving the gift of healing back to your dog familiar in the form of a spiritual cleanse with a blessed crystal elixir.

Crystal Elixir Dog Bath

Magical practitioners do bath spells to spiritually cleanse themselves, and this can be done with your dog familiar too. If you're giving them a bath, you can turn it into a magical ritual to bless them. Using a crystal elixir is a safe way to add some magic to your dog's rinse water without strong essential oils or chemicals that might cause an allergic reaction. Some elixir can be added to your dog's bath *and* your bath so that you and your familiar can build a deeper understanding of one another.

Because the crystals never come in direct contact with the bathwater, feel free to get creative and use crystals that will protect, calm, energize, or give whatever blessings you'd like to your dog. For a wide range of crystals and their use with animal familiars, check out Appendix C.

You don't need to limit this spell to just dogs. Any familiar that you bathe can benefit from this ritual.

What you will need:

- One or more crystals
- A small clean glass jar to hold your crystals
- A large glass or ceramic bowl to hold both the water and the jar of crystals
- Spring water (bottled spring water can be purchased, though ideally from a glass bottle), distilled water, rainwater, morning dew, or simple tap water
- Sunlight or moonlight

1. Program your crystals with your intention by holding each one between the palms of your hands and speaking out loud what it is that you would like the crystal to do for your dog.
2. Put your crystals in the small jar, fill it with water, close the jar, and place the jar in the large bowl.
3. Pour water into the large bowl without allowing any of the water to get into the jar containing your crystals.
4. State your intention once again over the bowl and jar.

5. Leave the containers in the sunlight or moonlight for at least an hour but preferably all day or overnight.
6. Remove the jar of crystals from the bowl, pour the water from the jar onto the earth, and remove your crystals to let them dry.
7. The water in the bowl has been programmed with the energy of the crystals and your intention.
8. Use this water in your and/or your dog's baths within the next 48 hours to receive the gentle yet powerful benefits of crystal healing.

Dog Fur and Toenail Clipping Spells

Every time you take your dog to the groomer, brush your dog, or give them a "pawdicure," you have an opportunity to collect some of their hair or nails to be used in magical spells. Unlike cats, dogs don't shed their toenails, so the only way to get them is to trim them. Make sure when collecting fur or nails that your dog is not in an agitated, fearful, or angry state, as this energy will be a part of the artifact. Most dogs are excellent runners, so their toenails can be used for spells of endurance, speed, and focus. Also think of the qualities of your dog's breed or personality. Are they a hunter? Energetic? Playful? Hardworking? Protective? Intelligent? Adding a toenail or fur with the characteristics of your dog to a charm bag or bottle spell can add that energy to your spell.

Dogs are wonderful protectors, so fur from your dog familiar can be used in protection spells around your home and property. If you have a garden, make pouches from burlap or old tights or pantyhose, and stuff your dog's fur in them. Place these little pouches around the garden with a blessing of protection for your plants. These little dog familiar charm bags can trick rabbits and other small animals into thinking that a dog is nearby and can keep them from nibbling your vegetables and flowers. You can also pack some loose fur around the roots of the plants, which can naturally discourage slugs, snails, and small bugs.

If you want to use your dog familiar's hair to help the wildlife around you, you can also wrap tufts of dog fur on the branches of bushes or trees in the early spring for birds to use to line their nests. This way, you can bless both your four-footed and winged friends or familiars.[3]

Spiritual Sniffari Ritual

One of the best ways to attune to your dog familiar is to go on a spiritual walk, allowing their nose to guide you. I like to call this a *sniffari*. Before setting out, ask your dog to show you the way that they see the world, teach you to open your own senses, and protect you as you both wander. These scent walks can really be a spiritual and emotional treat for both of you.

Canines are incredibly scent oriented. The part of the dog's brain responsible for processing scent is approximately 40 percent larger than a human's, and they have up to 300 million scent receptors inside their nose, compared to only 6 million for us.[4] You truly can learn to stop and smell the roses from your dog familiar.

If possible, choose a route that is quiet and nature-filled, away from traffic, people, and other dogs, and then let them show you the way. If you are in an area where there are trees, rocks, and paths that they can explore and new and interesting scents to smell, all the better. As long as it's safe, be willing to go off the path and explore the things that are intriguing to them. Dogs are constantly collecting information through scent and sound. Pay attention to what captures their attention, and try to hear and smell what they do. Yes, it might mean barking at a squirrel once in a while, but your canine familiar can teach you mindfulness and magic. Follow with curiosity, and your pup can refine your intuition and teach you new ways of seeing the wonder that is in front of you.

The benefits of these dog-led walks in nature are immense for both you and your familiar. Being in nature has a grounding effect, which can reduce inflammation and improve sleep and mood. Exploring new areas will bring positive stimulation and help you and your dog to focus and can distract you from anxiety, worry, and unwanted self-talk that may be going through your head.[5] Sniffing actually has stress-reducing benefits for your dog, so it can also be a great way for your dog to decompress after a stressful event, like going to the groomer or vet.[6]

Dogs as Mediums

Most dog lovers will tell you stories of their pet's psychic ability, such as their dog knowing that they were coming home even at an unexpected time or via a different mode of transportation. This sixth sense allows dogs to access information that may not be apparent to us. In many myths around the world, dogs travel between the world of the living and the world of spirit, so naturally they have the ability to sense spirits. How many times have you seen your dog staring at what appears to be nothing? This ability to recognize spirits also makes them the perfect messengers to the spirit world. If you want to pass on a message to a deceased friend or ancestor, tell your dog familiar the message and whom you'd like to contact, and they will gladly pass it along for you.

Dog Familiar Spiritual Protector Ritual

Your dog will naturally take on the role of protector to guard you and your home, but you can also call on this natural trait of theirs when doing your magic. Train your dog to sit quietly beside you when you are casting a circle or doing spellwork. If you are doing astral projection, meditation, or dream work, keep your dog familiar near to offer protection when you go into these vulnerable states.

Notice the signals your dog gives when they are being protective in your day-to-day life. Do they prick up their ears, suddenly stand at attention, bark, or growl? Note if they do these things when you are doing your spiritual work. They may be warning you of a spiritual intrusion of some kind. Take a moment to cleanse the space by ringing a tinkling bell in the direction where their attention is going or lighting some incense or an herb bundle and wafting the smoke around the room. When your dog settles back down again, you know that your space is clear and you can proceed.

Dog Collar Amulet

Your dog familiar is so good at protecting you and your shared home, it's natural that you would want to do the same for them. You can turn your dog's collar, leash, tag, or bandana into a protective amulet in many creative ways. An easy and totally safe way that you can bless your dog's amulet is by waving it through incense smoke along with an incantation such as:

Four-footed friend, familiar of mine,
May you be guarded by the divine,
With protection and safety, by night and by day.
May all that is harmful stay far away.

You can do this ritual once and be done or, if you wish, you can recharge the talisman every time you wash and groom your dog.

If you would like to create an even stronger bond between you and your dog familiar, you can wear matching talismans. Add a protective charm or special crystal to their collar and wear an identical one as a necklace yourself. Bless them both by waving them through incense smoke. While any incense can be used as a medium for blessing an item, you can add extra support by choosing a botanical incense that is aligned with the particular energy that you would like to bless your dog with. Refer to Appendix B for specific suggestions.

Dog Bandana Amulet

Can we all agree that a dog in a bandana is adorable? Even the toughest guard dog dials up the cuteness factor if they are wearing a colorful cloth around their neck. A bandana can be more than just a fashion statement, it can be an opportunity to give your dog an extra dose of magic.

You can choose a bandana with symbols printed on it or, if you're a crafty witch, you can embroider a custom selection of symbols into very fancy canine couture. You can use protective symbols such as a pentacle, evil eye charm, six-petaled rosette, or Egyptian eye of Horus. You might want deeply magical symbols such as a triple moon, which stands for the blessings of the goddess; a protective witch's knot; a *triskele*, symbolizing divine connection; a *vegvísir*, which can help them always find their way home; or a *triquetra*, representing protection of land, sea, and sky. Think about the blessings you'd like to give your pup, and speak these wishes aloud as you embroider to add that energy to their talisman. Finish it off by waving it through incense smoke before tying it around their neck with a kiss on their forehead to seal the spell.

Dog Familiar Blessing Massage

Just as a massage relaxes, soothes, and heals us witches, so can it have a similar effect on our dog familiars. Hands-on contact with our canine companion can reduce their stress and anxiety (as well as ours), increase their circulation, decrease pain, and help you identify any health issues your dog might have at an early stage. Massage can also be turned into a magical ritual to bless your dog with health and happiness.

Massage is a give-and-take. If you're massaging a person, they can tell you to press harder or ease up on your touch if something is sore. Pay attention to your dog's signals. Make sure that your dog is in a calm, submissive state before you begin. If your dog is wound up in any way, try going for a long walk before you start. Begin with a light touch, and stop if your dog nips, growls, flinches, or moves away.

1. Start by choosing a mindful and peaceful space to perform this ritual.

2. Close your eyes and visualize what blessing you would like to give your dog. If your dog is ill, for example, you might visualize them romping around with vigor and happiness. If you want your dog to be safe, you can imagine them with a pink bubble of protection around them.

3. Gently pet your dog all over while speaking soothing phrases of your blessing such as, "Your body heals completely and your energy returns," or "You are safe and protected."

4. If your dog responds positively to this petting, you can begin massaging your dog's neck with light circular strokes. You can customize the blessings to the different parts of the body that you're focusing on too. For example, you can say, "May you always hold your head up with pride."
5. Work your massage down toward your dog's shoulders, then the chest, then front legs, and then paws. Be very gentle with the sensitive paw pads or skip massaging them altogether.
6. Using circular motions, go up and down on both sides of the spine, then move to the back legs and the base of the tail.
7. When you are finished, your dog should be thoroughly relaxed. Take a moment to lay your hands once again on your dog and visualize the blessing you wish for them to receive.

Magically Bonding with Your Dog Familiar

When you have a dog in your life that you love and adore, it's hard to even imagine that the relationship could get any closer. However, if you are a witch with a dog who wants to help you with your magic, that relationship *can* get even richer and deeper. If you are lucky enough to have a dog familiar, you can have even more wonderful adventures and make magical memories that will last lifetimes.

CHAPTER 9

Cat Familiars

Lessons from Your Cat Familiar

When you think of a witch's familiar, if the first thing you think of is a cat, you are not alone. For millennia, cats have been intimately entwined with magic and spirituality. They were honored in ancient Egypt through the worship of the cat goddess Bastet; there are stories of the prophet Muhammad and his love of cats; and in Japan, the lucky cat, Maneki Neko, brings fortune to both homes and businesses.

The association of cats specifically with witches might go back to Greek mythology and a story of Hekate, the goddess who is considered the queen of the witches. When she was attacked by the monster Typhon, she escaped to Egypt and shapeshifted into a cat. Of course, during the Middle Ages, when the Catholic Church declared that cats were satanic, people who had close cat companions had this relationship turned on them as they were suspected of practicing witchcraft. The cunning folk and their cat companions shared an independence that we can admire today but was seen as dangerous by those who wanted to control the population.

This true self-reliance is just one of the lessons that our cats can offer us. Working with a feline familiar can also teach us about patience. Just as your kitten will learn to sit and wait until the perfect moment to attack the hapless catnip toy in the corner, so our cats can teach us to spring on an opportunity at just the right time. They offer the skill of resilience, or "landing on our feet," when we're in an emotional free fall. Cats can show us how to use our psychic senses just as they use their whiskers and their reflective eyes to sense what isn't visible to us. Another lesson they have to offer is the gift of silence and invisibility and how this inconspicuousness can help our magical practice. Furthermore, feline familiars show us the power of honoring our personal cycles, taking time for play but making sure to indulge in plenty of restorative cat naps.

How Your Cat Familiar Can Help You

If you're a witch lucky enough to have a cat familiar, you may be reaping some benefits of this relationship without even knowing it. Being around happy cats is shown to significantly reduce stress. Even watching a video of a playful cat has been scientifically shown to improve mood, as if we needed *more* reasons to watch cat videos on our social media feed.[1] You can lean on your cat familiars to help you with spells to bring more joy into your life.

These little healing companions also improve our mental health. If you have a cat in your home, you have an in-house healer who, along with traditional modalities, can improve symptoms of depression, anxiety, and PTSD. Cats can also be helpers for neurodivergent children, such as those with autism or ADHD. Cats won't put up with bad behavior, and so they can teach give-and-take and other positive social behaviors that can help us improve our human relationships.[2]

How Your Cat Familiar Can Heal You

Sound affects more than our ears. Have you ever had the experience of being near a car with a booming bass or standing on the sidelines as the bass drum in a parade goes by? Then you know that you can feel sound in your body—from the thumpingest low notes to the gentlest tinkle of a bell. If you've ever taken a sound bath, you know the therapeutic benefits of auditory frequencies.

It's clear that sound waves can have a positive impact on you, and a cat's purr is no different. While cats often purr when they are feeling pleasure, curiously they also purr when under duress, such as healing from an injury. Studies have confirmed that purring falls between 25 and 240 Hz. This frequency has been shown to increase bone density and speed up the healing process of wounds, broken bones, and tendon and joint injuries.[3]

Purring releases endorphins in cats. And, as any witch who's had a cat curl up on their lap will attest, our human endorphins get activated by hearing and feeling a cat's purr as well. Endorphins lower stress and blood pressure, which in turn can improve your mental well-being and physical health. A study of over 4,000 people over a 20-year span discovered that cat owners are 40 percent less likely to die of a heart attack and 30 percent less likely to die of another cardiovascular disease (including strokes) than people without cats.[4]

If you have a cat familiar, you may find them snuggling up and purring next to you in times of intense stress or ill health. To maximize the benefits of this familiar doctoring, close your eyes and try to sync up your inhale and exhale to the rhythm of their breathing. Visualize your stress melting away and returning to the earth to be recycled into something better. Or simply see your body healing itself, cell by cell, in your mind's eye.

Whenever your cat purrs, you can attune to the rhythm they create and chant along with your cat. Think of a short positive affirmation that matches that rhythm. For example, you can chant "All is well" in time with each of your cat's purrs and work together to bring peace, stability, and contentment to you both.

Magical Artifacts of the Cat Familiar

Fur can be obtained through brushing your cat. Claws and whiskers can often be found around the home, if you look carefully. Whiskers should never be trimmed, as they are sensitive tools for helping cats navigate the world around them. These gifts from your cat, given freely and with pleasure, will have more positive power than nails trimmed, whiskers cut, or fur shaved off a fussy and struggling cat.

Cat Familiar Brushing Ritual

Cats groom each other to build mutual trust and show affection. By brushing your cat familiar, you can deepen your bond as well as receive the gift of their fur, which can be used in spells.

You can adapt this spell to any animal familiar that enjoys a good brushing.

What you will need:

- Incense or herb bundle (See Appendix B for specific suggestions.)
- A cat comb or brush
- A small bowl or box (to collect the fur)

1. Start by blessing your cat comb or brush by waving it through incense smoke with the intention of receiving the gifts of your cat before brushing them. You can add extra support by choosing a botanical incense that is aligned with the particular energy that you would like to bless your cat with.
2. Make sure your cat is comfortable and receptive to being touched. Pet them with your hand and ask them if they are willing to share some fur with you in exchange for some cuddly grooming time. If they agree, you will get a positive response from them, such as purring and slow blinking. If they fuss or play bite, it means, "Not now."

3. Start with the areas that they like being petted, such as the top of the head, along the back, or under the chin. As you brush them here, speak positive and reinforcing words to them. You can verbally admire their beauty and disposition, or thank them for all they do for you, including sharing their magical fur with you.
4. Collect the fur off the brush and set it aside in a small box or bowl.
5. If your cat is enjoying the grooming, venture to more sensitive areas such as the belly and see if your cat responds favorably. If not, go back to the "safe areas" of the head and back.
6. Usually, your cat will let you know when the grooming session is done, but you can also wrap it up when you have collected enough fur for your spellwork.
7. Sit with your cat for a moment, look them in the eyes and blink slowly at them. Thank them for sharing their magical fur with you.
8. Finish your ritual with some play or a special treat as an offering to your familiar and to reinforce the positive feelings of this exchange.

Obtain Whiskers and Claws from Your Cat Familiar Spell

Occasionally, a cat will shed a whisker or a claw. If you're lucky enough to find one of these special gifts from your familiar, it can be used in your spellwork. Claws that are shed are more powerful than claw trimmings because they are given freely and do not hold the energy of distress that most cats experience when getting a pawdicure. The following ritual will help you communicate to your familiar that you'd like to receive one of these gifts, if they're willing.

1. Sit with your cat familiar and pet them. If your cat is not open to touch, you can sit calmly nearby and send loving thoughts to them.
2. As your cat becomes receptive to your interaction, let them know about your desire for a whisker or claw that you can use in your magic.
3. In your mind's eye, sense, see, or feel finding a claw or whisker around the house or remember a time when you did find a claw or whisker. This imagery will let your familiar know you want them to leave it somewhere in the house where you can find it.
4. Let the petting or sitting session wrap up normally.
5. Over the next seven days, look for whiskers and claws as you clean up around the house.
6. If you don't find a whisker or claw, it may not be the ideal time for them to shed one. Be patient. You can repeat these steps once a week until you find your treasured gift from them.

Cat Fur, Claws, and Whiskers Spells

The fur, claws, and whiskers of your familiar can be used in a myriad of spells. Add them as an ingredient to a spell bottle used to protect your home, a spell box where you can charge up other items with their energy, or a spell bag that you carry in your pocket or purse to keep your feline familiar's magic flowing all around you.

Feline artifacts are often used in spells to bring second sight (cats can see in the dark), to sense and work with the spirit realm (cats can see spirits that we humans can't perceive), for longevity (cats have "nine lives"), or to turn bad luck to good (cats are able to magically land on their feet when falling). They can also be used as a link to your familiar when the two of you are apart or as a ritual object to bless them.

A cat's fur coat is their crowning glory, and they will take great care to groom themselves to make themselves beautiful. Fur also allows them to camouflage and blend in with their surroundings. These attributes can be used for your spellwork. Consider using their fur in spells for beauty, grace, or making yourself energetically invisible to your enemies.

Cat claws can be used in spells of fiery protection. They are used for catching prey and climbing, so they can also be used for hunting down and holding on to something that you desire or climbing to higher success. Cats tend to move silently (unless, of course, they are knocking over the tchotchkes on your dresser), so consider using their claws in spells to avoid detection or maintain secrecy.

Whiskers are a cat's sensitive receptors of the world around them. They can be used in your spells for strengthening empathic skills and developing your sixth sense or intuition. Because they provide information about the environment that can protect a cat from harm, they can be used in protection and shielding spells too. Since cats also use them for navigation, consider adding them to travel spells or spells to remove blocks and avoid obstacles.

Cat Fur Poppet

Your cat's fur can be felted just like wool to create a poppet that can then be used in spells to bless, protect, and bring your cat back home if they go missing. (If you're new to felting or would like more detailed guidance, consider looking for felting video tutorials online.) You'll be creating an oval ball for the body, a smaller ball for the head, two small triangles for the ears, and a long cylinder for the tail.

What you will need:

- A large handful of your cat's fur
- A felting needle

1. Start with the body. Roll half the fur into a loose oval-shaped ball between your hands. Rolling between your hands will begin to mat the fur and will form the beginnings of your shape.
2. Poke the felting needle into the ball and pull it out repeatedly. Poking the felting needle will cause the fur to mat and compact into the desired shape. Be patient with this process, as felting is slow and meditative. As you do this poking/felting, you can chant an incantation such as:

Four-footed fur friend, I love you, I do.
This poppet I'm crafting's a stand-in for you.
May it guard and protect you from any mean foe,
And bless your adventures wherever you go.

3. When the matted fur feels firm with few hairs sticking out, you are done.
4. Repeat this process with a smaller amount of fur to create a round head.
5. Attach the head to the body by holding them in place and repeatedly poking the felting needle at the spot where the head joins the body.
6. Felt two small cone shapes for the ears and attach to the head in the same way.
7. Create a tail and attach it to the body.
8. Your felted cat poppet is complete. Wave the poppet through incense smoke (a great incense would be to burn catnip on charcoal, but you can use botanical incense from any of the recommendations found in Appendix B) and say:

   I link this poppet to (name of cat)
   for their safety and protection.

9. Place the poppet on an altar or keep it in a safe place until needed.
10. When you want to protect your cat from a distance, you can burn incense and wave the poppet through the smoke. This poppet can also be used anytime you are separated and need to

communicate with them. For example, you can pet and talk to the poppet to calm your cat's nerves when they are at the vet or groomer, or, if they are lost, you can speak to the poppet to call them back home again.

Whisker Wishing Spell

It is said that burning a cat's whisker while wishing will ensure that the wish comes true. You can burn the whisker by itself or add the whisker to a burning charcoal along with herbs and resins that are aligned with your wish. (Refer to Appendix B for specific suggestions.)

What you will need:

- A found cat whisker
- Matches
- Piece of foil

1. Hold the whisker between your thumb and forefinger.
2. Whisper your wishes into the whisker.
3. Finish your wish with the phrase, "It is already done!"
4. Light the tip of the whisker with a match over the foil, then drop it onto the foil when the flame gets close to your fingers.
5. If the flame goes out before burning completely, just light the whisker again.

6. Once the foil cools, take the ashes outside to be lifted by the wind and float wherever they need to go to manifest your wish.
7. Recycle the piece of foil with a blessing of protection for the earth.

Catnip Psychic Link Potion

If your cat is a catnip lover (about 50 to 70 percent of cats are), consider a catnip tea party for the two of you. One of the magical uses of catnip is to increase the psychic connection between you and a cat. This ritual can be used to strengthen your psychic link to your familiar or to initiate the bond between you and a cat you wish to be your familiar.

Catnip can make cats livelier but for humans it has the opposite effect. It contains the terpene nepetalactone, which can improve relaxation and mood and reduce anxiety, restlessness, and nervousness in humans.[5] Catnip can make you drowsy, so this is a brew best consumed toward the end of the day. While catnip is generally safe for most humans and cats, as with all medicinal herbs, you should research catnip before ingesting to make sure it is compatible with your body, your cat's body, and any health conditions that either of you may have.

What you will need:

- 4 teaspoons dried catnip (*Nepeta cataria*) leaves or flowers
- Teacup or mug
- *Optional:* teapot

- *Optional:* tea strainer
- Saucer
- *Optional:* lemon or honey, to taste

1. Pour 2 cups of boiling water over the dried catnip in your mug (or teapot, if using).
2. As the tea steeps, hold your hands over the steam and speak the words of this incantation to increase the connection between you and your cat familiar:

   Magical cat! Oh, feline friend!
   May the link between us never end.
   Make our bond be stronger here tonight,
   And join us with our second sight.

3. Allow the potion to brew for 5 to 15 minutes. The longer the brewing time, the stronger the flavor, but the magical strength of the potion is unaffected.
4. Use a tea strainer if desired to remove the leafy bits as you pour some of this brew into a saucer for your cat and portion some for yourself. Allow the potion to cool to room temperature.
5. You may add lemon and honey to your cup but leave your cat's saucer of tea plain. Catnip tea has a woodsy, grassy taste, but the longer it sits with lemon in it, the more you'll taste its natural underlying minty, citrusy flavor.
6. Drink your potion together as you sit in each other's company, and enjoy this cozy familiar bonding ritual.

You may discover after doing this ritual a few times that you can sense what your cat needs or wants more easily and that, if your cat is away, you can telepathically call them back to you.

Cat Omens (Ailuromancy)

It wouldn't be a surprise to most cat owners to discover that their pet has a secret double life, but you might be surprised to find out that your cat familiar is also a fortune teller. *Ailuromancy* is a folkloric method of divination by the action of cats. Even nonmagical people in times past saw that cats had a knack for sensing events that were to come, especially when it comes to predicting rain. Observing the actions of your familiar can be an enlightening way for your cat to communicate with you. Pay attention when your cat does any of these actions to get signs for what lies ahead:[6]

- **Curled up with their forehead touching the ground:** stormy weather is coming
- **Following you as you walk:** money is coming your way
- **Looking out the window for a long time:** rain is coming
- **Sitting with their back toward a fire/heater:** cold weather is coming
- **Sleeping with all their paws tucked under their body:** rain on the way
- **Sneezing once:** luck is coming to the house

- **Sneezing the day before a wedding:** a happy marriage
- **Sneezing three times:** someone in the house will catch a cold
- **Unknown cat coming into the house:** birth and fertility or good luck
- **Washing their face on your front doorstep:** a spiritual person will pay a call
- **Washing their face vigorously:** rain is coming
- **Washing their ear:** a visit from a stranger*
- **Washing their ear three times:** a visitor coming from the direction that the cat is looking*
- **Wildly running through the house:** a storm is coming

*If it's the right ear, it means a man; the left ear means a woman.

Inviting Your Cat Familiar into Your Magic

Cats by their nature are mysterious and magical creatures, which makes them a natural when it comes to working with them as familiars. Like most familiars, you both must agree to this partnership, but if your cat has indicated that they are willing to help you with your magic, you will find that they enhance your practice in special and surprising ways. Enjoy the fun, enchantment, and bewitchery that your feline familiar brings to everything you do.

— CHAPTER 10 —

Horse Familiars

Lessons from Your Horse Familiar

If you have a horse familiar, you have a very special magical companion indeed. Anyone who is close to horses can tell you that there is nothing like the power, affection, and trust that you learn from allying with these majestic beings. In every ancient culture where horses existed, they were revered as special creatures, embodying grace, beauty, strength, independence, and mutual trust.

Humans have had a deep connection to horses for millennia. Cave paintings made tens of thousands of years ago feature animals of all kinds, but the animal most often depicted is the horse. Even though horses have been domesticated for 6,000 years, we still sense their wild and free nature. If you ride horses, you most definitely have had the experience of tapping into that freedom. It isn't uncommon for horse riders to experience the sensation that they and their horse galloping in unison are one being. This feeling of merging may have been the inspiration for the centaur, a being that is half-human and half-horse. It's not a stretch to say that human culture as we know it would not exist if it weren't for the close relationship between human and horse. It is no wonder that the equine familiar is a special favorite of witches.

How Your Horse Familiar Can Help You

The bond between you and your horse familiar can be exceptionally rewarding. Horses are herd animals, and in the wild they rely on one another and form deep, long-term friendships with others in their group. Horse buddies will play together, groom each other, and stand together to sleep. If one is separated from their friends, they can show signs of anxiety and depression. They are also open to forming new bonds when an unfamiliar horse joins the herd. This natural friendliness means that when you gain the trust of a horse, you gain a loyal and lifelong partner. A horse familiar will eagerly lend you their magic, assist you in attracting good people into your life, and help you deepen your bond with other animals.

Any horse-owning witch can tell you that horses are smart. Their intelligence is what allows humans and horses to work closely together. They respond particularly well to training with the positive reinforcement of treats and loving strokes. They can even understand and respond to words in human language. They have excellent memories and can recall complex, problem-solving strategies that they learned 10 or more years earlier. They also remember friends from the past and can recognize and respond to horses and people who have treated them with kindness even after years of separation. Of course, they can lend us their energy to reinforce our intelligence and memory, but they can also teach us how to use these qualities for strengthening loving connections. With their ability to work together with a caring witch companion, they can be lovingly trained to assist in ritual as well.

How Your Horse Familiar Can Heal You

An emerging body of scientific evidence confirms that interacting with horses can help people with a wide array of physical, emotional, and mental health conditions. People who grapple with everything from motor disabilities to PTSD can see improvement by participating in equine therapy.[1] If you are facing your own challenges, big or small, you can work with a licensed equine therapist, but you can also invite your horse familiar to send you healing simply by asking them to share their energy with you.

Position yourself next to your horse familiar when they are calm and contented, then gently place your hands on them and close your eyes. See, sense, or feel the energy that your horse is sharing with you; imagine it going to the places in your heart, mind, or body where it is needed. After receiving this healing energy for as long as you and your familiar are comfortable, open your eyes and thank your wonderful familiar for their generous gift.

Horse Familiar Communication

Horses are great communicators and express themselves through both body language and a wide range of vocalizations. A horse's whinnies, neighs, snorts, and sighs are not just random noises; they are filled with deep meaning. Learning their language can open up rewarding conversations and deepen your connection.

You can even learn to speak "horse" yourself. For example, when a horse makes a long, contented, drawn-out snort, blowing air through their nose when eating, resting, or playing, they are expressing enjoyment and well-being. When horses get together and make this sound to each other, it is a sign of love and affection. If you make this sound back at your horse familiar, they can understand that you're saying, "I love you too, friend."[2]

Horses also use their ears, tail, and posture to express themselves. When a horse's tail is hanging loosely behind them, they are relaxed or possibly even bored. A tail that is slightly raised indicates contentment. However, if they are switching their tail forcefully, they are sending you a big no and expressing resistance and dissatisfaction. Horses' ears also are also quite expressive. If your familiar's ears are alert and pointed forward, they are expressing curiosity and attentiveness; if they are pinned back, they are telling you that they are angry or fearful.

Horses can even be trained to communicate in quite specific ways. In a Norwegian study, horses were trained to touch a board in their stall with three different images to express if they wanted their blanket on, blanket off, or no change. The horses understood the meaning of the three symbols and were able to communicate appropriate desires based on the temperature of their stall.[3] This opens up some wonderful possibilities in terms of how you and your horse familiar can communicate, make magic, and even perform divination.

Divination with Horses (Hippomancy)

The ancient and widespread practice of using horses for divination, or *hippomancy*, holds a prominent place in ancient Persian, Celtic, Slavic, Germanic, and other cultures of antiquity. Sacred horses were seen as intermediaries and messengers between deities and humankind and were bred specifically as oracles who could predict future events. The movements, vocalizations, and traces that sacred horses left would be interpreted by diviners who would convey the message to the querent. If you have a sacred horse (and if a horse is your familiar, they are *very* sacred), then you might want to try some of this method to let your horse advise you on decisions you have to make.

Slavic Hippomancy

Slavic people in antiquity had quite formal divination rituals connected with the horse. A special sacred all-black or all-white horse would be kept in a temple associated with a specific god and used solely for forecasting the future. When a tribe was contemplating going to war, a holy incantation would be spoken, and the hallowed horse would be led over spears to foretell the outcome of the battle.

Different temples had variations on the details of this rite. In one temple, the practice was to place three pairs of crossed spears stuck into the ground and lead the sacred horse over them. If the horse stepped over all three with their right foot first, then the battle would be a success. If they led with their left foot over even one of the pairs, going into battle was inadvisable. In another example, nine spears were laid flat on the ground and the horse would be led over the nine spears three times. If the horse stumbled on any of the spears, then the battle was fated to be lost.[4]

If you like, you can adapt this ritual, and perform divination with your horse familiar. Rather than spears, use broomstick-sized dowels. If you have access to ground poles, you can use them instead, as this method is very similar to training your horse to walk over ground poles. You can start with mastering walking over one pole, and then eventually work your way up to nine.

What you will need:

- 9 broomstick-sized dowels or ground poles

1. Think of an endeavor that you would like to pursue, such as a job, a relationship, or an opportunity of some kind.
2. Lay nine poles down about one yard (1m) apart in a parallel horizontal path—like stepping over cracks so you don't break your mother's back.
3. Ask your question aloud to your horse familiar, and then recite the following incantation:

   Sacred horse, familiar of mine,
   I open the doors to advice divine.
   Share your wisdom, please confess
   If my endeavor will bring success.

4. Lead your horse over the poles in one direction.
5. Turn them around and lead them back over the poles.
6. Turn them around a third time and lead them forward over the poles one more time.
7. If they step over all the poles without stumbling, then the answer is a yes to your endeavor.
8. If they stumble over any of the poles, then now is not the time for this endeavor.
9. You can ask about a different endeavor and do the ritual again, or ask about the same endeavor again at a later date.
10. Thank your horse for sharing their wisdom with you and give them a treat to show your gratitude.

Horsehair Fairy Knots

The mane and tail of a horse are filled with magic. If you have a horse familiar, you probably have noticed that you can leave your horse perfectly combed at night and return the next morning to find their mane and tail has knots and tangles. The phenomenon of these mysterious knots is filled with lore. For many cultures, the belief is that these tangles, called *elf locks* or *fairy knots,* are made by the fae folk overnight. While you are sleeping, the good folk look for the most magical horses in the stable and twist their manes to form tiny stirrups and reins so that they can ride them on otherworldly adventures throughout the night. When they return them to the stable in the morning, the evidence of their nighttime rides can be found in these knots that they leave behind.

When you find these on your horse, you know that they have been blessed by the fairies. Some folks believe that if you untangle the knots, you upset the fairies, because they must do all their hard work over again. So, if you do take these knots out, leave the fairies an offering of a saucer of milk or a little porridge sweetened with honey near the stall to placate them.

Horsehair Braiding Charm

You can create blessings for your horse familiar by making your own neat braids in the mane and tail. Braiding hair, either your own or your horse's, is a magical act. When you braid three tresses together, you are combining the forces of the Lower World, Middle World, and Upper World for a powerful spell. These three otherworldly realms are the segments of the mythical World Tree and where we connect to a variety of spirits. The Lower World is ruled by nature spirits, animal spirits, and ancestor guides. The Middle World is inhabited by us humans, animals, and other tangible beings, as well as the hidden folk such as elves, fairies, and gnomes. The Upper World is the home of deities, ascended masters, and other rarified spirits. By braiding three tresses, we can invite the blessings from all these worlds.

As you braid, speak, sing, or think of an incantation that will bring the blessings that you would like to give your horse familiar.[5] Tie the braid off with a ribbon in the color that is most aligned with your wish. See Appendix D for a list of colors and their magical properties.

Nine-Knot Horsehair Charm

A long hair from a horse's tail can also be turned into a very powerful charm that you can carry with you. As with all familiar charms, this should be freely given, either one that your horse has shed on their own or one you get from brushing them. Carrying a plain horsehair in a small pouch can help you access the blessing of your horse familiar: freedom, success, strength, motivation, and vitality. It can also strengthen the bond between you and your familiar.

If you would like the help of your familiar in a particular intention, however, you can create a traditional nine-knot charm.

What you will need:

- A horsetail hair from your familiar that is at least 13 inches (33cm) long
- Cloth pouch
- Matches

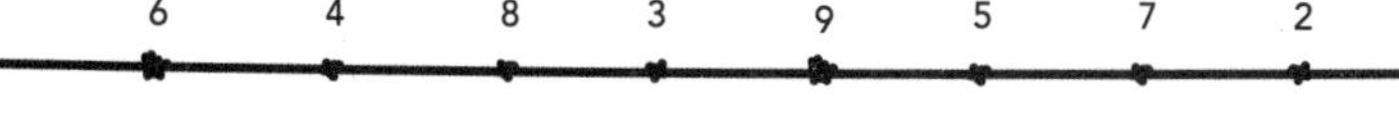

1. Hold the tail hair in your hands and focus on the intention or goal that you would like to manifest. You may whisper it into the horsehair, speak it aloud, or visualize having the result.
2. Tie the knots in the order shown in the image. The first knot is made on the far left, the second knot on the far right, the third in the middle, and so on.

3. As you make each knot, recite the following incantation, one line for each knot:

   By the knot of one, the spell's begun.
   By the knot of two, it cometh true.
   By the knot of three, thus shall it be.
   By the knot of four, 'tis strengthened more.
   By the knot of five, so may it thrive.
   By the knot of six, the spell we fix.
   By the knot of seven, the Stars of Heaven.
   By the knot of eight, the hand of fate.
   By the knot of nine, the thing is mine.[6]

4. Place the horsehair in a cloth pouch and carry it with you in a pocket or purse until your wish comes true.
5. After you receive your wish, burn the horsehair and thank your familiar for lending their magic by giving them an extra treat.

Horseshoes

Probably the most familiar amulet that the horse brings to us is the horseshoe. In cultures throughout Europe, the Middle East, and the Americas, horseshoes are seen as luck-bringers. It is believed that horseshoes, with their crescent shape, bring luck because they represent the protection of the moon goddess.

There is an ongoing debate on how you should hang a horseshoe, whether the ends should point up, like the letter *U*, or down. The points-up people believe that all your luck will run out if the ends are down; the points-down folks think that the luck flowing out is the whole idea, so the horseshoe will pour luck on you every time you walk under it.

My advice to you is to experiment with both. If you have a strong intuition or cultural tradition for one direction, follow that. Personally, I have horseshoes pointed both up and down in my home and my office. You might think that I'm just covering my bases, but I have seen a genuine outpouring of luck from both. Go with whichever one feels right for you.

Horseshoe Talisman

If you own a horse, then using a horseshoe that they have worn can add some extra magic and connect you even more deeply to your familiar. It is believed that a horseshoe that has been worn has much more power than simply a decorative one, so a shoe from your companion can bring even more magic. Make sure that the horseshoe that you use is one removed by a farrier, not one that your horse has thrown. Throwing a shoe is bad luck for your horse familiar so is less likely to bring luck to you.

Hammer a horseshoe above the door to your house and over your horse's stall to protect them too. Horseshoes also have a protective element, as they are made of iron, which is believed to keep mischievous spirits at bay. If you'd like to amp that up even more, you can rub a drop of a spiritual oil on them from time to time for protection, power, or luck. (See the protection oil recipe in Chapter 5). Touch the horseshoe as you pass under it to receive an extra blessing.

Horseshoes can impart their power even when they are not hung up. You can charm a tree by burying horseshoes under them. The people of rural Lincolnshire, England, would bury horseshoes under ash trees. The protective and curative power of the horseshoe would be absorbed by the tree, and the twigs of this blessed tree could be stroked over livestock to remove hexes and the evil eye.[7]

The Magic of the Horse Familiar

The connection between you and your horse familiar is unique and powerful. When you ride your familiar, the two of you can move in unison, feeling the sense of freedom, power, and pure joy. Your majestic horse familiar can lend you its energy to heal you and make you brave, confident, and strong. Lean on your horse familiar for magic as well as friendship and enjoy the ride.

CHAPTER 11

Rodent and Rabbit Familiars

The Magic of Rodent and Rabbit Familiars

Fuzzy, nibbly, lovable little critters like rabbits and rodents are some of the most popular pets out there. If you've ever read Beatrix Potter's tales of Peter Rabbit or Mrs. Tittlemouse, you're probably just as enchanted as she was with these adorable and affectionate creatures. When one of these cuddly beasties agrees to be your familiar, the two of you will discover exciting worlds, explore new ways of casting spells, and make incredible magic together, having fun all the while.

Lessons from Your Rodent Familiar

Squirrels, rats, mice, hamsters, gerbils, guinea pigs, and chinchillas are little bundles of fluff that can co-create an animal familiar bond that is delightfully close and infinitely entertaining. Nowadays, you might get a look of slight surprise when playing with your pet rat or mouse, but a person who had a pet rodent in centuries past would have been viewed as truly breaking the rules of society. Prior to large-scale industrialization, rodents were viewed as vermin who carried disease and destroyed crops. Nevertheless, there are documented confessions of accused witches having mouse and rat familiars. Even though these confessions were undoubtedly forced or coerced, they give us a hint that people may have had close connections to wild rodents in a time when this would have been seen as truly rebellious.

What people without experience don't know is how bright, friendly, and entertaining these special familiars can be. Some of these rodent familiars can be quite portable and adaptable, allowing you to take your "pocket pet" with you wherever you do your spell casting. They lend their playful nature to your magic, helping you to lighten up, have fun, and not get so anxious about the little things. When you frolic with your rodent familiar, you'll discover the magic in play and the play in magic.

Making Magic with Your Rodent Familiar

Some rodents, such as squirrels, should always be considered wild familiars. Others, such as hamsters, gerbils, guinea pigs, and chinchillas, are almost always domestic pets, unless you live in the areas where they are wild. And mice and rats can be found both domestically and in the wild. When you care for your rodent familiar in your home, consider the following rituals for working with them and developing your relationship.

Rodent Familiar Magic Pouch

Getting a domestic rodent to like being cozy with a human takes time and patience, but a bonding pouch may speed up the process. This is a specially made fuzzy sack that you can hold or wear on your body to help your rodent get used to your smell, being handled and touched, your movements, and the sounds you make. Inside that comforting, cozy space, your familiar will feel safe next to you so that eventually you feel safe to them too.

You can make a pouch from one of the many patterns available online, or you can purchase one that is already made. Once you have it, you can make it a magical pouch to bless and protect your familiar, as well as create a closer familiar bond.

Embroider or use nontoxic fabric paint or fabric ink on the exterior of the pouch to add magical symbols such as pentacles, triple moons, triskeles, witch's knots, or six-petaled rosettes. (You'll find some examples of magical designs in the "Dog Bandana Amulet" section of Chapter 8.) After it is decorated, hold the pouch in your hand, close your eyes, and visualize your familiar and you bonding.

Rodents are scent-oriented, so if you can put the pouch (or the cloth before you make the pouch) in their cage, it will seem homier to them, so they will be more eager to go inside. Let your familiar get used to going in the pouch on their own, then progress to removing the pouch from the cage with the animal in it, then holding it in your lap. Once your familiar is comfortable in their pouch in your lap, you can start wearing the pouch as you move around the house. If you want to create that trust bond, don't rush it. The process should be a slow and gentle one over many sessions, always led by the familiar.

Rodent Familiar Blessing Ritual

Pet rodents can be quite sociable and, with a little encouragement, will happily crawl on your arms and shoulders or sit on your lap. If your familiar has gotten friendly with you, this trust bond can be turned into a blessing ritual that will bring the two of you even closer.

This ritual requires that your familiar crawl through a tube. If your rodent is not used to doing so, you can train them by putting a small treat inside and offering one at the exit. Repeat until they are comfortable going through the tube.

What you will need:

- Empty paper towel tube, toilet paper tube, or similar
- Pen or marker

1. Think of a wish or a blessing that you would like for yourself, your familiar, or for both of you. It can be very simple, such as "I am prosperous," or "Bless my familiar bond."
2. Write the blessing on the outside of the tube. You can write individual words, an incantation, sigils, or symbols representing your wish.

3. Place the tube in your rodent's enclosure and encourage them to walk through the tube. As they do, hold your hands over the tube and speak or visualize the blessing.
4. At the exit of the tube, hold out your hand and let your familiar crawl on you. As they touch your body, imagine each little touch of their tiny paws spreading the blessings you are envisioning over you.

Rodent and Rabbit Familiar Wand

One of the most remarkable things about your rabbit or rodent familiar is their teeth. Rodents have two long incisors and rabbits have four, and these teeth grow continuously throughout their lives. These powerful choppers can cut through cables, plastic, fiberglass, and even sheet metal. Of course, it is a terrible idea to let your familiar chew on these harmful materials, but you can and should provide them with healthy ways to trim down and sharpen their teeth.

You can help your familiar keep their teeth in perfect shape and even make some magic with them by giving them a natural wand made of nontoxic wood to chew on. Wands are used in magic to focus our intentions, and the material it's made of can add extra energy. Refer to Appendix F to see how you can harness the energy of different trees and plants for distinct types of magic. You can purchase many of these woods from pet supply stores or you can harvest them yourself if you can positively identify the plant and know that it is growing in a pesticide-free area.

1. Select a wood that is in alignment with your magical goals according to the list in Appendix F.
2. Purchase untreated wood sticks made for rodents and rabbits or harvest fresh, pesticide-free branches. Always thank the tree or bush for the gift and give it an offering in return. Water is always appreciated by plants, but you can also offer a pretty crystal or some biodegradable food that is safe for the earth and any animals around.
3. *If using fresh branches:* Check the wands, remove any thorns, and discard any branches that exhibit disease, infestations, or rot. Dip the fresh branches in boiling water and then bake in an oven on a low setting (about 200°F to 250°F/90°C to 120°C) for 2 to 3 hours to dry and sanitize them.
4. *Optional:* Carve or use a wood-burning tool to inscribe a short wish or intention on the stick, if you desire, such as "true love" or "abundance."
5. Ask your pet familiar to assist you with your goal. Envision each nibble that they make on the wand being like a little boost of energy to your intention.

Chinchillas

The shy little chinchilla has the softest fur of all the rodents, which can make them absolutely irresistible for cuddling, but you'll have to earn that privilege. It may take a year or two for your chinchilla to warm up to you, but with a lifespan of 10 to 20 years, you'll be able to enjoy that closeness for quite a long time.

Chinchillas are used to jumping around in the high mountains of Peru and when your chinchilla familiar is feeling comfortable in their surroundings, they will zip around, throwing in jumps, twists, turns, and hops like an athlete doing parkour off your walls and furniture. If you need more physical strength or energy, your chinchilla familiar has lots to spare. They can also help you find the free spirit inside of you. If you are lacking zest for life, ask your chinchilla to lend their energy and do a spell for more *joie de vivre*. (Refer to "Exchanging Energy with Your Familiar" in Chapter 4.)

Chinchilla Protection Bath

One of their favorite activities is taking a dust bath, which is their method of self-grooming. Watching them twist, turn, and flip in the blink of an eye, kicking up dust everywhere, you can sense their pure joy. Chinchilla dust is made from ground pumice, a stone known for its magical ability to absorb negativity as well as clean your familiar.

Hold your hands over the dust and bless it with the intention that all stress, sadness, and anxiety is removed every time your chinchilla does their self-care routine. Deepen your connection by using a pumice stone to rub away your own rough skin in the bath.

Gerbils

Gerbils are about the same size as hamsters but with pointy, ratlike noses, long hind legs that they can extend and stand up on, and long furry tails with a tuft at the end. They are inquisitive, active, and incredibly interested in the people around them. When kept where the action is, they will easily adapt to the routine of the witches they live with.

Gerbils are highly social and need daily interaction and handling. Most love being held and don't even mind you waking them up, as they are always ready for some play and fun. They like to be social and will be happiest living in even-numbered groups or pairs of gerbils. Their love of socializing can also help you in any magic you do to feel comfortable around other people and attract quality friendships and relationships. If you are looking for a partner, whether a best friend or a lover, your gerbil familiar will be happy to share their special magic.

Gerbil Willow Ball Spell

Balls made from woven willow branches are a favorite gerbil toy and can be turned into a magical tool. Willow attracts love, protects against negativity, and aids in healing magic. Before giving your gerbil familiar a new willow ball, hold it in both hands and make one wish for your gerbil and one wish for yourself. As your gerbil gnaws away at the ball, envision the wish being sent out into the Universe to be activated.

Most other rodents and rabbits enjoy playing with a willow ball too, so this spell can be adapted to your pocket pet.

Guinea Pigs

Unlike the other rodents in this chapter, guinea pigs have been domesticated in South America for more than 7,000 years. While they were initially domesticated as a food source, they began to be viewed as pets when they were introduced in Europe by Spanish and Portuguese soldier-colonizers who brought them from Peru, Ecuador, Columbia, Argentina, and Bolivia in the 16th century. These novel pets became favorites of the nobility, and Queen Elizabeth I was one of the early adopters of this trend. When you have a guinea pig, you really do have a familiar fit for a queen.

While generally quiet like all rodents, guinea pigs do have special vocalizations that have different meanings. Squeaks, tweets, and squeals are their way of saying, "Help! I'm in danger!" "Wheek, wheek" means "Hey, witch friend, feed me!" Whining is their way of saying, "This sucks!" Their "chutt" or chortle means, "Everything's awesome!"

Start imitating the positive sounds your familiar makes when they are happy, calm, and content. By speaking to them in their language, you can start to understand them more and get even closer. Guinea pigs can help you with spells of communication, when you need to speak your truth and be heard by others. As your familiar sings their joyful squeaky tune, you can sing or whistle along too.

Guinea Pig High-Five Spell

Guinea pigs like to have all four feet on the ground in case they need to make a quick getaway. However, you can train them to place one or both front paws on your hand by offering them a small treat. If your familiar is accustomed to you, you can slowly hold your hand out to them palm up like a ramp for them to step on. Hold a treat with your other hand just far enough away that they have to place one of their paws on your hand to reach it.

Whether your familiar is a guinea pig or another domestic familiar, anytime you are preparing to do some spellwork with your hands, take a moment to offer them a treat and get a high five from them to add their magical energy to your spellwork.

Hamsters

While hamsters are not as avid for human company as some other rodents are, they are generally independent, clean, low-maintenance and, with patience and kindness, can develop a bond with their witch. Watching your hamster familiar run on their wheel or energetically dig, you can see how they can add lightheartedness, moxie, and a touch of whimsy to your magic.

If you have a hamster familiar, you will learn how to be adaptive. Hamsters are nocturnal and *you* will definitely have to learn to work around *their* schedule. Wake up a sleeping hamster, and you will get a grumpy little familiar who will most likely not want to make magic with you. But, if you like casting spells at the witching hour, you'll have a charming little dynamo who will delight you as they party all night long.

The name "hamster" comes from the German word *hamstern*, which means "to hoard" and undoubtedly came about because of the adorable way they store their snacks in their chubby cheeks. In your magical practice, a hamster can share their energy to bring abundance.

Hamster Abundance Spell

Hamsters love the special treat of a dried flower or herb every now and then, and many of their favorites are also herbs that are used in prosperity spells. Chamomile (*Matricaria chamomilla*), sunflower (*Helianthus annuus*), calendula (*Calendula officinalis*), hazelnut leaves (*Corylus americana*), apple leaves (*Malus domestica*), and peppermint (*Mentha x piperita*) are all safe for your hamster and can be sprinkled in their cage for them to forage.

When you offer your hamster their treat, bless the herbs for abundance in your home. Doing a prosperity candle spell will amp up the power. Simply sprinkle one or more of these herbs around the base of a green candle, then light it for a prosperity wish to bring more abundance into both your lives.

Other rodent and rabbit familiars enjoy herbs and flowers too, so you can adapt this spell to them with herbs that are safe for their species.

Mice

If you are inviting a mouse familiar, you are most likely going to be working with a domesticated or fancy mouse. If you are working with a wild mouse, treat them with respect as to their nature. It is harmful to the mouse and potentially to you too, to trap a wild mouse in a cage or train it to become dependent on you. Mice are delicate, and their tiny size makes them more vulnerable, so they must be handled with gentleness. Still, you may find that your mouse takes a long time to get comfortable with humans.

When it comes to human touch and companionship, mice can be a little particular. Female mice are just fine socializing with other female mice and may or may not desire a relationship with a human. Male mice, on the other hand, will battle with other males or impregnate females, so they do best when housed on their own and getting their socialization needs met through contact with you.

In the spiritual realm, a mouse familiar can teach us about focus, abundance, humility, precision with details, and living in the moment. Work with your mouse to calm your worries about the future, to focus on the present, and cherish the simple things in life. Your little mouse will be happy to share their energy with you to give you a sense of purpose for even the smallest actions.

Mouse Treasure Hunt Spell

Mice love to dig and burrow. Invite them to do a special spell with you, and their diligence can add the energy of achievement to your magic. Set up a digging box filled with moistened coconut fiber substrate and bury a few toys, seeds, or chewing sticks for them to discover. As you bury each item, add a blessing, such as, "Sunflower seed, may our abundance grow" or "Applewood stick, bring us luck." Then let your mouse find the treasure and add their energy to your wishes. (This spell can easily be adapted for use with another rodent or rabbit.)

Rats

Like snake and spider familiars, rat familiars get a bad rap. While those who don't have experience with rats might think that your pet is the same as the rodents digging in the trash and stealing slices of pizza in subway stations, they are not the same. It is not recommended to trap or keep any wild animal, including a rat. Wild rats have certain problematic characteristics that domestic rats do not, and they can transmit diseases, making it inadvisable to physically work with them. You can, however, work with their energy as you do with all wild animals—at a respectful distance that honors their wild nature.

Fancy or domestic rats, on the other hand, are ideal for familiar magic because they are calmer, less aggressive, sociable with people, and exceptionally clean. They are also highly intelligent and inquisitive, and can be trained to play games and even solve puzzles, all of which support a close, loving connection that makes a familiar bond even cozier.

In the spiritual realm, rats symbolize wealth, wisdom, opportunity, and intuition. Let your rat familiar lend its energy to your magic. As your rat crawls over your shoulder or snuggles in your lap when casting a spell or during a meditation session, imagine them lending you insight, enhancing your psychic skills, attracting prosperity, or opening new opportunities for you.

Rat Familiar Fetch Spell

Smarty-pants rats are one of the easiest rodents to train. They love the challenge as well as the treats you give them when they succeed. You can train your rat to fetch a small object and bring it to you. Start with an easy item, like a plastic water bottle cap. Reward them with a treat for picking up the item, then for running a short distance to the item, and then finally getting the item across the room and dropping it in front of you. Once they have mastered the bottle cap, you can move on to having them fetch a small, slotted cat ball or small wiffle ball.

Once your rat is trained to fetch, you can create a fetch spell. Toss the ball across the room and speak a word of intention, such as "Love!" "Abundance!" or "Success!" As your rat brings the ball back to you, they are lending you their energy so that you attract more of these blessings.

Squirrels

Have you ever gotten a chance to watch squirrels as they go about their business, rushing here and there, carrying food from one place to another, or chasing one another up and down a tree? If you are growing fruit in your backyard or are trying to lure birds with a bird feeder, a crafty squirrel can be a nuisance. But if you take a moment to observe and appreciate them, their energetic comings and goings can be fascinating.

Squirrels are highly intelligent and communicate with a complex language, using multiple sounds and intonations to express many different ideas. They also have excellent memories that help them as they cache the nuts that they retrieve later. Tricky squirrels can even engage in deceptive caching. They pretend to bury nuts in a certain place while being watched, then actually bury them in a different place when they think they are not being observed.

Squirrel Familiar Abundance Spell

If you've had the joy of observing your squirrel familiar, you'll have noticed how they industriously run back and forth, collecting food—some for eating now and storing some of it for later. This habit of saving for a rainy day can be something they lend you for building your own future. Whether you are putting money away for a big purchase, socking away for your retirement, or simply building a healthy savings account, your squirrel familiar can be your magical partner.

You can also adapt this spell for other familiars who like to cache, such as corvids, wild mice, woodpeckers, or ants.

What you will need:

- One gallon (4 liter) glass jar
- Photo or drawing of a squirrel
- Photo or drawing of your financial goal (for example, an image of your dream house, a slip of paper with an amount you'd like in your bank account, the perfect vacation, or happy retired people)
- Cash in the form of bills or coins

1. Place the images of the squirrel and the goal inside the jar facing outward so they can be seen through the glass.
2. Place the jar near the window closest to where you usually see your squirrel familiar.
3. Hold your hands palms down over the top of the jar as you say the following incantation:

Little squirrel, so smart and brave,
Help me set aside and save.
We work together, soul to soul.
Side by side we reach our goal.

4. When your squirrel familiar makes an appearance, ask them to help you to remember to save as efficiently as they do.
5. Determine an amount that you would like to put in the jar each time you see your familiar.
6. Place your jar in a hidden, out-of-the-way place near the window.
7. Each time you see your squirrel familiar (or one of their kin), put that amount of money from your wallet into the jar.
8. Each month around the time of the full moon, honor your squirrel and yourself by taking the money out of the jar and putting 90 percent in a dedicated savings account for your future goal, and using 10 percent to buy a special treat to reward yourself.
9. Thank your squirrel familiar for their assistance, and repeat the process until you reach your goal.

Rabbits and Hares

The rabbit and its larger, faster cousin, the hare or jackrabbit, have long held a place as sacred and magical creatures in the ancient lore of many cultures. If you join forces with a rabbit familiar, it could be with a wild rabbit or a domesticated one that you care for. For hares, however, the relationship must only be with a wild hare, as they are too skittish and aggressive to make good house pets.

While a rabbit's foot has long been considered a good luck charm, why not spare the rabbit and quadruple your luck by working with the four feet attached to a living rabbit familiar?

Lessons from Your Rabbit or Hare Familiar

Rabbits, and even more so hares, are fast, with some species sprinting over 45 miles per hour (72 km/h) with leaps and zigzags that elude predators. Rather than this quality being seen as timidity, both hares and rabbits are depicted in folklore as sacred trickster figures who can outwit their more powerful antagonists. Sassy Bugs Bunny besting Elmer Fudd with his shotgun is one of the more recent in a long line of legendary rabbits who outmaneuver their opponents. When you partner with a rabbit or hare, they can lend you their energy to get out of tricky situations.

Rabbits and hares can get pregnant within hours after giving birth, and hares can even get pregnant with a new litter while they are in late-stage pregnancy. This energy can be added to your magic for human fertility, of course, but fertility doesn't have to be about giving birth to children. Their prolific nature can aid you in amplifying your creative output, giving birth to abundant new projects.

Rabbit Moon Magic Ritual

As nocturnal animals, hares became affiliated with the night. In Egyptian mythology, hares were strongly associated with both the masculine waxing moon and feminine waning moon. It was also believed that hares would shift back and forth between the masculine and feminine genders, a belief that also existed in European folklore up until the 18th century.[1]

The dark patches on the full moon are seen in East Asian, Mesoamerican, and Native American mythology as a sacred hare or rabbit. In China, for example, the Jade Hare is thought to be depicted with a mortar and pestle in which he pounds the elixir of life for the moon goddess Chang'e.[2] In Japan and Korea, the Rabbit in the Moon is said to be pounding rice into tasty mochi.

In ancient Mayan spirituality the moon goddess, Ixchel, was often depicted with a rabbit at her side. There is a legend from the Cree people about a young rabbit who wished to ride the moon and a crane who took him up there. In the process, the weight of the rabbit stretched the crane's legs and left a bloody paw print on his forehead, both of which can be seen in the long legs and the red spot on the crane to this day. On clear nights, however, you can still see the rabbit up there riding on the moon.

To honor your rabbit familiar, you can take them outside on the night of a full moon and show them their ancient ancestor up there in the sky. If your familiar is an indoor-only rabbit, you can open the curtains and let the light of the full moon shine down and bless them.

Rabbit Fur in Spells

Young rabbits molt at about the age of five months, and adult rabbits shed their fur twice a year, in spring and fall, to gain the appropriate coat for the upcoming season. Gently brushing your rabbit at this time with a very soft brush can help you gather some of this fur for your spells. If you own an Angora rabbit and feel crafty, you can spin their fur sheds into a soft yarn that can then be used for weaving, knitting, or crocheting. Refer to "Spinning Magic Talisman" and "Spinning Divination" in Chapter 7.

Even the fur of shorter-haired rabbits can be felted, as described in "Cat Fur Poppet" in Chapter 9. Rabbit fur felt is often used in making hats, so creating a hat or other piece of clothing out of felted fur can be another way to bring you and your rabbit familiar closer. You don't need to be a clothing designer to do this, however. Even a small necklace or bracelet of rabbit fur felted balls strung together on thread can be a special talisman that you can wear to bring in the support of your rabbit familiar when doing magic.

Rabbit Otherworld Journey

In Celtic mythology and folklore, the Otherworld is a supernatural realm of everlasting beauty, youth, abundance, and happiness that exists alongside our own ordinary reality and is inhabited by faeries, spirits, and deities. One of the ways to reach the Otherworld was through entering one of the many ancient mounds with underground passages of these lands called *sídhe* (Old Irish) or *sìth* (Scots). The hare, who had the ability to burrow underground, was believed to be able to easily travel to the Otherworld. As sacred animals, hares were revered and protected and often seen as messengers between these worlds of ordinary and nonordinary reality.

People with magical gifts could shapeshift into the form of a hare to move back and forth between these spirit realms as well.[3] This practice, also called hedge riding, trance journeying, or astral projection, is the act of entering into a trance for the express purpose of journeying to the Otherworlds. Mystics throughout history have used altered states of consciousness for ecstatic experiences that reveal deep spiritual wisdom. In many ways, hedge riding is similar to shamanic journeys in that you are able to access worlds that are invisible to those who only focus on the mundane.

Trance states can be achieved in many ways. Dancing, chanting, sex, breath work, or physical activity are some of the ways that trance can be induced. These states allow us to enter the realms of the Otherworlds, what is known in many cultures as the World Tree. This concept depicts multiple coexisting realities in the framework of a tree with the Lower World being the roots; the Middle World, the trunk; and the Upper World, the leafy canopy. The Lower World is a wild and natural place with animals, ancestors, spirit teachers, and nature spirits. You won't find much human impact in the Lower World, although human and humanlike spirits may appear here. The Middle World is our world with the overlay of being able to see the invisible spirits who dwell here. The Upper World is the Summerland, the place to meet deities, masters, spirit guides, and other ascended beings.

This hedge-riding journey can be adapted to the spirit of any animal familiar, but is extra special when done with the ancient spirit of your rabbit familiar.

1. Set your intention. If you have never done hedge riding before, it is best to set the intention to go to the Lower World first. This is where you can meet magical animals and your familiar can comfortably guide you.
2. Sit with your rabbit familiar and ask them if they will take you on a safe and protected tour of the Otherworld.
3. If you get an assent from your rabbit (cuddles, rubs, nudging, or coming closer to you), you can proceed. If not, you can try another time.
4. If you have a talisman or ritual clothing made from the fur of your rabbit familiar, dress or adorn yourself with it to protect and assist you in traversing through these other realms.
5. *Optional:* Put on some gentle instrumental music if it helps you to enter into a meditative state.
6. Sit or lie in a comfortable position. See, sense, or feel yourself near a magical mound with an opening or door. (If it helps you to visualize, you can do an image search for "Celtic mounds" beforehand to give you a reference.)
7. Imagine your rabbit or hare familiar at your side as you stand in front of the mound.

8. As you stand there, sense your familiar rubbing against you and the two of you becoming infused with a protective shimmer.
9. Sense an opening in the mound, and observe your rabbit bounding forward into the mound as you follow behind.
10. As you both walk deep through the earthen tunnel, see the shimmers on the two of you casting a faint light to help you make your way.
11. Sense the tunnel opening onto the Otherworld in all its mystical beauty. Let your rabbit familiar lead you to the sights and sacred spots they want to show you.
12. While you are in the Otherworld, you may find that your rabbit familiar can send you psychic messages or even speak human language to you to teach you about the Otherworld.
13. When you have completed your exploration, let your rabbit familiar guide you back through the tunnel to the opening of the mound.
14. Thank your familiar for this journey and then open your eyes to return to ordinary reality.
15. Once you return, you may want to journal to integrate and process all that you have experienced.

Rabbit Incantation

There is a long-held belief in English-speaking countries that saying "rabbit, rabbit" (or alternatively, "rabbit, rabbit, rabbit" or "white rabbit") as your first words on the first day of the month will ensure an entire month of good luck. The first record of this little incantation traces back to a letter in the 1909 English periodical *Notes and Queries*, where a contributor stated, "My two daughters are in the habit of saying 'Rabbits!' on the first day of each month. The word must be spoken aloud and be the first word said in the month. It brings luck for that month. Other children, I find, use the same formula."[4] Another charm that can add additional magic can be to say "hare, hare" as your last words before going to sleep on the last night of the month.[5]

If you have a rabbit familiar, you can empower this charm by envisioning what it is that you would like to receive in the month ahead and then speak "hare, hare" and "rabbit, rabbit" out loud to your familiar, letting them lend their energy as you call these intentions forth.

The Magic of Rodent and Rabbit Familiars

Rodents and rabbits are charming little familiars that can lend big magic to your spellwork. Take the time to build a trust bond with these fun and furry familiars and they will reward you by becoming a special magical partner who can bring energy, enthusiasm, fun, and excitement to your life and your spells.

—— CHAPTER 12 ——

Bird Familiars

Lessons from Your Bird Familiar

Since ancient times, birds have captivated our imagination with their magical and otherworldly abilities. Before the invention of the hot-air balloon, the bird's ability to defy the laws of gravity and soar up into the sky was seen as divine. Even now, with our planes, helicopters, and other modes of air transit, you can still feel the wonder, and perhaps even a bit of envy, as you watch birds effortlessly flap their wings and head up into the clouds.

Birds are also the originators of music. Prehistoric people listened to the sound of the birds and learned about rhythm, tone, and melody. To imitate the songs of the birds, these ancient people did the magical act of creating flutes and pipes from animal bones, including the delicate hollow bones of birds, to mimic their sounds.[1]

To hunters and gatherers, birds gave information about where food could be found, and their migrations were also a source of information about the changes of the seasons and the weather. When spiritual practices moved from animism and ancestor worship toward gods and goddesses, birds, with their ability to soar into the upper realms, were seen as messengers and companions of the sky deities.[2] Some of the earliest records show goddesses who were part bird and part human or gods who were fully human and had bird companions. These alliances demonstrated the deep connection that humans have had to birds in all spiritual paths. Even today, the Christian Holy Spirit is depicted as a dove and angels are depicted with bird wings.

If you connect to a bird familiar, you are allying with a powerful being able to break the bonds of our earthly existence and access the highest reaches of the heavens. While a few domestic birds were touched upon in Chapter 7, this chapter dives deeper into the world of birds.

How Your Bird Familiar Can Help You

Whether your bird familiar is a pet in your home, a farm animal, or a creature that you encounter in the wild, they have so much to offer you. Step outside to get in touch with the collective energy of birds. Notice the birds you see and hear when you go for a walk. Watch your feathered friends as they dart around in the sky with grace, land skillfully on a branch with ease, or squabble over the treats in a bird feeder. Are they tending to nests, finding food, or simply observing what is going on around them? Attune to their energy of self-sufficiency to give yourself a dose of "You got this!"

Listen to the calls of the birds around you. See if you can imitate their songs. Their music is sometimes the only clue you get that a shy nighttime bird, such as the nightingale or owl, is near. If you step into the world of the birds, you can even appreciate the harsh caw of the crow, the insistent honk of the goose, the screech of the parrot, or the high-pitched *kee-kee* of the hawk. Birdsong brings joy, so pay attention to their songs to top off your tank of optimism.

Bird Call Magic

Apart from the few species that are silent, all birds have a secret language in their calls. Some are for mating, some may be a warning, and others communicate even more nuanced messages. If your bird familiar has some distinct calls, listen to their songs and learn what they mean. Imitating their songs can draw you in even closer to your familiar and will allow you to communicate with them. Hutsul shepherds high in the Carpathian Mountains are known for their skill in imitating the sounds of the mountain songbirds with a small wooden flute called a *sopilka*. If you'd like to connect more deeply to your bird familiar, you could learn to play a few notes on an instrument that can imitate the sounds of their calls.

Before the advent of recorded sound, people made note of the music that birds made by giving words to their calls, in essence putting lyrics to the music. The whippoorwill, for example, was named for the trill of its call, which sounds a bit like *WHIP poor WILL.* When you hear a birdsong, pay attention to the cadence and notes of the tune and see if some words bubble up for you. When they do, try to refine those words to make up a spell or affirmation that can be associated with their calls. Then, when you hear the call, it will be a message and trigger your memory so you can repeat it with them.

Working with Feathers

Throughout human history, feathers have been used for comfort, adornment, and magic. In Chapters 4 and 7, you'll find some suggestions for working with feathers in your magic, but those are just scratching the surface of all that is possible.

Feather Mindfulness

Are you the type of magic maker who notices feathers that you find on your walks out in nature? How amazingly generous our bird companions are to leave us these little surprises so frequently.

Please remember that throughout North America there are laws in place, such as the Migratory Bird Treaty Act, that forbid picking up feathers from protected species. In the early 1900s, the popularity of feathers in fashionable ladies' hats threatened many species with extinction, so strict laws were enacted to protect these birds. Since it is hard to prove whether feathers, nests, eggs, or other artifacts were collected via destructive means or not, the law forbids anyone from possessing any artifacts from these species even if they are dropped naturally by the birds. The U.S. Fish and Wildlife Service has a Feather Atlas online (www.fws.gov/lab/feath-eratlas) that can help you identify your feather, but if you are in doubt, leave the feather where it is.[3] However, the law does not forbid touching, looking at, and photographing these feathers, so if you come across an amazing feather, take a photo and do some found feather divination.

Found Feather Divination

When you come across a feather, you can look at these offerings as a message that your spirits or your magical birds wish to convey to you. Of course, you can read every single feather that you encounter, but my method of bird feather divination is to read feathers that are unusual in size, shape, or color. After all, I could find gray pigeon feathers all day, every day in my city, so instead I just focus on the standouts: the iridescent black of a crow tail feather, the royal blue of a scrub jay's flight feather, a lime-green parrot plume, or a pure-white puff of swan's down. I'm not even picky about their provenance. I've found hot-pink ostrich plumes and stumbled upon long, elegant pheasant feathers dyed green on my walks. Yes, I know that these feathers were not dropped by Day-Glo birds, but I still interpret them as messages that can reveal something to me.

When you find an unusual feather on your travels, pay attention. If you know what kind of bird it came from, you can research the characteristics of that bird and interpret a message from them. For example, if you find a seagull feather and discover the unusual ability seagulls have to drink seawater, you might interpret that as an encouraging message that you can turn the salty comments of your co-worker into something positive.

Whether you know the species of bird or not, you can also look at the colors of the feather and let those guide you. When using this form of divination, you can look at the main color of the feather as the main message and any other colors as additional secondary notes. For the meaning of different colors and the messages the animal is conveying, refer to Appendix E.

The Magic of the Egg

When considering working with eggs, remember that, just like feathers, the eggs of wild migratory birds are protected. Leave them where you find them and don't disturb any nest or eggs, even if you think they may be abandoned. Unless you are working with domesticated fowl, it's also a good idea not to encourage pet birds to lay eggs, because it can cause some serious health issues if they lay excessively. If you own a female bird, however, it is inevitable that they will lay at least one egg in their lifetime and this unique treasure can be used in your spells. For ways to work with these special, sacred eggs, check out "The Magic of the Egg" in Chapter 7.

Bird Omens (Ornithomancy)

Ornithomancy is the fancy word for reading bird omens. This practice is cross-cultural and goes back to antiquity. People of long ago had numerous forms of divination associated with birds. Our modern-day word for fortune telling, *augury*, was the same word Romans used for the practice of observing the movement of birds to predict the outcome of events. Seers in ancient Mesopotamia, Greece, and Rome would observe the flight of birds, bird behavior, and the way birds interacted with animals, humans, and each other, and interpret these as messages from the gods. There are Hittite texts that are over 3,000 years old describing bird augury.[4]

Hittite oracles believed that birds flying into view from the right to the left were good omens, while movement in the opposite direction was negative.[5] You can try this divination method yourself if your familiar is a wild bird.

Traditional Bird Divination

Sit in a place where you can observe your bird familiar and their flock, if applicable, when they are settled down. Ask a yes/no question and wait to see which direction the birds fly when they take off.

- If they fly to the left, the answer is yes.
- If they fly to the right, the answer is no.
- If they fly straight toward you or away from you, the answer is maybe or ask again later.

Birdhouse and Bird Feeder Magic

Birdhouses and bird feeders can be a wonderful way to connect to wild birds. If you would like to encourage a specific type of bird to nest, you can choose a house that is optimized for that species or fill a feeder with their favorite food. Research the species in your area, the specifications on the type of house or treats that are most inviting, and where they should be placed.

Having a birdhouse near your home not only provides a sanctuary for a possible new familiar but also brings the blessings of these birds right to your door. The birdhouse can be a talisman that invites harmony, prosperity, and spiritual protection to your home and family. Providing a birdhouse is an offering to our wild, winged friends and they will reciprocate by sharing their loving energy with you.

You can make your birdhouse and bird feeder even more magical by painting them in colors corresponding to the type of blessings you would like to invite and decorating them with sigils, symbols, or words that reinforce those blessings. See "Bat House Spell" in Chapter 6 for some suggestions. Every time your birds go in or out of their little home, or settle in for a snack, they'll be spreading that energy with each flap of their wings.

Making Magic with Your Bird Familiar

Of course, every single bird is magical and can make a very special familiar, but with thousands of species of birds, it would take an encyclopedia to cover each one of them as they deserve. All birds are part of the scientific class Aves, and below are a few of the more popular orders of the dozens that encompass the most common bird species that you are likely to encounter. Feel free to take the spells from any of these birds and adapt them to your own bird familiar. If you are looking for chickens, ducks, and geese, you'll be able to find out more about them in Chapter 7.

Doves

Doves and pigeons, who are simply larger doves with their own name, come from the *Columbiformes* order. Doves represent peace, love, harmony, and communication. In pre-telephone times, "pigeon post" was developed using pigeons specifically bred to find their way home over long distances. These homing pigeons were used as tiny telegram couriers by attaching a capsule to their leg containing a small scroll with a short message inside. In ancient times, the dove was seen as a divine messenger, so you can work with your dove or pigeon familiar whenever you want to receive spiritual messages or empower your own communication skills, especially if you'd like to imbue them with love and gentleness.

Dove Offering Spell

From the Greek Aphrodite to the Mesopotamian Innana, doves have had a long history of representing mother goddesses and love goddesses in ancient Near East and Mediterranean cultures. At one time, doves were sacrificed as offerings to these deities, but even in antiquity, dove-shaped figurines were seen as worthy substitutes for the real thing. If you have a wish for peace, love, or simply want to make an offering to a goddess, your pigeon or dove familiar can lend their energy to a figurine you craft to make it even more empowered. If your familiar is a protected species, you can collect a feather from a rock pigeon, the common feral pigeon found in the city. This species is not protected by the Migratory Bird Treaty Act, and their feathers can stand in for species that are protected.

When crafting your dove figurine, be sure to use all-natural clay and not air-dry clay, modeling clay, polymer clay, plasticine, or other artificial materials, as you will be leaving this offering in nature. Natural clay is made of organic materials and will harmlessly break down back into the environment. If you live near rivers or streams, or places where rivers and streams once flowed, you may be able to source your own natural clay for free.

What you will need:

- Natural clay
- A feather from your familiar or a rock pigeon
- Herbs associated with your wish (see Appendix B)

1. Flatten a piece of clay, and place the feather and herbs in the center. Roll the clay into a ball.
2. As you form the ball into an egg shape, reflect on the magic of the egg as the potential for all things. Envision your outcome in its brightest and highest form as you hold the egg in your hands.
3. Form the egg into the shape of a nesting dove or pigeon. It does not have to be a work of art, just a loose representation of a bird.
4. Allow your clay figurine to dry for three weeks. During this time, you can place the drying figurine near your pigeon or dove or in their habitat so they can lend their energy to your wish.
5. Once your clay figurine is completely dried, thank your familiar and take the figurine to a natural body of water or another wild place of a peaceful nature.
6. Drop the figurine into the water or bury in the land while envisioning your wish coming true, saying, "It is done."

Landfowl

Landfowl come from the *Galliformes* order and are the family of heavy-bodied, ground-feeding birds that includes turkeys, chickens, quail, grouse, pheasants, and peacocks. These adorable landlubbers are probably best known for running from danger rather than flying from it. They are also famous for being the dandies of the bird world. The males are almost always dressed to the nines with bright and beautiful feathers as well as loud, strutting courtship behaviors. If you're a witch who's a little extra, especially if you identify as masculine, you'll find a familiar who truly gets your need to bask in the spotlight. (If you have a chicken familiar, see Chapter 7 for more about these special birds.)

Peacocks

The fanciest of the fancy landfowl is undoubtedly the peacock. The male peacock is a bird of regal extravagance, with his display of iridescent and otherworldly blue-green feathers capturing the imagination of humanity for thousands of years. If you are fortunate enough to have a peacock as a familiar, you are quite aware that they are just as loud as they are beautiful. Their cacophonous screeches help them to communicate with each other over the din of their noisy jungle habitat. Your peacock familiar can assist you in both being seen *and* heard.

Peacocks are native to India and Sri Lanka and were domesticated to be kept in temple complexes, not only for their beauty but because these omnivores can eat snakes, including deadly cobras. A peacock familiar can be a powerful guardian protector from negativity of all kinds.

Peacock Feather Magic

Male peacocks, with their fan-shaped trains of gorgeous feathers, develop their brilliant colors in adulthood to attract a mate. The female peahen is much more discreet, with feathers that are primarily brown with a touch of iridescent blue-green only on their chest. Every year, after mating season, the peacock sheds his long train feathers and grows a new set. So peacock feathers can be ethically harvested without harming the birds at all, and if you have a peacock familiar in your life, they will generously give you feathers regularly.

Peacock feathers are recognizable for the spectacular iridescent eye at the center. You can use a peacock feather in spells for empowerment, beauty, expression, abundance, higher consciousness, psychic awareness, and protection from the evil eye. If you have a turkey, pheasant, or another elegantly plumed familiar, feel free to adapt these spells.

- Use a peacock feather as a quill for writing petition papers, making notes in your grimoire, or crafting sigil papers.
- Display peacock feathers in your home to ward off the evil eye and bring in luxurious abundance.
- Lightly brush a peacock feather over your third eye, the spot between your eyebrows, to open up psychic ability and clairvoyance.
- Keep a peacock feather next to your bed to prevent nightmares. If you have a bad dream, brush the peacock feather over yourself from head to toe to restore peaceful feelings that allow you to go back to sleep.

- Make a peacock feather fan and open it just like a peacock train to wave it over yourself for a magical dose of beauty, self-confidence, and empowerment.

Nonperching Birds

While the name of the order *Apodiformes* may not seem immediately familiar, it encompasses all the hummingbird and swift species of the world. These birds are the fast fliers who do their eating in flight and, in the case of swifts, even their mating. Although apobirds do have feet, they rarely use them to stand and never use them to walk. If you need more get-up-and-go and zest for life, or if you simply have a lot to accomplish, your hummingbird or swift familiar can add their ample energy to your magic.

Hummingbirds

These little speed demons zip around and hover over flowers like fairies blessing your garden. Hummingbirds need to eat more than twice their body weight daily, so when you provide them with a little extra nourishment, you are being a true ally. If you have a yard, research nectar-rich flowers to plant and give them food sources throughout the season.

A hummingbird feeder can supplement their diet. Hummers are very territorial and will fight other hummingbirds that try to drink from what they think of as *their* personal soda fountain, so if you are planning on getting more than one feeder, make sure that you place them at a distance and ideally out of the sight of each other. With their territorial energy, your hummingbird familiar reminds you that size doesn't matter when it comes to standing up for yourself.

Hummingbird Familiar Sweetening Spell

To make your own nectar to fill your hummingbird feeder, combine one part sugar to four parts boiling water. Continue heating and stirring until combined.

Sugar is used in spells for sweetening up a situation, so as you make this nectar, stir it in a clockwise direction and speak the words of blessing that you would like to give to your familiar and the sweetness you would like your hummingbird to add to your life.

Owls

Beautiful, stealthy, mysterious owls are categorized as the *Strigiformes* order. Owls have been both revered and feared by people throughout history. In ancient Egypt and Rome, medieval and renaissance Europe, and even today in some, but not all, indigenous traditions, the owl is seen as an omen of death. However, there are also less ominous beliefs that owls are guides who lead the soul to the afterlife, are messengers from the spirit world, or are the embodiment of the spirits of those who have died. Even in popular culture, owls and their eerie hoots at night are a part of a spooky Halloween. An owl is a classic witch's familiar who can connect you to the world of the spirits and help you to develop a closer relationship to your ancestors.

One of the reasons owls may be thought of as spooky could be because of their ability to sneak up without a noise.

Owls have unique feathers that allow them to fly without making a sound, giving them the advantage of surprise when it comes to catching prey. This stealth also allows them to hear small mammals as they skitter around at night, helping them to be even more effective hunters. When you and an owl partner in a familiar relationship, they can teach you the power of being silent and keeping your magic hidden from others.

There are also the "wise, old owls" that represent intelligence, studiousness, and academic success. For Athena, the Greek goddess of wisdom, the owl was her sacred companion, providing her with insight that would help her to strategize effectively. The wide-eyed owl that can see at night must have inspired the ancients who viewed them as discerning and astute. Owls' eyes are amazing in their own right, though. Their tubular-shaped eyes can only stare straight ahead, like binoculars, but this shape aids them in their depth perception, so that they can gauge distance to perfectly aim their strikes. To compensate for the fact that their eyes don't move, owls have the ability to rotate their head 270 degrees. If an owl is your familiar, you can call upon them to lend their traits to develop your own inner vision and perceptivity to wisely assess any situation that may come your way.

Owl Hoot Divination

The number of times an owl hoots can foretell an event to come. If your owl familiar is near, ask them to bring you a numerological message about the future and then count the number of times they hoot to discover what they predict for you.

- One hoot means success in a solo endeavor
- Two, love is near
- Three, a creative opportunity
- Four, money is coming
- Five, an adventure ahead
- Six, a gathering with good friends
- Seven, luck takes a turn for the better
- Eight, a prize will be won
- Nine, the end of one chapter and the beginning of a new one

Parrots

Macaws, cockatoos, cockatiels, parakeets—like a parade at Carnival, the world of the parrot familiar is fun, festive, noisy, and full of bright colors, loud squawks, and flapping feathers. In the era of Middle English, parrots were called *popinjays*, a name that was also applied to people as a compliment on their beauty. By the 1500s, the bird had become perceived as gaudy and loud instead, and the meaning of the word similarly shifted to become derogatory. Parrots, and these other birds from the *Psittaciformes* order, are most often pets, but parrots are quite adaptable. You can find feral parrot colonies in California, Florida, and Texas that all began with pet parrots that escaped and bred in the wild.

In Hindu mythology, Kamadeva, the god of love, desire, and infatuation, rides on the back of a parrot as he shoots fragrant flowers instead of arrows from a bow made of sugarcane and honeybees. You might astutely see a connection between Kamadeva and the Roman god Cupid or Greek god Eros, both of whom arrived on the scene hundreds of years later. Kamadeva's beautiful, extravagant parrot, Suka, represents the rebirth of spring and, as parrots often pair up, the ideals of romantic love. If you have a parrot familiar, you might not be able to ride on their back, but you can invite them to enhance the romance in your life.

Parrots also have incredibly long lives, with some species having a lifespan of 80 years or more. When you bond with a parrot, you have a long-term familiar relationship that can get deeper and closer with every passing year.

Parrot Affirmation Spell

Some species of parrots are incredible mimics and can amuse us with their ability to copy the sounds around them, like doorbells ringing, sirens going by, or even a drippy faucet. Parrot familiars who have this gift of gab and spend lots of quality time with their witch can learn to mimic human speech as well and even use their words in context to communicate, like the classic example of saying, "Polly want a cracker," when they would like a treat. Parrots often repeat a phrase over and over again, so you can train your familiar to repeat positive affirmations to cast spells on your behalf and remind you to say them too.

Perching Birds (Passerines)

Passerines, or perching birds, are any birds of the *Passeriformes* order and can be identified by their three toes pointing forward and one pointing backward, which allow them to easily hang onto branches. Corvids, swallows, mockingbirds, wrens, sparrows, finches, cardinals, larks—more than half of all bird species belong to this order. All songbirds are passerines, so whether your familiar is a virtuoso thrush or a raven who could be the singer of a death metal band, your familiar can lend you energy to empower your voice, enhance your creativity, and make your own music.

Corvids

Crows, ravens, rooks, magpies, jackdaws, jays—the corvids are a family of birds that are whip-smart, brassy, sassy, and endlessly fascinating. Even if you wanted to ignore them, they won't let you with their loud vocalizations, but why would you? Once a corvid familiar enters your life, it's like making friends with the smart-alecky, wisecracking class clown who will constantly keep you on your toes with their antics.

Never cross your corvid familiar. They not only remember faces but also hold grudges—and even talk behind your back. This remarkable memory works both ways; if you show kindness to your crow familiar, they will remember you and start reciprocating your good deeds by leaving behind found bits and bobs for you. These presents from your familiar can be used as magical talismans, placed on your altar, or used in your spells. (See "Animal Familiar Offerings" and "Animal Offering Magic" in Chapter 4.) There are plenty of stories of crows bringing gifts to people who leave them food. However, the question remains: Are the crows saying thank you or training their benefactors to leave more food for them? With corvids being as smart as they are, I say that's a matter best discussed between you and your familiar.

Counting Crows Divination

There is a wonderful old nursery rhyme divination that you can use whenever you see a group of crows, magpies, or any other social corvid. Count the number of birds and then say the poem. The number of birds will tell you what fortune to expect for the upcoming days. There are many nursery rhyme variations, so the meanings here are an amalgam of the best of these rhymes:

One for sorrow,
Two for mirth,
Three for a wedding,
Four for a birth,
Five for silver,
Six for gold,
Seven for a secret, not to be told.
Eight for a wish,
Nine for a kiss,
Ten, a surprise that you don't want to miss,
Eleven for health,
Twelve for wealth,
Thirteen beware, it's the devil himself.[6]

Raptors

Birds of prey from the *Accipitriformes* and *Falconiformes* orders are the carnivores of the bird kingdom and include hawks, eagles, vultures, and falcons. Strong and fast, these keen-eyed hunters have razor-sharp talons that make them the apex predators of the skies. While most raptors are found in the wild, they have also been domesticated and trained as hunting birds for thousands of years. Falconers create a true partnership with their birds that is based on respect and trust, especially because a hunting bird has the freedom to end the relationship by flying off and never coming back. Whether you are working closely with a raptor or admiring one from a distance, they can teach you patience and genuine cooperation and share their energy to bring you gifts of keen observation, speed, and decisiveness.

Hawks

Hawks are found on every continent of the world, except Antarctica, and are legendary for their spectacular abilities. There is a reason we call someone with great visual acuity a "hawkeye." A hawk's superior vision is eight times better than the average human and allows them to see the ultraviolet wavelengths. They also have a 280-degree view up, down, and side to side and can spot small prey from distances of up to a mile (1.6 km) away. If you want to work on your own abilities of perception, whether in assessing a situation, for visionary work, or for increasing your clairvoyance, your hawk familiar has gifts to share.

Hawk Clairvoyance Spell

Your hawk familiar can assist you when you want to increase your "second sight," the ability to see otherworldly visions, or ascertain future events. Prepare this potion any time you are preparing to go on a vision journey or prior to a meditation where you will seek insight. This spell can easily be done with any raptor familiar or another animal with keen eyesight.

For this spell you will need to prepare some roasted dandelion root tea. Roasted dandelion root has a pleasant taste somewhat akin to coffee, but feel free to add sweetener, lemon, milk, or milk substitute to your preference. While dandelion root is considered safe to drink, as with any ingestible herb, please research to make sure it is safe for your particular health conditions.

What you will need:

- A photo or drawing of your hawk familiar or any hawk
- A clear glass mug, teacup, or heavy drinking glass
- 2 teaspoons (4 to 6 g) roasted dandelion root tea (*Taraxacum officinale*)
- Pot or teapot
- Dried wormwood (*Artemesia absinthium*) herb bundle (smudge stick)
- Matches
- Tea strainer
- *Optional:* sweetener, lemon, milk, or milk substitute

1. Place the hawk image beneath your cup so that you can see it through the glass.
2. Add the roasted dandelion root and 1 cup water to a pot on the stove.
3. Bring the water to a simmer, then turn off the heat and allow to steep for 5 to 15 minutes. Leaving the

potion to steep longer will give it a stronger flavor but will not change the power of the potion.

4. As the tea steeps, light your wormwood bundle and waft the smoke over yourself, the cup, and the image of the hawk, reciting the following incantation:

Flock, squawk, gawk, stalk,
Give me vision of the hawk.
Razor talon, feathered tail,
Let me see beyond the veil.

5. When the potion has cooled slightly, strain out the pieces as you pour the tea into your cup. Add sweetener, if desired.
6. Drink the tea and then enter into your meditation vision journey. If you are just delving into meditation and vision journey work, use a guided meditation track to assist you.

Seabirds

Sandpipers, gulls, puffins, terns, and other shorebirds from the *Charadriiformes* order and pelicans of the order *Pelecaniformes* live in coastal areas and fly, walk, or wade in the water while feeding. Whether they are found at the shore or, in the case of seagulls, far inland, seabirds evoke the magic of oceans, skies, and seaside vacations. Some shorebirds stay in one place but others are globetrotting travelers who migrate thousands of miles each year as they follow the sun (and food). If you have a seabird familiar, you have an ally who brings the relaxed energy of summers at the beach or an old salt's thirst to explore the seven seas. With a familiar that is equally comfortable on land, sea, or sky, the magical possibilities with your seabird familiar are as vast as the big blue ocean.

Seagulls

Anyone who has had their bag of chips stolen by a seagull can testify that they are the bold and crafty tricksters of the bird realm. In Irish legend, the god of the sea, Manannan Mac Lir, the trickster god known for intelligence, creativity, and playfulness, takes the form of a gull. A seagull's ingenuity doesn't just help them figure out how to get a sandwich out of a plastic bag. Groups of seagulls will do a special dance, stamping on the ground to trick worms into thinking it's raining so they come to the surface and the gulls can gobble them up. If you want to work together with others to solve problems or boldly take advantage of opportunities that come your way, the gull is your guy.

Seagull Gliding Spell

When you spot your gull familiar gliding overhead without breaking a sweat, it's your opportunity to catch that wave of easy breezy energy to make your own life as effortless. Envision a long, imaginary silver kite string connecting your heart to your familiar in the sky above you. Feel the vicarious sensations gliding and then whisper to the gull what area of your life you would like to be as easy. They will lend you that energy to make everything as smooth.

Waterfowl

Wild ducks, geese, swans, grebes, loons, and other waterfowl from the *Anseriformes*, *Gaviiformes*, and *Podicipediformes* orders are the serene lake and pond dwellers. Have you ever seen a waterfowl floating on a pond on a frosty day? How is it that they don't get waterlogged or freeze their cute little feathered butts off? Waterfowl were made for swimming and have surface feathers with a waxy coating that repels water and an inner layer of downy feathers that keep them warm and dry even if they dive underwater. Even their featherless webbed feet can tolerate chilly water because the blood vessels in their feet are specially designed so that they don't lose heat. If you are an empath who unwittingly picks up the negative energy around you, this insulation is something that your waterfowl familiar can lend you for gentle protection from anything unwanted.

Swans

For many witches, we may feel a special kinship with the swan in "The Ugly Duckling." Hans Christian Andersen's story champions those of us who feel like we don't quite fit in and lets us know that what others might call odd, we can see as unique and beautiful. Stories of deities, spirits, and humans shape-shifting into the form of the swan come to us from areas as diverse as ancient Babylon, India, Greece, Egypt, Rome, Ireland, and Scotland, as well as from the Inuit people of Greenland and the Buryats of Siberia. If you have a swan familiar, you can do a visualization and feel yourself turning into a powerful and refined swan flying over the land and floating gracefully on the water.

Because of their elegant beauty and lifelong monogamous pairing, swans are often linked to love and romance. Swans can also be incredibly feisty, territorial, and downright aggressive, especially when they are protecting a nest. This dual nature appears in Norse mythology, where swans are associated with the love goddess Freya, but also the fierce but beautiful Valkyries that guide the war dead to Valhalla. If you have a swan familiar, they can lend you their energy to likewise be formidable, fascinating, and fabulous.

Swan Mirror Spell

When you see a pair of swans float so majestically on the still surface of a lake with their enchanting reflection on the water, you can truly become mesmerized. You can do a swan mirror spell with your familiar, so that they can lend you both their aristocratic elegance and help you to invite a lasting love into your life.

What you will need:

- Hand mirror, the more beautiful and elegant the better

1. Visit your swan familiar on a day when they are peaceful, calm, and serene. You don't need to get close; you just need to be able to see them from where you are.

2. Face your back to the swan and hold up the mirror so that you see both your face and the swan in the background.
3. First, focus on looking at your swan familiar in the mirror as you say this incantation:

Swan familiar, elegant and free
Bring beauty, strength, and love to me.

4. Now focus on your face in the mirror as you say the rest of the incantation:

Light my way by sun and star
That I may be just as you are.

5. Repeat this spell anytime you need a boost of self-confidence and empowerment or would like to attract a meaningful romantic relationship into your life.

The Magic of the Bird Familiar

Birds are all around us, yet they are so otherworldly. These creatures that are so different from us are often so willing to connect with us when we approach them with the reverence that they deserve. When you have a bird familiar, they can help you to step out of your mundane life to see things from a "bird's-eye view." Befriend a bird familiar, and your spirit can soar as high as the skies above.

CHAPTER 13

Amphibian and Fish Familiars

The Magic of Amphibian and Fish Familiars

When you invite an amphibian or fish familiar into your practice, it's as if you wave a wand and magically become a mermaid yourself, entering into a completely new underwater world. In magic, water is the element of emotions, intuition, and spirituality, so when you partner with a familiar who lives in watery environments, you open up to a wonderful realm where magic rises like the rushing of a river or the ebb and flow of the tides.

Lessons from Your Amphibian Familiar

Long before Shakespeare wrote about the witches of MacBeth throwing "eye of newt and toe of frog" into their cauldron, magic makers have cavorted with amphibians. (By the way, the "eye of newt" was witchcode for yellow mustard seed and the "toe of frog" a type of buttercup, so even back in Elizabethan England, witches were looking out for their familiars, not cooking them.)[1] For generations, frogs, toads, newts, salamanders, and other amphibians were seen as magical beings. You only have to look at the number of folk tales revolving around these delightful and mystical creatures. If you've heard the stories of the Frog Princess, the Frog Prince, or any of the many other fairy tales involving amphibians, you know how truly special they can be.

Amphibians have the remarkable gift of being able to absorb water and breathe oxygen through their skin. They also secrete mucous that allows them to stay hydrated as they move between these two worlds. Some amphibians have evolved the ability to eat and exude poisons through their skin as well, causing irregular heart rhythm, dizziness, cardiac arrest, paralysis, and even death to any creature who touches them, including humans. One of the most poisonous animals in the world is a golden poison frog, which can exude enough toxin to kill 10 people.

How Your Amphibian Familiar Can Help You

The word *amphibian* comes from the Greek root "amphibios," which translates to "living a double life." Most amphibians go through metamorphosis, beginning their lives as eggs and evolving into tadpoles that live entirely underwater. When they finally grow legs and lungs and become adults, they move as easily on land as in the water. For a witch who has to keep her practice under wraps or has to adapt by code-switching her way through multiple cultures, an amphibian familiar can be a true ally.

Amphibian pets require deep commitment, patience, and dedication. Some species, like the small cave salamander called the *olm*, can live over 100 years. Even an average toad can live for up to 20 years. However, the length of their lives also allows you to create a powerful, meaningful bond of love and magical connection. If one of your magical goals is to live a long and prosperous life, your amphibian familiar can lend you their ancient energy.

Just as there are fairy tales of people being bespelled to appear as amphibians or characters who change their form between human and frog, you can tap into this ancient magic of transfiguration. If you want to learn the art of shapeshifting, a frog familiar can offer you deep wisdom.

Taking Care of Your Amphibian Familiar

You might want to think twice before kissing a frog—even the most innocent, nonpoisonous pet amphibian can spread salmonella to humans. If you meet an amphibian familiar in the wild, you can admire it from a distance, but don't touch it. While there's a risk of you picking up poison or unhealthy bacteria and harming yourself, you're also likely to transmit things that can be harmful to the amphibian when absorbed through their sensitive skin. Handling them with dry hands can cause their skin's delicate protective layer to rub off, putting them in contact with deadly human bacteria, toxic chemicals, or even simply your skin's natural salts and oils.

When acquiring a pet, it is important to do your research and only adopt or purchase animals from an ethical source. Look for captive-bred rather than wild-caught amphibians. Amphibians are one of the most threatened classes of vertebrates worldwide, with over 40 percent being endangered or vulnerable, and it is illegal in many areas to capture them. It is also unkind to keep a wild animal confined and will do little to build the relationship between you two. Instead, help wild amphibians to thrive by creating friendly habitats for those that live outside.

If you want to honor your familiar, you can become an activist for their endangered cousins and support organizations that protect the amphibians that are struggling to survive.

Frogs and Toads

For millennia, frogs have been a part of mythology, lore, and legend. Throughout the world, they have been associated with fertility, shapeshifting, and the primeval waters out of which life emerged. Frogs encapsulate the evolution of the animal kingdom in their individual lifetimes, from water to land, and so can reveal deep and ancient mysteries to you. This gift of metamorphosis can allow the frog to assist you in creating revolutionary transformation in your own life as well as tapping into the magic of transfiguration to learn the art of shapeshifting.

While popular Western culture might describe frogs and toads (who are just frogs who tend to be more terrestrial) as slimy and dirty, there are many cultures where they are associated with cleansing and purity. There are long-standing beliefs that a frog in a well means that the water is fresh and safe to drink. A frog familiar can lend you their energy in spiritual cleansing magic.

Frogs also symbolize the fertility of the land and therefore abundance. In ancient Egypt, for example, the flooding of the Nile coincided with the appearance of numerous frogs, so frogs became associated with the growth of the crops and the sustenance of the community. In *feng shui,* the *jin chan,* or money frog, is a charm for good luck and wealth. This mythical golden toad is said to appear during the full moon near houses or businesses that will soon receive good news about their finances. The charm is depicted as a three-legged frog sitting atop a pile of coins and holding a coin in its mouth. Having this figurine in your home or workplace ensures that wealth and luck will come to all who live or work there. Your frog familiar might not have three legs or be golden, but they can still assist you in amplifying your wealth and abundance.

Attracting a Frog or Toad Familiar

If a frog or toad is indicating that they would like to start a familiar relationship with you, there are a few ways you can nurture this kinship, depending on whether the relationship is with an animal in your home or in the wild.

If you do choose to keep a frog familiar in a terrarium, ensure that it was raised in captivity by an ethical breeder. Make sure to get a large terrarium that mimics their natural habitat. If you have a tree frog, make sure your terrarium has ample space for climbing; if your familiar is ground dwelling, they should have plenty of horizontal space.

If you are bonding with a wild frog, create an inviting space for them in your yard. A small pond or fountain can attract and protect your frog familiar, simultaneously giving them freedom and support. To keep them healthy and happy, avoid the use of any chemicals in the garden or water, which can be absorbed through their sensitive skin. If your familiar is a ground-dwelling toad, consider creating a *toad abode* from an overturned terracotta pot or stack of stones, a dark little cave where your toad can hide from predators and stay cool and moist.

Like most animals that can be eaten by predators, frogs are shy creatures. Make offerings to your frog to build trust. Research what species they are and what they like to eat. When you feed your familiar on a regular basis, it will begin associating you with food and will be more likely to feel safe in your presence. When you have developed this bond, you can begin to do spells with them.

Frog Familiar Croaking Spell

If you are working with frogs in the wild or have a male frog at home, then you have heard their rhythmic croaking when it's mating season or they are establishing their territory. Listening to repetitive sounds, like the croaking of frogs, can be hypnotic and relaxing. You can use the rhythm and music of the frog's magical chorus to enter into an altered state where you can envision whatever you want to manifest.

This spell can be done with any animal that has a repetitive song, such as crickets or birds. If you have a noncroaking female frog or it isn't the right season, your chant can also be done with recorded sounds of frogs croaking.

1. Get within earshot of your croaking frog or frogs, taking care not to disturb or frighten them. Sit or lie in a comfortable position, and close your eyes.
2. Focus on the sound of the frogs, and breathe in a similar rhythm.
3. When you reach a state of relaxation, envision your wish or whisper a short and snappy chant for what you'd like to manifest, for example, "true love" or "more money."
4. Keep the chant going for several minutes or as long as your frog familiar is croaking.

Salamanders and Newts

Salamanders are amphibians that have moist skin, similar to a frog, but are shaped like a lizard. Just as toads are a form of frog, newts are a more terrestrial form of salamander with a drier, wartier skin. Salamanders have been misunderstood for centuries with all kinds of mythical powers attributed to them. It was believed they were born out of fire, ate fire instead of food, had fire-resistant skin, and could put out fires with their clammy hides. The root of these myths probably stemmed from the fact that salamanders hang out in moist forest places, including rotting wood. When these rotting logs were thrown on the fire, the fleeing salamanders appeared as if they were born out of the flame. For ancient people who wanted to classify everything under the four elements, salamanders became one of the only creatures that could be classified as a fire animal and the tall tales about their fire-resistant abilities took off from there.

Salamanders are among the quietest of animals. Occasionally, they may make a click or a sigh, but otherwise they make no noise. Most salamanders can't hear sound in the way that most typical land animals do, but they are highly attuned to sensing vibration. These qualities make salamanders excellent magical allies for attuning your more subtle psychic senses.

Salamander Healing Magic

One of the most remarkable features about the salamander is their ability to regrow their body parts. If they lose a toe, it will grow back. Even if a part of the heart or spinal cord is removed, a salamander can grow new tissue and survive. This astounding ability to regenerate is intriguing to scientists who hope to discover the secrets of this mechanism and apply it to humans and other species.

This energy of regeneration can be used magically, and your salamander familiar can assist you. They can be called on for spiritual support in a healing spell for alleviating grief or for mending a broken heart. You can also do a healing spell for physical healing with the intent of finding the right health care providers, the most accurate and helpful information, and the perfect treatments to reach your health goals.

To do this healing spell, you will need to sit in the energy field of your salamander familiar. All natural beings and things have an energy field, also called an *aura*, which is the electric and magnetic field around each of us. Animals that are healthy and happy have large energy fields, so to access your salamander familiar's field, you can be anywhere within several yards of them. Since amphibians don't like to be handled, this is a great way to exchange energy with your familiar in a respectful way.

If your familiar is in the wild, you don't need to even have visual contact with them. If you know where your salamander likes to hide out, position yourself nearby but not too close as to disturb them.

1. Seat yourself comfortably within the energy field of your salamander familiar.
2. Close your eyes and hold your hands in prayer pose over your heart to bring the focus to yourself and your familiar.
3. In your mind's eye, sense, see, or feel your familiar in front of you.
4. Choose a color that appeals to you or that has a magical correspondence that you would like to invoke. (Check out the list in Appendix D.) Imagine your heart glowing with an iridescent light of love in the color that you chose.
5. Imagine this light growing, extending out toward your salamander, bathing them in a gentle glow.
6. Feel the regenerative energy of your familiar. The salamander doesn't worry about whether or not they can survive. They have the confidence of knowing that if they lose a body part, they can grow a new one.
7. Now, picture the part of you that needs regeneration. If you are healing a broken heart, for example, picture your heart.

8. Ask your familiar to lend you its regenerative energy to heal the area.
9. Sense, see, or feel your familiar sending you a gentle light of its own back to you and focusing that energy on the area that needs regeneration.
10. Picture the part of you that needs healing growing stronger and stronger. See your salamander lovingly lending you all the energy you need for strength and wholeness. Bathe in this light for as long as you like.
11. When you are finished, thank your salamander for lending you their energy.
12. Open your eyes and feel the radiant energy of your wholeness and wellness.

Lessons from Your Fish Familiar

Fish familiars invite us into a completely instinctual realm where going with the flow is the norm. Among all the creatures, it can be challenging, but not impossible, to form a relationship with a wild fish familiar. Fish move from place to place or swim in schools with dozens of relations that look just like them, so you are much more likely to have a familiar relationship with a pet fish than one in nature. If you do connect to fish in the wild, you can connect to them collectively as familiars, developing a partnership with the entire family of that animal. Think of them as animal guides who can perform some of the functions of a familiar.

With a pet fish, however, you can enjoy repeated interactions that will allow them to trust you and build a bond. Simply watching your fish as they swim in their environment can have a profoundly positive effect on your mental well-being—helping you de-stress and getting your mind into the meditative and focused state that is so good for casting spells and making magic.

Whether your familiar is a guppy in a fishbowl, a flashy tropical fish in an aquarium, or a big, beautiful koi in a pond, your fish familiar can bring you a sense of peace and harmony as they move through their watery world.

Bonding with Your Fish Familiars

When you choose to bond with a fish familiar, the options of the species of fish are practically as numerous as there are fish in the sea. It seems like there is a different personality for every type of witch. There are puppy-like oscars and unearthly puffer fish. Some, like bettas, are quite territorial, while others, like guppies and tetras, feel more at home when there's a large group of them around.

If you do have a little school of fish under your care, you can discover if one is your familiar by finding the individual who is most collaborative with you. Try some of these techniques to interact with your pet fish familiar to see if they want to make magic with you. If your familiar is in the wild, you might not be able to connect to an individual fish in these ways, but you can connect to them collectively as familiars, developing a partnership with the entire family of that animal.

Fish Familiar Blessing

You can train your fish to follow a stick or your finger in the water. While there is a popular belief that fish can only remember things for a few seconds, most fish can actually remember things for a couple of weeks or even longer. If you train your fish consistently and in small doses, you can get them to trust you and start to develop that closer relationship.

1. Hold your finger (or a stick) close to your aquarium. Be patient, allowing your familiar's curiosity to draw them in.
2. Every time they come close to your finger, feed them a little nibble of food.
3. Move your finger, offering more food if they continue to follow.
4. Repeat the training at least daily. Once your fish is following the stick or your finger, you can bless your fish.
5. Say a brief blessing as your fish follows, such as: "As you follow this stick/my finger, may you always follow happiness."

Fish Familiar Empowerment Spell

Bettas and goldfish can also be trained to jump out of the water. Your fish familiar will be happy to share the energy of their big leaps of faith with you.

Try this once they become comfortable with your finger or the stick near them. Pick a time when your fish are hungry, as they'll be extra motivated to get out of their comfort zone for a snack.

1. Wet your finger (or the stick) and affix a small piece of food on the end.
2. Hold your finger just above the surface of the water, so your familiar pokes out their mouth to get a bite.
3. Repeat the training at least daily. Over time, raise the target higher and higher to get them to jump out to get a bite. As they jump, tap into their adventurous energy and bless yourself for climbing higher and achieving more.
4. Cast a positive spell for your success when they jump out of the water. Say a short incantation or affirmation such as "I can do it!" or, my personal favorite, "You got this, girl!" every time they jump.

Fish Familiar Divination

You can also train your fish to push a Ping-Pong ball around as a divination ritual.

1. Place a clean ping pong ball, or other light floating ball, into your familiar's aquarium.
2. Every time your fish touches the ball, give them a treat.

3. Repeat the training at least daily. When they begin associating pushing the ball with getting something to eat, you'll find a playful familiar who will perform tricks practically on command.
4. Once you have trained your fish to push the ball, you can do a little fishy divination. Ask your familiar a yes/no question. Tell them that if they move the ball to the left side of the tank, it means no, to the right means yes, and around the middle means maybe.
5. Drop the ball in the middle and watch which direction your familiar pushes it.
6. Be sure to tip your fishy fortune teller with a little treat once they give their answer.

Tip: Always put the ball in the tank when you are there to reward them. If you leave the ball in the tank all the time, they will not be as likely to associate it with a tasty snack.

Fish Decor Magic

Fish in the wild live in an ever-changing environment, so fish in a tank can get bored with the same items arranged in the same way over extended periods of time. To keep your fish happy and stimulated, give their home a makeover every time you change the water. Move the ornaments and hiding places around, take out some, and add others. Keep their underwater environment fresh and fun with caves to explore and new things to discover.

Whenever you go browsing for new decor for your fish familiar's home, think of the magic that it can add to your partnership. Think of the qualities that you would like them to bless you with and choose a gravel or other decor in the color that corresponds to that intention. (See Appendix D for magical color correspondences.) Choose objects that represent the magic that you want to make with your familiar. You can add a little bubbling volcano to represent big breakthroughs, a castle for moving to a new home, a ship to go on a cruise, mushrooms for travelling to fairy realms, or a treasure chest to bring in prosperity. When you place it in the aquarium, you can even use a variation of the incantation from the fairy tale of *The Magic Fish*:

Fish of mine,
Familiar divine,
Grant me a wish,
O, magic fish!

A fish familiar so lovingly cared for by you is sure to lend you their energy so that your wishes come true.

The Magic of Amphibian and Fish Familiars

Amphibians invite us to reach back in our ancestral line. They open the door to mystical realms and can help us find our way to wholeness. An amphibian familiar will teach us respect and boundaries and to meet nature on its own terms. Fish invite us to dive deeply into their intuitive, spiritual, watery realm to make some enlightening magic. Invite your amphibian or fish familiar to open your awareness and you will see life from exciting new perspectives.

CHAPTER 14

Reptile Familiars

Lessons from Your Reptile Familiar

Sleek snakes, lounging lizards, cranky crocs, tenacious tortoises—when it comes to the reptile familiar, you have so many interesting choices. They can be found in their natural habitat or kept as loving pets. When you find them in the wild, you can connect to them through observation. When you take on the responsibility of bringing a reptile familiar into your home as a companion, you can link up with a special soul for an extra-personal friendship.

While there are people who are repulsed or even fearful of them, if you're a reptile lover, you are able to see beyond what society rejects and find enchantment in their otherworldliness. Unlike other domesticated animals, reptiles can seem almost detached and aloof but their jewellike colors, tough hides, and penetrating gaze can hypnotize you with their beauty.

Apart from those fast little lizards that skitter around the garden in the summer sun, most reptiles tend to move on the slow side. A reptile familiar can remind you to take your time. "What's the rush?" they seem to say to you as they stretch out under their heat lamp. Unlike birds and mammals, reptiles do not maintain a constant internal body temperature and instead move into the sun or shade to regulate their metabolism. They can teach us to enjoy the warmth of the sun. When you are feeling depleted or in a low mood, get out under the sun and soak up some rays (and vitamin D).

How Your Reptile Familiar Can Help You

The cold-blooded quality of the reptile can help us achieve our own sense of calm when under stress. The word *sangfroid* translates as "cold blood" in French. Unlike our English phrase of *cold-blooded*, meaning "uncaring or emotionless," sangfroid means composure and coolness even when faced with challenges or danger. Bringing sangfroid into a situation allows you to think rationally and make good decisions under pressure, and your reptile familiar, with their slower pace and methodical ways, can help you remain collected when others are stressed.

Befriending a reptile allows us to enter their earthy world. Most reptiles make their homes underground and are associated with the element of earth. Even tree snakes, lizards, and sea turtles find shelter in or near the earth. The energy of these earth-dwellers can lend us grounding, stability, and rootedness. Many reptiles have an exceptionally long lifespan. Some can live up to 50 years or more. So, if you keep a reptile familiar in your home, they can teach you lessons about dependability and commitment.

Apart from a gentle hiss or click, reptiles don't make much noise and can remind you of the power of silence in your craft. There is a time to share and even shout out with pride, but your reptile familiar can remind you that sometimes it's appropriate to keep your magic to yourself instead of telling everyone about the spells that you are doing. That silence also extends to how your reptile familiar moves and so, along with their ability to camouflage themselves, they can teach you the power of blending in and hiding in plain sight.

How Your Reptile Familiar Can Heal You

Safely handling and gently petting your reptile familiar can be a source of healing energy for you. Some reptiles are docile and can be handled with relative ease, while others can be more skittish and prone to biting or scratching. Reptiles can be easy familiars for people with limited mobility or who otherwise can't leave their house. They provide a sense of companionship and can combat loneliness but don't require you to chase them down or take them for a walk. Caring for your reptile familiar can help create and maintain a routine, which is great for bringing you out of a funk.

Lizards

Lizards are popular as pets and familiars. Whether you invite an iguana, bearded dragon, gecko, chameleon, skink, or monitor into your life or are simply connecting with the lizards (or even crocodiles or alligators) that you find out in the wild, you are creating a bond with a creature who can teach you about taking time to enjoy life. When I think of them, I can't help but picture the lizards that I come across basking in the warmth of the sun. They are like those people who live for sitting on the beach on a summer's day with a piña colada in one hand and a great trashy novel in the other. Of all the animals around us, they seem to appreciate the sun the most, so when you come across them warming themselves, take a moment to honor the sun too.

Lizards sometimes get knocked just for being themselves. Think of a sleazy "lounge lizard" or the "lizard people" conspiracy floating around on the fringes. This distrust of lizards has been around since antiquity, but there are cultures that likewise see the lizard as beneficial. In Central Europe, for example, the lizard was seen as a protective spirit and among the Fang people of Central Africa and Diyari of Australia, the lizard was the first form of humanity.[1] If you love lizards, then you too have the witch's gift of seeing beauty in what mainstream society rejects.

Lizard Tail Talisman

Lizards also have the magical ability of regeneration. When captured or caught, a lizard can sever its tail with no blood loss. The severed tail will whip around and wiggle on the ground to distract predators and let the lizard get away. In 6 to 12 months, a new tail will grow in its place, although one that is less colorful and shorter.[2] This act of *autotomy*, or self-amputation, allows the lizard to not only get out of danger but also to have a fresh new start. Lizard familiars can lend that energy to your magic to cut ties with problematic or downright dangerous situations and start over again.

It is never kind to take a lizard's tail forcibly, but if you find one and don't feel too squeamish about preserving it, you can dry it out in a 1:1 mix of salt and borax and then place it on your altar or carry it in a charm bag for connecting to your lizard familiar. You can also use it in spells for escaping harm or getting out of sticky spots.

Snakes

From the Aztec feathered serpent, Quetzalcoatl, to the Australian Aboriginal Rainbow Serpent, the sensuous snake has been an alluring spirit and magical creature throughout history. It is primarily since the advent of Christianity that snakes have been maligned as tricky, dangerous, and an embodiment of evil itself. But if you go back further, snakes were revered for some of their amazing characteristics.

Snakes were often seen as the rulers of the Underworld or Lower World. Unlike the more modern concept of hell, the Lower World was seen as a place of spirits, filled with otherworldly nature and magic. As a snake emerged from their hole in the ground, ancient people imagined this entire underground land where they came from. Unlike the other beings of the lower realm, snakes could traverse between this world and our own Middle World at the surface and were often regarded as guardians of the Lower World or as messengers between the Upper, Middle, and Lower Worlds.

Snakes have also been a symbol of regeneration. Snakes shed their skin as they grow, always returning anew, just like the cycles of the seasons that people throughout history have observed. You can borrow this energy to bring fresh new starts or evolve to higher levels. In Egyptian iconography and the magic traditions of ancient Greece, the Ouroboros was a symbol of a snake eating its own tail, signifying the eternal cycle of life, death, and rebirth.

Snake Shed Collection Spell

Whenever snakes shed their skin, they usually leave large strips or even an entire casing. These snake sheds, as they are called, are often used in spells. As with all animal products used in magic, the most powerful artifact is one that your snake familiar leaves for you. This is unlike working with a snakeskin, which is taken by killing the animal. Instead, a shed is strong because you and the snake are working cooperatively.

Whether you collect these snake sheds in your vivarium or are lucky enough to find them out in the wild, you can use them as artifacts in your magic or to bond you and your snake familiar more closely.

If you find a snake shed out in nature, you can say a thank you to the snake who shared it with you as you pick it up, such as this traditional Ukrainian incantation:

Snake, what you were dressed in,
in both winter and hot summer,
What you took off and I put on,
let it serve my cause.

Snake Familiar Home Protection Spell

Wild snakes were seen as shapeshifters, with folklore from many cultures viewing them as human spirits taking on snake form. An example of this is found in Ukrainian folklore where the snake was one form that the *dvorovyk*, a humanoid spirit who protected the farm animals, could take. Instead of driving a snake out of their barn, a wise farmer would leave a saucer of milk out to feed the snake-dvorovyk in return for his protection. The fact that the snake ate rodents who ransacked the feed bins was just an extra benefit.

While your snake familiar should never drink milk, you can thank them with an extra treat when you want to show appreciation for their protective energy. Add this incantation over the treat to give your snake an extra blessing:

Snake who slithers on the ground,
Sense the goodness all around.
Swallow this that you may live,
And receive the blessings that I give.

Snake Dance Spell

Like the ancient Minoan priestesses or the voodoo queen of New Orleans, Marie Laveau, you can dance with your snakes. Belly dance performers are known to bring the sensuous snake into their performances, but you don't have to don a costume to play with your slithering familiar. Pop on some music and allow your snake to twine around you while you groove to the beat and feel the protective, healing energy that they share with you.

Snake Communication Spell

Your snake familiar can be a wise advisor who shares the mysteries of the Lower World with you. If you'd like to establish communication with your familiar to gain this deep wisdom, you can burn dried yarrow (*Achillea millefolium*) and allow the smoke to permeate the space where you and your snake are.[3]

1. Prepare any questions you may have for your familiar so that you are ready to ask once the link is made.
2. Light an incense charcoal and place some yarrow on it.
3. Let your snake twine around your arms or sit near their terrarium. Close your eyes and activate your strongest clair. (For information about the clairs, see Chapter 3.)
4. Envision your snake looking into your eyes. Ask your question and receive the message from them.

Be aware that the communication may come through symbolic visions or psychic messages. If you don't receive a message during the session, your familiar may answer you in your dreams that evening.

Turtles and Tortoises

All tortoises are turtles, but not all turtles are tortoises. All tortoises live exclusively on land, while other turtle species may be primarily water dwelling or exclusively land dwelling—it depends on the type. One thing many have in common is the quality of longevity. Depending on the species, they can have a lifespan of anywhere from 10 to 150 years. If you are taking a turtle as a familiar, you may have found a magical ally for life. While the responsibility of taking on a lifelong friend is a serious decision to make, think of all the energy you build up by deepening your relationship year after year.

Most of us are familiar with Aesop's fable of "The Tortoise and the Hare," where the slow and steady tortoise bests the speedy hare in a footrace. If you have a hare-like quality of always rushing to the finish line, the patience and endurance of the tortoise can remind you that you can achieve big goals by doing small things each day. The tortoise's long-range view of life can remind you that you don't always have to keep up a frenetic pace. Life in the slow lane can be more mindful, and being methodical means you don't have to fix mistakes that you make when you rush through the steps. The tortoise never allows anyone to rush them when they need to take things at their own pace and, with a tortoise familiar by your side, you can honor your own slower rhythm to reach your aims.

Tortoise Treat Divination

Tortoises have a naturally varied diet, eating lots of different plants with the occasional treat of a piece of fruit. Many of these plants have magical properties, so you can choose ones with specific meanings and do a spell divination with your tortoise.

1. Select a few different magical plants from the list below.
2. Offer them to your tortoise, and see which one they go for first. This will let you know what type of magic that the two of you should focus on.

   - Apple (*Malus domestica)*: immortality
   - Blueberry (*Vaccinium corymbosum, Vaccinium angustifolium*): protection
   - Cabbage (*Brassica oleracea*): luck
   - Carrot (*Daucus carota*): lust
   - Celery (*Apium graveolens*): psychic powers
   - Chicory (*Cichorium intybus*): invisibility
   - Clover (*Trifolium repens*): success
   - Collard greens (*Brassica oleracea*): money
   - Cucumber (*Cucumis sativus*): fertility
   - Dandelion (*Taraxacum officinale*): wishes (offer only young, tender leaves)
   - Grape (*Vitis vinifera*): abundance
   - Hibiscus flowers (*Hibiscus rosa-sinensis*): love
   - Mustard leaves (*Brassica juncea*): intellect
   - Peach (*Prunus persica*): longevity
   - Pear (*Pyrus communis*): employment
   - Plantain plant (*Plantago*): healing
   - Strawberry (*Fragaria* x *ananassa*): romance
   - Turnip leaves (*Brassica rapa*): endings

This divination technique can also be done with other vegetarian or omnivorous reptiles. As with all ingestible spells, make sure that the plants that you are offering are organic and safe for your specific species and their nutritional needs.

Magic with Your Reptile Familiar

Inviting a reptile familiar to join you is perfect for learning give-and-take. Unlike other familiars, with reptiles you must have patience and be willing to meet them on their own turf. The joy of this familiar relationship is that it gives you a gentle push to join them in their world. Take your time, bask in the sun, and let your reptile familiar take you to lands you never dreamed were possible to explore.

CHAPTER 15

Insect Familiars

Lessons from Your Insect Familiar

Butterflies, honeybees, ladybugs, dragonflies, and crickets—when a member of the *insecta* class steps up as your familiar, you have a magical and otherworldly connection. Bugs can teach us to be mindful and live in the moment, as most live out their lives within a single year (some live only days, or even minutes!).

For years, researchers believed that insects did not have any consciousness. However, science has caught up with what we witches who connect with insect familiars have always known: namely, that while insects have a decidedly different consciousness than humans, they are sentient beings that can express pain and suffering as well as feel emotions akin to joy and desire.[1] Think of the way most people think of bugs.

We say things like, "Don't be a pest," and "Stop bugging me," implying that an annoying person is like an insect. While there are fewer of us who want to take on a mosquito, tick, cockroach, or flea familiar, we shouldn't forget that there are many insects that are beautiful and beneficial. We rely on insects for life on earth. They are the diligent beings working hard in the background pollinating, recycling nutrients, controlling pests, and feeding other creatures. Without them, life as we know it would not exist.

How Your Insect Familiar Can Help You

Whenever you connect to the insect kingdom for magic, you are daring to enter into a realm that is very different than our human world. It's not by chance that the popular image of a fairy is often quite buglike. Both insects and fairies, with their iridescent gossamer wings, are tiny, delicate, and colorful. Just as fairies can invite us into the world of spirits, so can insects bring us into their fast-moving, live-in-the-moment energy. If you are feeling stagnant or in the doldrums, ruminating too much about the past or getting anxious about the future, your insect familiar can remind you to be here now.

Connecting with Your Insect Familiar

If you are keeping an insect in a terrarium, you can connect deeply to that one familiar, but you can also find a familiar out in the world. If you are working with insects in the wild you can connect to them collectively as familiars, developing a partnership with the entire family of that animal. It's a little bit like an animal guide dialed up to familiar status.

When you start paying attention to the animal kingdom, you might notice that insects are extremely responsive to magic. When you cast spells, meditate, or perform rituals, pay attention to the insects that appear; you might find more of them coming around to assist you. The insects that show up may want to work magically with you. You may accept or decline the invitation, but explore the magic that that insect has to offer before you say, "No thanks."

There are more than one million different species of insects, so the bugs that we will be focusing on are by no means a comprehensive list. I have chosen some of the most popular insect families and the familiar relationships that can be developed with them. Let these key insects start a familiar journey that expands into the many other bug familiars that can bring magic into your life.

Beetles

Beetles are by far the largest group of insects in the world. In fact, one out of every four animals on earth is a beetle. These tiny, armored warriors range from the magical glowing firefly to the industrious dung beetle revered as the scarab in ancient Egypt. Beetles can display an almost psychedelic variety of colors, which can reveal a special message when they appear. See Appendix E to interpret what these colors can mean for you.

Ladybugs

"Ladybug, Ladybug, fly away home. Your house is on fire, your children will burn." Almost everyone in the English-speaking world has said some variation of this children's poem when a ladybug has landed on them. Ladybugs eat crop-destroying aphids, and it is believed that this little poem was said by farmers in centuries past to warn the ladybugs to flee before they would burn their fields following the harvest.[2]

Ladybugs, or *ladybirds* if you are in Great Britain and Ireland, carry a name with great spiritual significance. It is said that in the Middle Ages farmers were facing a devastating infestation of insects eating their crops. They prayed to Mother Mary, and a cloud of red beetles with black spots came to eat these insects and were named "Our Lady's Beetle," which evolved into ladybird and ladybug.

If you have a ladybug familiar, you are a lucky one indeed. Even people who generally despise insects can't help but get excited about a ladybug landing on them, for in many cultures this is a sign that they are sharing their luck with you. How do you know if a ladybug is your familiar? One of the sure signs is that you see ladybugs often, have them land on you frequently, or feel a special excitement anytime you encounter one.

Ladybug Familiar Wishes

When a ladybug lands on you, it's a sign that luck is coming your way. Make a wish for the luck that you would like to have. Let the ladybug crawl on you for as long as they like.

The longer they stay on you, the more luck you will receive. When they fly away, say your wish out loud, and the ladybug will take that wish out to the realm of spirit to come true.

Ladybug Familiar Messages

Ancient people would see animal encounters as omens, and with ladybugs, you can do that too. While you might think of ladybugs as a single species, there are many different beetles that are called ladybugs. They can have no spots or up to 24 spots. Next time you see a ladybug, take a close look and count the number of spots on its back and then reflect on the message it is sending you.

- **Zero:** If you see a ladybug with no spots, it's a sign that you have a clean slate, and anything is possible. Think about all the possibilities and realize that you are limitless. If you think of limitations in your life, get past those imaginary barriers into your wildest dreams becoming realities.
- **One:** A ladybug with one spot is exceedingly rare and would only come from a mutation, so when it appears, it means that a once-in-a-lifetime opportunity is about to come your way. Taking a risk will lead to a great reward. In our lives we get many chances to make bold moves, but these individual opportunities may only come around once. Don't worry if you don't take advantage of all the opportunities. If you don't take one, a different one will come around.

- **Two:** A two-spot ladybug brings a message of love—a new love or a deepening of an existing relationship. This can be romantic love, of course, but it can also be a sign of friendship or even a message about your familiar relationships. What it does signify is your connection to another being will be more fulfilling and magical.
- **Three:** A ladybug with three spots reminds you that you are a never-ending fountain of creativity. If you have put creativity on the back burner, it's time to bring it to the forefront. If you are feeling stagnant, you can expect a new burst of inspiration. If you have always wanted to try a new creative and expressive endeavor, now is the time to get started. And don't be limited by your own beliefs about creativity. Creativity can show up in the arts, of course, but it can also be problem-solving and inventiveness of any kind.
- **Four:** When you encounter a ladybug with four spots, it's a sign of increase and abundance. Look for more financial flow, of course, but also look for abundance of other kinds, such as gifts and advantageous exchanges. Take a moment to reflect on and appreciate the abundance you already have in your life and invite even more in.
- **Five:** A ladybug with five spots is telling you that travel and adventure are ahead. I like to picture that ladybug holding a map and wearing a little backpack, with a protective hat on her head, and standing in teeny-tiny hiking boots. Adventure doesn't always mean climbing to the top of a

mountain in a distant land; it can mean exploring a nearby town or checking out that new club you've always wanted to join. Follow your curiosity and take the leap to explore new things.

- **Six:** When a ladybug with six spots appears, it's a sign of connection to groups and community and working harmoniously with others. She's giving us a reminder of the power in numbers. Have you been flying solo lately? Then it's time to reconnect with groups of friends, family (or found family), or finding new groups of mutual support. Do you have big projects and big dreams? Then you may need to bring together a group to see those dreams become reality.
- **Seven:** A seven-spot ladybug is a divine messenger of spirit. She is a reminder to deepen your spiritual connection through practice and study. If you've been slacking on your meditation routine, for example, she's reminding you to jump back in. If your spiritual practice is getting a little stale, research or learn a new skill that you have always wanted to explore.
- **Eight:** The ladybug with eight spots brings a message of success and achievement. If you are feeling like your goals are out of reach, she is here to remind you to keep going and that you will get there. She also tells you that your dreams and goals are worthy and that you are worthy of achieving them. How big, how high, and how far do you want to go? You've got this!

- **Nine:** Did you meet a ladybug with nine spots? This ladybug is sending you a message of completion. Time to wrap things up and move on to the next project. If things are feeling challenging right now, know that your hardships will soon be over.
- **Ten or More:** A ladybug with 10 or more spots represents having an abundance of options. Reflect on all the possibilities. You may have more choices than you realize.

Butterflies and Moths

Like seeing a rainbow in the sky, butterflies delight nearly everyone who encounters them. Like most insects, the butterfly familiar will most likely not be an individual butterfly but can be all butterflies collectively or a particular color or species.

However, one wonderful way to connect to an individual butterfly familiar is to make or purchase a butterfly nursery and larvae native to your region in the spring or summer and watch them go through their entire life cycle. Butterflies aren't domesticated creatures, but you can build a special familiar relationship by protecting a caterpillar as they go through the stages of metamorphosis and releasing them when they emerge as a butterfly from their cocoon. If you create a safe haven for a caterpillar, just make sure that you have access to the appropriate fresh food for the species that you are raising and that the butterfly it will become will be released in the proper season and environment to sustain them after they are free.

If you'd like less of the responsibility of rearing larvae in captivity, you can still give a gift to your butterfly familiar by planting host plants from your region that caterpillars like. If you plant some nectar plants that butterflies like in addition to your caterpillar host plants, you can create a magical garden where you can sit among these fluttering familiars and observe their entire life cycle. Bless the plants with the intention of bringing you and your butterfly familiars closer to share their magic with you.

The moth is like the butterfly's goth cousin, hanging out at night and dancing around at their lamppost nightclub. Heck, the death's-head hawkmoth even has a giant skull tattoo on its back. Despite moths being overshadowed by their daytime compatriots, they are just as remarkable, if not more so. There are moths, like the atlas moth, that are as big as birds and the male mandolin moth that scratches his leg against his wing to serenade his lady love. Moths are also masters of disguise, blending in with the vegetation around them, and can lend you that energy if you'd like an invisibility spell to make you unnoticeable.

Lessons from Your Butterfly or Moth Familiar

Observing the process of metamorphosis that a butterfly or moth goes through can be a thoroughly enlightening experience. You probably remember from elementary school science, or the book *The Very Hungry Caterpillar*, that a butterfly starts out as an egg that then hatches into a caterpillar, which then goes into a cocoon and emerges weeks later as a butterfly. Simple, huh? Before diving into the world of butterflies, I never gave the process much thought, but when I did, I discovered something shocking. When a caterpillar goes into its cocoon, it doesn't just sprout wings; it liquifies into a sort of caterpillar soup that then reassembles itself into a butterfly or moth. That process is much more extreme than what I casually imagined it to be.

With butterflies and moths representing true transformation, you can be sure that when you take on the butterfly as a familiar, you will have the resources at your side to move through trials with a special grace and ease and emerge more vibrant, beautiful, and glorious at the end.

Butterfly and Moth Familiar Messages

Butterflies and moths symbolize transformation, so when you see one of your fluttering familiars, they can remind you that positive change, growth, and evolution are coming. Pay attention to any concerns or topics that are at the top of your mind when you see a butterfly or moth.

The color of the butterflies or moths that you encounter can be a way for your familiar to communicate to you what this change will bring. When you see a butterfly or moth, note its primary color, refer to Appendix E to get a message, and then take time to reflect on what your messenger is saying to you.

Butterfly Familiar Wishing Spell

To commune more deeply with your butterfly familiars, you can encourage them to land on your hand. Butterflies are very delicate, so do not pick them up, touch them, or pet them, but you can certainly hand-feed them. Sit still near the flowers where butterflies are congregating and hold a piece of wet, overripe, sweet fruit such as watermelon or a banana moistened with some water and bless it as an offering to your familiar to bring the two of you closer. Hold the piece of fruit underneath where the butterflies are congregating. Butterflies taste through their feet and suck up nutritious nectar through their long proboscis, so let the butterfly land on the fruit and then slurp up the sweetness through their built-in boba straw.

Have patience as you embark on this practice. The butterflies may or may not choose to partake, but when they do, it will be a thrilling connection to these special insects. When your butterfly familiar lands on you, make a wish or set an intention and let the butterfly bless it with all its gratitude.

Dragonflies

Hang around a lake or pond in spring or summer, and you are bound to encounter one of these iridescent wonders. Dragonflies and damselflies have such remarkable abilities to fly forward, backward, side to side, or hover in place that engineers are studying them hoping to replicate their speed and coordination for drones and flying robots. If you need to amp up your physical or mental agility, tap into the energy your dragonfly familiar can give you. Dragonflies and damselflies spend most of their lives, up to two years, underwater as larva. When they emerge as adults, they live for a few short weeks. Your dragonfly familiar can remind you to savor every moment with mindfulness.

Dragonfly Warrior Magic

In Japan, dragonflies are revered not only for their beauty but also for their prowess as hunters. Dragonflies catch and eat smaller insects such as mosquitos and midges, deftly flying up and grabbing them. One of the old Japanese names for the dragonfly is *katsumushi*, which means "victory insect." Surprisingly, the delicate dragonfly was often emblazoned on samurai armor and swords. The hope for the soldier was that he too could quickly attack and kill his enemy and never retreat.[3]

If you are thrown into a competitive situation and need the courage of the dragonfly to come out on top, wear dragonfly jewelry or carry an image of the dragonfly with you and invite your dragonfly familiar to lend you its warrior spirit.

Musical Insects

The insects of the *Orthoptera* order—crickets, katydids, grasshoppers, locusts, and cicadas—are the musicians of the insect kingdom. When the males of this group want to attract a mate or establish their territory, they rub their wings together to make their music. When they call to you as a familiar, they are there to remind you of the power that music has in your life.

On a purely neurological level, listening to music causes your brain to release the happiness chemicals of dopamine and serotonin, and feeling joy does wonders for our magic as well as our well-being. Even Shakespeare saw this connection between crickets and happiness. "Shall we be merry?" Prince Henry asks in *Henry IV Part 1*. "As merry as crickets, my lad," comes the reply.

Play some of your favorite music in the background as you work, exercise, or relax. If you play an instrument, pick it up again for a quick dose of music therapy. If you've ever wanted to learn to play an instrument, your musical insect familiars will lend you inspiration and encouragement to remind you that you don't have to play perfectly to find joy in making sound.

Crickets

Crickets have a long spiritual history and are well-known for the chirping sound that they make. In China, Japan, and some indigenous cultures of North, Central, and South America, crickets are thought to bring good luck. As early as 500 BCE, there is evidence of people keeping crickets in cages to enjoy their song on a regular basis. They were also used as an ingenious alarm system. Crickets will stop singing when they feel the vibrations of anyone or anything approaching them, and so the sudden silence of these caged crickets could warn the people of a home about unexpected guests or intruders.[4]

Cricket Familiar Sound Bath Spell

If you are developing a relationship with cricket familiars, you don't need to keep a cricket in a cage. You can enjoy an entire chorus of crickets playing their music on a summer's evening, giving you a peaceful and relaxing concert and allowing the cricket musicians their freedom. There are studies that show that listening to the sounds of nature, such as crickets, can help calm and focus our minds—the perfect state for making magic.

1. Listen to the rhythm and cadence of the crickets' chirps, and tap into their resonance and frequency. If the time isn't right for your cricket familiar to be chirping, then listening to recorded cricket chirps can be a great substitute.
2. Imagine your cricket familiars giving you a lovely healing sound bath and receive their energy.
3. If there is a special wish for a change in your life, imagine that the chirps are a chant and chant along with them aloud or in your mind for a few minutes to empower your incantation.

Social Insects

Bees, wasps, ants, and termites are the insects who work together in social groups. The big teamwork energy of their colonies reveals an interesting paradox. The colony is made of individual insects, but they only survive by working as a collective that functions as an organism itself. Each insect in the colony has a role to fulfill, and they work together for the good of all, finding food and other resources and communicating that information to others. If their home is attacked, they can amass an army and mount a vigorous defense. They know that there is power in numbers, outcompeting other insects and even larger animals for territory and resources.

If you are in the process of discovering your role in a group or want to build groups that are harmonious and effective, your social insect familiar can lend you their energy to make things hum along like a beehive.

Honeybees

In so many cultures, bees are thought to be divine messengers who traverse between the world of spirit and the world of the living. In ancient Greece, this association may have come about from observing bees coming and going from wild hives created in the cracks in rock walls and caves, which were believed to be entrances to the Underworld. We also see this connection referenced in Celtic mythology where the presence of a bee after a death signified the soul leaving the body.[5] For thousands of years, it has been believed that bees were the spirits of departed ancestors, a folk belief which is still held by traditional beekeepers in Europe and places where European people emigrated.

Honeybees in particular can also be familiar-helpers when you need to communicate with a group. A typical beehive can have up to 50,000 honeybees. They communicate with each other using pheromones and a "waggle dance" that is performed by the scout bees to tell the rest of the hive where a good source of nectar can be found. You don't have to shake your booty to be a public speaker, but if you routinely do presentations, a group of honeybee familiars could lend their communication energy to you. They can also teach us to share opportunities with others in our community and to get out of habits of fear, greed, and hoarding.

With bees of all kinds, you can work them in the wild or bring them a little closer. If a honeybee is your familiar, you can start keeping a hive. If you get called to work with other types of bees, you can buy or build housing for them. Social bees, such as bumblebees, love a nest box while solitary bees, like mason bees or leafcutter bees, will flock to a bee hotel. These important pollinators might not make honey or beeswax, but they can make your garden thrive and are fun to watch and connect with, just as you would with wild birds in a birdhouse.

Telling the Bees Spell

There is an ancient European folkloric tradition of "telling the bees" that is still practiced today. The bees are informed of births, marriages, and deaths in the family of the beekeeper. It was believed that if you did not tell the bees of these major life events, they would stop producing honey or abandon the hive entirely. If there was a wedding taking place, the hives might be decorated with flowers, and a slice of wedding cake would be placed near the hive to keep the bees making abundant honey. Queen Elizabeth II's royal beekeeper performed the ritual of telling the bees when she passed away, placing black ribbons on the hives and informing them, in hushed tones, of the Queen's passing and King Charles's ascension. He related that, "You knock on each hive and say, 'The mistress is dead, but don't you go. Your master will be a good master to you.'"[6]

If you have bee familiars, you can speak to them too, and not just about marriages and deaths in the family. Sit next to the hive or near wild bees collecting nectar and share what is going on in your life and listen to their reply. If you follow the old tradition, then hearing an increased buzzing after the news is delivered is a good sign that your bee familiars are going to assist you as you make your way through life.

Listening to the Bees Spell

Not only can you tell the bees, but you can also listen to them too. If you are working with your bee familiars in a hive, spend some time resting near the hive and listen to the golden hum of thousands of buzzing bees. Researchers have discovered that bees emit a healing frequency that can help with calming anxiety, bringing relief from PTSD, relieving pain, calming inflammation flares, and even boosting the immune system.[7] In addition, the buzz frequency has been shown to increase the production of serotonin, which is a neurotransmitter that helps to regulate mood, appetite, and sleep.

If you don't have a hive, you can still benefit from listening to recorded sounds of beehives for a sweet sound bath that connects you to your bee familiars even when they're not nearby.

Honey Spells

Honey, especially honey collected from bees that you have befriended as familiars, can be a powerful spell ingredient. Honey itself has been treated as a magical substance for millennia. Not only has it been used to sweeten food and make delicious, fermented beverages like mead, it was used for medicine due to its antimicrobial and antibiotic properties. In ancient Egypt, honey was used in magic to repel ghosts.[8] In ancient Greece, honey and the beeswax honeycomb were used as a special offering to the gods and used in spells and potions for love, purity, abundance, blessings, knowledge, and wisdom. In your own magic, you can use your bee familiar honey as a powerful ingredient in potions to make the outcome sweeter.

Other Kinds of Insect Familiars

There are so many other wonderful insects that you can interact with that may be around you: ants, cicadas, inchworms, grasshoppers, pill bugs, earthworms, snails, and so many more bugs that are ready to assist you in your magic. Look for the insects that sing to your heart. If you feel drawn to them, there is no judgment. Look for ways that you can protect and honor that species of insect, and pay attention to their special characteristics and how you can receive and share in their energy.

— CHAPTER 16 —

Spider Familiars

Lessons from Your Spider Familiar

If you are a witch who sees the beauty in a delicate gossamer web, are fascinated by anything with eight legs, and appreciates nature's weavers and spinners, then a spider familiar may be waiting to work with you. Unlike their cousins, the insects, spiders seem to straddle the world of the domestic and wild familiar. A spider will set up their home in your house or garden and usually stay put for a while. This means that, just like Wilbur the pig in the book *Charlotte's Web*, you have the possibility of developing a friendship with an individual spider.

You can even set up a cozy home for your arachnid, creating a spider terrarium (can we call it a *spiderarium*?) where you can observe your spinning familiar more closely. Spider-loving witches have been known to keep certain species, such as tarantulas, as familiar pets. While these larger spiders might seem more intimidating to some, they can be fascinating companions who can even be gently handled to bring the two of you even closer.

How Your Spider Familiar Can Help You

Spiders have been revered by spiritual people for thousands of years. In ancient Slavic lore, spiders were the creators of the world, a belief shared by many cultures. There are tales throughout the world of spider deities such as Anansi the Spider from the Akan-Ashanti people of Ghana and the Ivory Coast; Grandmother Spider in Hopi, Pueblo, and Navajo/Diné traditions; and Ariadne in Greek mythology, just to name a few.

Spiders are seen as diligent spinners and skillful weavers, and so, in the past, they were the special animals of the people who created textiles. The webs that they weave are incredibly strong as well as elastic. The design of the web can be refined as well as functional. The delicate lace of a web can be a focal point for meditating on the web of life or even a metaphor for the delicate yet powerful spiritual threads that connect each living thing to all others.

Spiders can also teach you about manifestation with your spellwork. A spinning spider carefully crafts their web and then waits for an insect to come to them. You can use this as a model for your own magic. Cast a good spell and then wait for the opportunity to come to you. When the chance does come your way, pounce on it.

Making Magic with Your Spider Familiar

Because they are so adaptable, you can choose where to work with your spider familiar—inside or outside. If you find a spider in your home but would rather have them outside, it is easy to scoop them up and bring them to the great outdoors, but if you are open to allowing them to share your space, they can be an adept helper who can bring luck to your home and power to your magic.

Spider Shed Spell

Spiders shed their exoskeleton as they grow, and this delicate little shell can be a gift given to you to use in your magic. In the case of big spiders, like tarantulas, this shedding can be very dramatic. I once babysat a tarantula for a friend, and one evening I came home from work and looked in the terrarium to see not one spider, but two full-grown tarantulas. I was so confused. *How did this happen? Were there already two and I just didn't notice? Did another tarantula find its way into the enclosure?* It wasn't until I tried to touch the doppelgänger that I realized it was the exoskeleton of the tarantula that I had been caring for—perfectly intact and looking like the spider's twin.

These spider sheds are an offering that your spider familiar can give you to use in your magic. Think of the qualities of the spider and how you would like to bring them into your spellwork. You can add them to spells to become more skillful at a craft or to tap into the energetic connection of all things. You can use them for spells of growth and transformation. It is simple to powder the sheds with a mortar and pestle and sprinkle them on your candle spells. Likewise, you can leave the entire shed intact and place it on an altar to bring all that spidery goodness to your magic.

Spiderweb Spell

Webs are also another offering that spiders give to us. It's important that you never take the web of a spider who is actively using it. Imagine someone commandeering your house as a party pad. Even if they were your closest friend, you would feel a tad resentful if you had to rebuild your house after they burned it to the ground. However, most spiders weave new webs every day, so find cobwebs or other abandoned spider silk and use them in your magic to keep the relationship between you and your spider familiar balanced and positive.

Any abandoned webs that you find can be used in your spells, but if you have a special familiar relationship with the spider who created them, they can be even more powerful. I often do visioning work for manifestation where I picture pulling on gossamer spider threads to bring in my biggest dreams and wishes. Real cobwebs can also be used for calling in your heart's desire. Wrap them around your candle spells and envision them drawing in and capturing what it is that you're wishing for. You can also simply leave them where they are to trap and transform negative energies before they affect you, your home, or your loved ones.

Spiderweb Charm

Romans carried amulets with spider images for success in business. If you'd like to draw and bind prosperity to you, you can use webs abandoned by your familiar as an ingredient in this charm. This recipe is for attracting and keeping money, but you can substitute another intention such as luck, success, fame, love, protection, and so on. If so, change the combination of herbs and swap out the word *money* for the new intention in the incantation.

What you will need:

- About 1 teaspoon of beeswax (If you like, this can be the beeswax remains from a money candle spell that you have completed).
- A piece of web from your spider familiar
- 1 allspice berry (*Pimenta dioica*)
- 1 dried chamomile flower (*Matricaria chamomilla*)
- 3 fenugreek seeds (*Trigonella foenum-graecum*)
- A small piece of paper with your name on it, curled into a scroll
- A piece of your own hair

1. Hold the piece of beeswax in your hands and stretch it to soften it until it becomes the consistency of taffy.
2. Form the beeswax into a sheet and place the web, herbs, name paper, and hair in the center of the wax.

3. Fold the wax over the items, and then roll it between your palms into a ball as you say the following incantation:

Spider familiar, flow and ebb,
Share with me your magic web.
May money come, may money stay,
Attract, increase, by night, by day.

4. Set the ball aside to harden, and then place it on your altar or carry it in a pocket or pouch.
5. Anytime you want to reactivate the charm to bring more money to you, just roll it between your hands and recite the incantation.

Nggàm Dù Spider Divination

In Cameroon and Nigeria, the Mambila people have a very unique form of fortune telling called *Nggàm dù*. Diviners do this work with a large ground-dwelling spider or a crab and beautiful "cards" made from dried leaves with patterns cut and woven into them. The diviner asks the spider a question with a two-option answer. A stick that represents one option and a stone that represents the other are placed to the left and right of the spider's hole. The leaf cards are placed over and around the hole and all are covered with an overturned pot. The spider emerges from their hole and moves the cards. After some time, the diviner removes the pot and interprets the position of the leaves that the spider has moved to give a nuanced answer to the question.[1, 2, 3]

If you have a large spider familiar in a terrarium, you can do a similar but simpler divination by placing two items in your spider's home and assigning one as yes and one as no. Place a third object, such as a leaf, that is easy for them to move, then ask a yes/no question. Look at their terrarium the next day and see whether they moved the leaf to touch the yes item or the no item.

Spider Omens

Good things *do* come in small packages. There is a tiny brown or black spider known as the money spider in the UK, Ireland, Australia, New Zealand, and Portugal. These lucky spiders can be found in just about every country throughout the world. If you discover one of these little weavers crawling on you, it is said that they are "spinning you a new set of clothes," meaning that you are about to come into some financial luck. This may seem like just another legend, but one woman in England won the lottery when a money spider crawling on her prompted her to buy a ticket.[4]

When a spider appears, pay attention to the message they give you and thank them for conveying that information. Pay close attention if you see any of these special omens. If your spider familiar does any of these, they are making some potent magic with you.

- Spiders are harbingers of good luck: the bigger the spider, the greater your fortune.
- A white spider means changes for the better, increased luck, and money coming your way.

- A spider crawling into your pocket is a sign that you will always have money.
- A spider hanging over your head means an important message (such as a letter or text or e-mail) is coming your way.
- A spider on your Yule tree will bring blessings to your home for the coming year.
- A spider descending from the ceiling is good luck.
- Seeing a spider on your wedding day is a positive omen of a happy marriage.
- A spider crawling on their web in the afternoon means you'll go on a journey.
- If you see a spider crawling on the wall, make a wish and it will come true.
- If you unexpectedly come across a spider spinning a web, it indicates that your income will increase from your hard work.
- If a spider makes a web across your door, it means a visitor is coming.

It's considered bad luck to kill a spider, so if you don't want one in your house, gently take it outside. If you do kill one, it is said that you must atone by killing 53 flies, and then your good luck will return. All that fly slaughtering may make you rethink smashing a spider carelessly.

The Magic of Spider Familiars

Spiders are not everyone's cup of tea, but if you are that special witch who sees the beauty and ancient magic of these spinning spirits, then a spider familiar might just crawl into your life. Spiders are a low-maintenance familiar who can keep your space insect-free and make some extraordinary magic with you. When you welcome this friendly familiar, they will weave a web of bewitching enchantment over all the spells that you do.

CONCLUSION

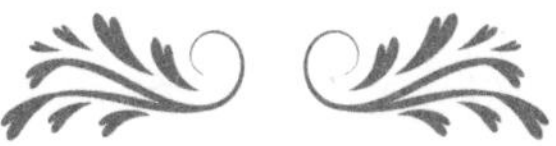

The Power of Animal Familiars

If you have delved into this book, enriched your understanding of the spiritual nature of your special animals, and tried some of the spells, rituals, and recipes, then undoubtedly you understand the power of the union between a witch and her animal familiar. When you partner with an animal familiar, you have an eager magical accomplice with a direct access point to the powers of nature. They will help you connect to the wild world that the seemingly irresistible magnet of technology tries to pull us away from.

Remember that part of your responsibility as a witch is to rectify the distortions, bad propaganda, and outright lies that have been told about us for hundreds of years and are sadly still swirling around out there. We don't deal with the devil, sacrifice babies (or animals), or have an entourage of demons disguised as Fluffy and Rover. There is a bumper sticker that has been around since the 1980s and perfectly sums up what it means to be a witch. It simply says, "Witches Heal." Historically, we *are* the healers, the midwives, the potion makers, the wise advisors, and the ones who cavort in nature and treat animals with respect and love.

You, dear witch, have the power to develop a unique bond with animals that few people will ever experience. You can make magic with them in the mundane world or fly, swim, slither, and run with them on the ethereal plane. You can meet them in the wild or create a cozy home for them right next to you. Your little furry, scaly, slimy, or downy companion is a witch in their own right. They can teach you life lessons, empathy, patience, strategy, courage, and how to experience true, unbridled joy. They can enhance your intuition and send you messages. They can take you on adventures and show you how to truly live in the moment.

After mastering the skills in this book, I know that you too will tell your own story of the familiars who have blessed your life, how they arrived in such surprising and unexpected ways, the wondrous unforeseen talents they revealed to you, and the priceless gifts that they gave to you. I look forward to hearing your tales of the magic that you and your animals make and the adventures that you have. May all witches and familiars work together to heal the world.

APPENDIX A

Western Astrology Correspondences

You can find an affinity to certain animals by referring to your astrological chart. Look up the zodiac signs of your "big three" (sun sign, moon sign, and rising sign) on this chart and see what animals you may build special relationships with. If you don't know your astrological information, there are many sites online, such as Astrology.com, that offer free charts.

Aries: sheep, lizard, dragonfly, hawk, rooster, hummingbird, hare

Taurus: cattle, pelican, ants, scarab, earthworm, salmon, bear

Gemini: eagle, parrot, chinchilla, goose, parakeet, grasshopper, pigeon

Cancer: crab, ladybug, wolf, otter, chicken, whale, octopus

Leo: lion, cat, peacock, turkey, macaw, chameleon, elephant

Virgo: rabbit, guinea pig, cricket, mouse, quail, honeybee, chimpanzee

Libra: swan, butterfly, spider, gerbil, pheasant, dove, mantis

Scorpio: scorpion, owl, bat, dog, snake, moth, hamster

Sagittarius: horse, salamander, rat, deer, duck, tern, shark

Capricorn: goat, beaver, tortoise, squirrel, pig, toad, goldfish

Aquarius: fox, corvid, coyote, swift, cockatoo, raccoon, dolphin

Pisces: fish, frog, seahorse, seagull, turtle, seal, jellyfish

APPENDIX B

Herbs for Familiar Spells

Please note that these herbs are recommended to be used in spells but not fed to animals. Each animal has its own health needs, so do thorough research before allowing an animal to have contact with a particular herb.

Animal Communication: cloth-of-gold, valerian root

Attraction: catnip, cedar, cinnamon, coriander, damiana, juniper, orris root

Beauty: catnip, elecampane, ginseng, rosemary, yerba santa

Blessing: angelica root, cedar, copal, frankincense, passionflower, red clover

Calming: elecampane, mugwort, St. John's wort

Communication: apple blossom, deer's tongue, pomegranate, valerian

Courage: borage, mullein, tea, thyme, yarrow

Dreamwork: camphor, celery seed, chamomile, cinquefoil, flax, frankincense, hibiscus, jasmine, rosemary, star anise

Fame: orris root, passionflower, sunflower

Familiar Commitment: juniper

Fertility: black mustard seed, fig, hawthorn, myrtle, mistletoe, patchouli, pine, white oak, yellow dock

Fidelity: basil, comfrey, cumin, hawthorn, magnolia, periwinkle, raspberry, rosemary, senna, skullcap, spikenard

Happiness: allspice, basil, benzoin, cacao, catnip, lavender, marjoram, thyme, vanilla

Healing (Emotional): balm of Gilead, marjoram, vanilla

Healing (General): allspice, althea, angelica root, calamus root, caraway, chickweed, coltsfoot, goldenseal, grains of paradise, lemon balm, myrrh, rue, sunflower

Health/Strength: acorn, bay leaf, coriander, dill, masterwort, peony, pine, thyme, white oak, white sage

Love (New): cardamom, catnip, coriander, cubeb, lemon balm, lovage, sandalwood, senna

Love (Platonic): acacia, catnip, clove, passionflower

Love (Romantic): caraway, catnip, cinnamon, cumin, damiana, deer's tongue, dill, dragon's blood, elecampane, gentian, ginger, hibiscus, jasmine, lavender, lemongrass, lovage, marjoram, myrtle, orris root, passion flower, patchouli, red clover, rose, saffron, sandalwood, tonka bean, vanilla, violet leaf, yellow mustard seed

Luck: acorn, alkanet, basil, benzoin, calamus root, catnip, cumin, devil's shoe string, ginger, gravel root, peony, star anise

Marriage: blood root, caraway, coriander, deer's tongue, hawthorn, lavender, magnolia, marjoram, myrtle, orange, periwinkle, raspberry, red clover, rosemary, spikenard

Mental Wellness/Clarity: cacao beans, caraway, coltsfoot, mustard seed, periwinkle, rosemary, rue, smartweed, spearmint

New Ventures: acorn, cinnamon, ginger, lemon balm, lemongrass

Peace: allspice, basil, benzoin, blood root, comfrey, cornflower, lavender, marjoram, myrrh, periwinkle, rosemary, sandalwood, valerian root

Personal Power: bergamot, carnation, devil's shoestring, echinacea, gentian, ginger, masterwort, orris root

Prosperity/Money: acorn, alfalfa, alkanet, allspice, basil, bayberry, blue flag root, calendula, cascara sagrada, cinnamon, cinquefoil, clove, comfrey, dragon's blood, fenugreek, ginger, Irish moss, nutmeg, patchouli, pine, sarsaparilla, sassafras, skullcap, smartweed

Protection from Wild Animals: holly, juniper, mullein, roots

Protection (General): acacia, agrimony, althaea, angelica, balm of Gilead, barberry, basil, bay leaf, benzoin, black pepper, blessed thistle, blue cohosh, calamus root, cascara sagrada, cinquefoil, coriander, devil's shoe string, dragon's blood, elderflower, eucalyptus, fennel, feverfew, flax, ginger, grains of paradise, lemon, lemongrass, marjoram, mistletoe, mugwort, mullein, mustard seed, myrrh, oregano, pennyroyal, peony, pine, poke, red clover, rue, salt, sandalwood, slippery elm, Solomon's seal, verbena, white sage, willow

Protection (Spirits): angelica, anise, asafoetida, basil, bay leaf, caraway, dragon's blood, elder, frankincense, holly, mistletoe, pine, rue, star anise, white oak

Psychic Ability: acacia, althaea, anise, bay leaf, camphor, celery seed, cinnamon, coltsfoot, dandelion, flax, gravel root, jasmine, mugwort, peppermint, spearmint

Self-Confidence: bergamot, cinquefoil, echinacea, ginger, orris root, tobacco, yarrow

Shapeshifting: mistletoe, yucca

Spirit Work (Connection to Spirits): acacia, althaea, anise, balm of Gilead, cascara sagrada, celery seed, copal, dandelion, frankincense, grains of paradise, holly, sweetgrass, thistle, tobacco, wormwood

Spiritual Cleansing: agrimony, alkanet, angelica root, anise, asafoetida, bay leaf, benzoin, blue cohosh, calamus root, camphor, chamomile, cinnamon, cinquefoil, dill, dragon's blood, feverfew, galangal, hyssop, lemon balm, lemon verbena, lemongrass, nettle, patchouli, peony, peppermint, pine, poke, rosemary, rue, salt, slippery elm, Solomon's seal, spearmint, sulfur, valerian, verbena, white oak, white sage

Success: cinnamon, clover, echinacea, ginger, lemon balm, masterwort, orris root, sunflower, woodruff

Wisdom: bay leaf, Solomon's seal, sunflower, white sage

Wishes: bay leaf, buckthorn, dandelion, elderflower, fava bean, ginseng, grains of paradise, Job's tears, sage, sandalwood, sunflower, tonka bean

APPENDIX C

Crystals for Animals

Any crystal can provide healing and support to your animal familiar, just as they do for us humans. However, there are some crystals that are particularly aligned with animals and can be used in your practice to heal your animal and support the familiar relationship.

Animal Communication: agate, Dalmatian stone

Animal Training: agate

Familiar Commitment: Boji stone, Herkimer diamond

Happiness: amber, carnelian, gold, hematite

Healing: aventurine, malachite, rose quartz, ruby

Mental Acuity: fluorite, ruby

Peace: amethyst, ametrine, aventurine, blue calcite, blue lace agate, chrysoprase, citrine, hematite, jade, rhodolite, rose quartz, smokey quartz, sodalite

Protection: black obsidian, black onyx, black tourmaline

Psychic Ability: Boji stone, clear quartz, Herkimer diamond

Self-Confidence: emerald, jasper, ruby

Strength: bloodstone, peridot

APPENDIX D

Color Correspondences for Spells

You can add support for spellwork by adding color to your spells. Work with colorful candles in your spells or add color magic to items your familiar uses such as collars, leashes, bandanas, water or food dishes, toys, or other items.

Black: banishing, transformation, uncrossing, endings, domination, protection, reversing, security, emotional safety, closure, breaking patterns, grief, mourning, the unconscious, mystery, shielding from the evil eye

Blue: reconciliation, harmony, peace, kindness, healing, ideas, intelligence, wisdom, meditation, communication, creativity, dreamwork, trust, blessings, forgiveness, truth, bliss, inspiration, honesty

Brown: justice, balance, fidelity, practical matters, seriousness, reliability, support, stability, safety, earth, nature, animals, home, needs being met, balance

Gray: neutrality, invisibility, working in "gray areas," anonymity, working in between worlds, secrets, the occult, arcane wisdom

Green: prosperity, abundance, wealth, generosity, money luck, career, growth, fertility, business, healing, self-love, altruism, universal love, contact with fae and nature spirits

Lavender: healing, calming, tranquility, spirituality, meditation, pacification, cooperation, sensitivity, compassion, empathy, selflessness

Orange: new opportunities, new ventures, beginnings, change, encouragement, opening the way, removing blocks, warmth, security, ambition, creativity, courage, optimism

Pink: romantic love, friendship, emotional healing, heart connection, affection, family love, admiration, youthfulness, healing grief, compassion, forgiveness, beauty, unconditional love

Purple: empowerment, mastery, ambition, achievement, charisma, psychic ability, spirituality, authenticity, spiritual truth, transformation, insight, wisdom, divination, ESP, intuition, wishes

Red: passionate love, energy, action, attraction, sexuality, magnetism, will, force, anger, fire within, courage, warmth, lust, drive, pleasure, vitality, vigor, excitement, desire

White: cleansing, clarity, blessing, healing, innocence, connection to spirits or the spiritual world, divine connection, consecration, purity, prayer, peace, purification, universal truths. White can also be used as an all-purpose color for your intention when the color you want is not available.

Yellow: optimism, prosperity, happiness, good luck, success, confidence, fame, self-esteem, communication, concentration, focus, inspiration, intellect, logic, memory, knowledge, learning

APPENDIX E

Color Messages from Animal Familiars

Colorful animals, such as birds, reptiles, and insects, can communicate with us through their hues. Look to the color of their scales, fur, carapace, or feathers to see the special message they have for you.

Beige/Tan: Beige and tan speak of grace and humility. Remember that we are all just trying to find our way and that there are others who can help you navigate whatever you are going through.

Black: Black indicates that it is a time of stepping into the unknown. You have an opportunity for discovery and will be protected as you explore.

Blue: Blue signifies a joyful release of some kind, getting rid of stuck energy and feeling a sense of freedom from what has been weighing you down. If you are feeling overwrought or are in conflict, a blue animal is letting you know that peace and reconciliation are around the corner.

Brown: Brown reminds us to connect to nature and the earth to find inner stability. Get back to basics and take some time to re-wild by immersing yourself in the natural world around you.

Gray: Gray symbolizes the ability to adapt to any situation. You may observe without being noticed and perhaps develop your ability to shapeshift.

Green: Green symbolizes a period of expressive growth, expansion, and fruitfulness. This could be personal growth but also could be a message of expansive career movement or an increase in abundance. It can also be a message to work with the plant kingdom or go on a visualization journey to the lush Lower World.

Iridescent: Iridescence is an invitation to step into magical realms. There is an opportunity to commune with fae folk and other nature spirits and learn from them.

Orange: Orange indicates a robust burst of creativity and problem-solving. Ideas can come faster than you can implement them, so be sure to jot them down for future reference. Keep your eye open for unexpected opportunities coming your way.

Pink: Pink feathers signify frivolity and fun and remind you that spontaneity can open the doors to love and friendship.

Purple: Purple is the color of self-empowerment and nobility. Remember your worthiness and that you have everything that you need to succeed. If you have been feeling unappreciated or disempowered in some way, you have more control over your situation than you may realize.

Red: Red represents life force and passion. New energy, vigor, and motivation is headed your way. If you have been having trouble getting started with a project, your familiar will lend you its power to get going or get moving again.

White: White feathers symbolize new beginnings, do-overs and fresh starts. There is an opportunity to wipe the slate clean and create from scratch. If you have a dream that feels distant or have had a series of events that are causing you to consider giving up hope, your familiar is telling you that brighter days are coming.

Yellow: Yellow symbolizes optimism, confidence, and success. It's time to go for big goals and fulfill even bigger dreams. Chase after your joy and catch happiness in both hands with gentleness and appreciation.

APPENDIX F

Magical Rodent Woods

This list contains woods that are generally safe for rodents. As with all ingestible materials, do your research to ensure that the wood that you choose is safe for your familiar's species.

Apple (*Malus domestica*): love, healing, immortality

Arbutus/Madrone (*Arbutus menziesii*): protection, spiritual cleansing

Ash (*Fraxinus americana, F. excelsior*): romance, protection, prosperity, health, clairvoyance, blessings

Bamboo Cane (*Bambusa vulgaris*): luck, wishes, removing negativity, protection

Beech (*Fagus sylvatica*): wishing, wisdom, divination

Birch (*Betula*): youth, beauty, healing, vigor, optimism, rebirth, fertility, happiness, well-being, protection, purification (White, grey, broadleaf, silver, and common birch are safe. All others are unsafe.)

Blackberry (*Rubus fruticosus*, R. *villosus*): healing, money, return evil to enemies, protection

Blackcurrant (*Ribes nigrum*): protection from evil, driving out fear, protection of the soul, protection when traveling, healing

Blackthorn/Sloe (*Prunus spinosa*): protection against evil, purification, boundaries, banishing negativity

Butterfly Bush (*Buddleia davidii*): faerie realms, courage, resilience, adaptability, freedom, rebuilding (Use the older woody growth rather than newer green growth.)

Cholla Wood (*Cylindropuntia fulgida*): protection, endurance, survival

Coconut Shell (*Cocos nucifera*): purification, protection (While not wand-shaped, a half shell can be a magical chalice for rodents to nibble on.)

Coffee Wood (*Coffea arabica*, C. *canephora*): energy boost, motivation, speed, focus, clear blockages

Cottonwood (*Populus deltoide*, P. *fremontii*): calmness, encouragement, healing, prosperity, hope, transformation

Crabapple (*Malus sylvestris*): ancestors, immortality, health, prosperity, love, rebirth

Dogwood (*Cornus florida*): wishes, protection, loyalty, keeping secrets, fertility

Grapevine (*Vitis vinifera*): fertility, money, mental acuity, binding

Hawthorn (*Crataegus monogyna*): fertility, happiness, protection

Hazelnut (*Corylus avellana*): luck, protection, wishes

Hemp (*Cannabis sativa*, C. *indica*, C. *ruderalis*): meditation, visions, healing, love, divine realms

Hornbeam (*Carpinus betulus*): strength, protection from negativity, moving between worlds, confidence

Kiwi Vine (*Actinidia deliciosa*): family love, health, ancestors, rejuvenation, transformation, fresh starts

Linden/Basswood (*Tilia sp.*): immortality, luck, protection, love (In the U.K., these are commonly called lime trees, but they are not to be confused with the citrus lime—all citrus woods are harmful to rodents.)

Manzanita (*Arctostaphylos manzanita*): self-love, acceptance, magnetism, attraction

Mulberry (*Morus sp.*): strength, protection, willpower

Pear (*Pyrus communis*): lust, love, divination, healing

Pecan (*Carya illinoinensis*): prosperity, career, abundance

Poplar (*Populus sp.*): prosperity, money, traveling to other realms, protection, strength

Quince (*Cydonia oblonga*): happiness, protection, love, marriage

Raspberry (*Rubus idaeus*): love, protection, pregnancy, childbirth, luck, fidelity, marriage

Rowan/Whitebeam/Mountain Ash (*Sorbus sp.*): power, success, protection, psychic ability, healing

Sycamore (*Platanus occidentalis*, P. *racemosa*, P. *mexicana*, P. *wrightii*, P. *orientalis*, P. *acerifolia*): immortality, strength, protection, perseverance, vitality, longevity

White Pine (*Pinus strobus*): prosperity, healing, protection, fertility, longevity, purification (Only kiln-dried white pine is safe for rodents. If the white pine has no scent, it can be considered safe.)

Willow (*Salix caprea*, S. *babylonica*, S. *discolor*): healing, love, protection

Yucca (*Yucca sp.*): protection, purification, control, transmutation

RECOMMENDED READING

Melissa Alvarez, *Llewellyn's Little Book of Spirit Animals*, 2018: Handy guide to animal messages

Erika Buenaflor, M.A., J.D., *Animal Medicine*, Bear & Company, 2015: Animal messages and shapeshifting from a Curanderismo perspective

D.J. Conway, *The Mysterious, Magickal Cat*, Llewellyn Worldwide, 1998: Cat lore and spiritual traditions

Liz Dean, *Nature's Hidden Charms*, Wellbeck Balance, 2021: Spells with natural items, including shells, feathers, and eggshells

Steven D. Farmer, *Animal Spirit Guides*, Hay House, 2006: Handy guide to animal message meanings

Miranda Green, *Animals in Celtic Life and Myth*, Routledge, 1992: Scholarly book on ancient Celtic animal spirituality

Raven Grimassi, *The Witch's Familiar*, Llewellyn Worldwide, 2003: Ceremonial magic exercises and methods for working with familiar spirits

Kit & George Harrison, *America's Favorite Backyard Wildlife*, Simon & Schuster, 1985: Guide to the behavior and amazing facts about wild animals you may encounter

Pea Horsley, *Animal Communication Made Easy*, Hay House, 2018: Introduction to psychic animal communication

M. Oldfield Howey, *The Cat in Magic*, Bracken Books, 1993: History of cats and magic from ancient Egypt to the twentieth century

Victoria Hunt, *Animal Omens*, Llewellyn Worldwide, 2008: Guide to animal messages along with personal stories

Buffie Johnson, *Lady of the Beasts*, Inner Traditions, 1994: Ancient connections between animals and goddesses

Sandra Kynes, *Bird Magic*, Llewellyn, 2021: Traditional and modern magic with a wide variety of birds

John Matthews, *Celtic Totem Animals*, Eddison Books Ltd., 2002: Celtic animal legends, includes a deck for divination

Regula Meyer, *Animal Messengers*, Bear & Company, 2015: Guide to animal messages

Peter Tate, *Flights of Fancy*, Random House, 2007: Bird legends and superstitions

Patricia Telesco, *Cat Magic*, Destiny Books, 1997: Cat mythology and spiritual history

Patricia Telesco and Rowan Hall, *Animal Spirit*, New Page Books, 2002: A sampling of various animal magic techniques from many cultures

INDEX OF SPELLS

ENDNOTES

Chapter 1

1. Maral Deyrmenjian, "Pope Innocent VIII (1484–1492) and the *Summis Desiderantes Affectibus*," *Malleus Maleficarum*, 1 (2020). https://pdxscholar.library.pdx.edu/mmft_malleus/1.
2. Helen Parish, "'Paltrie Vermin, Cats, Mise, Toads, and Weasils': Witches, Familiars, and Human-Animal Interactions in the English Witch Trials," *Religions* 10, no. 2 (2019):134. https://www.mdpi.com/2077-1444/10/2/134.
3. Kathleen Walker-Meikle, *Medieval Pets* (Suffolk, UK: Boydell Press, 2021).

Chapter 4

1. Emily Doolittle, "Crickets in the Concert Hall: A History of Animals in Western Music," *Trans* 12 (2008). https://www.sibetrans.com/trans/article/94/crickets-in-the-concert-hall-a-history-of-animals-in-western-music.

Chapter 6

1. "Bats 101," *Bat Conservation International*. https://www.batcon.org/about-bats/bats-101.
2. Andreas Tjernshaugen. *Finding the Fox: Encounters with an Enigmatic Animal* (Vancouver, CA: Greystone Books, 2024).
3. Elisa Bandini, Margherita Bandini, and Claudio Tennie, "A Short Report on the Extent of Stone Handling Behavior across Otter Species," *Animal Behavior Cognition* 8, no. 1 (August 2021): 15–22. https:/animalbehaviorandcognition.org/article.php?id=1249.
4. Fred H. Harrington, L. David Mech, and Steven H. Fritts, "Pack Size and Wolf Pup Survival: Their Relationship Under Various Ecological Conditions," *Behavioral Ecology and Sociobiology* 13, no. 1 (1983): 19–26. https://www.jstor.org/stable/4599604.
5. Jane P. Davidson and Bob Canino, "Wolves, Witches, and Werewolves: Lycanthropy and Witchcraft from 1423 to 1700," *Journal of the Fantastic in the Arts* 2, no. 4 (8) (1990): 47–73. https://www.jstor.org/stable/43308065.

Chapter 7

1. Brianna Artz and Doris Bitler Davis, "Green Care: A Review of the Benefits and Potential of Animal-Assisted Care Farming Globally and in Rural America," *Animals* 7, no. 4 (2017): 31. https://www.mdpi.com/2076-2615/7/4/31.
2. Christian Nawroth, Jemma M. Brett, and Alan G. McElligott, "Goats Display Audience-Dependent Human-Directed Gazing Behaviour in a Problem-Solving Task," *Biology Letters* 12, no. 7 (July 2016). https://royalsocietypublishing.org/doi/full/10.1098/rsbl.2016.0283.
3. Page Smith and Charles Daniel, *The Chicken Book* (Athens, GA: University of Georgia Press, 1975).
4. Vorozhinnja na svjatki na pivni, https://jak.koshachek.com/articles/vorozhinnja-na-svjatki-na-pivni.html.
5. "Rozpovily pro naydyvnishi metody vorozhinnia na Andriia," Bug.org.ua, 2024, https://bug.org.ua/news/rozpovily-pro-naydyvnishi-metody-vorozhinnia-na-andriia-497017.
6. Helen Macdonald, "How to Imprint Ducklings," *New York Times*, June 22, 2022, https://www.nytimes.com/2022/06/22/magazine/how-to-imprint-ducklings.html.

Chapter 8

1. Nikolai D. Ovodov, Susan J. Crockford, and Yaroslav V. Kuzmin, "A 33,000-year-old Incipient Dog from the Altai Mountains of Siberia: Evidence of the Earliest Domestication Disrupted by the Last Glacial Maximum," *PLOS ONE* 6, no. 7 (July 2011). https://journals.plos.org/plosone/article?id=10.1371/journal.pone.0022821.
2. McNicholas et al., "Pet Ownership and Human Health: A Brief Review of Evidence and Issues," *BMJ* 331, no. 7527 (November 2005): 1252–1254. https://www.ncbi.nlm.nih.gov/pmc/articles/PMC1289326.
3. "7 Things You Can Do with Your Dog's Fur," *American Kennel Club*, https://www.akc.org/expert-advice/lifestyle/things-you-can-do-with-dog-fur.
4. "Mindful Dog Walking: Create Calmer Walks for You & Your Dog," *Psychologies*, May 5, 2022, https://www.psychologies.co.uk/mindful-dog-walking.
5. Stephanie Weaver, "How to Have a More Mindful Walk for You and Your Dog," *This Dog's Life*, March 11, 2022, https://www.thisdogslife.co/how-to-have-a-more-mindful-walk-for-both-you-and-your-dog.
6. "Mindful Dog Walking: Create Calmer Walks for You & Your Dog," *Psychologies*.

Chapter 9

1. Jessica Gall Myrick, "Emotion Regulation, Procrastination, and Watching Cat Videos Online: Who Watches Internet Cats, Why, and to What Effect?" *Computers in Human Behavior* 52, (June 2015): 168–176. https://www.sciencedirect.com/science/article/abs/pii/S0747563215004343.

2. "Cats Are the Unsung Heroes of Mental Health," *The Establishment*, https://theestablishment.co/cats-are-the-unsung-heroes-of-mental-health-2a78398f9f3/index.html.

3. Leslie A. Lyons, "Why Do Cats Purr?," *Scientific American*, April 3, 2006, https://www.scientificamerican.com/article/why-do-cats-purr.

4. Qureshi et al., "Cat Ownership and the Risk of Fatal Cardiovascular Diseases. Results from the Second National Health and Nutrition Examination Study Mortality Follow-Up Study." *J Vasc Interv Neurol* 2, no. 1 (January 2009):132–5. PMID: 22518240; PMCID: PMC3317329. https://www.ncbi.nlm.nih.gov/pmc/articles/PMC3317329.

5. Jeff Grognet, "Catnip: Its Uses and Effects, Past and Present," *Canadian Veterinarian Journal* 31 (June 1990): 455–456. https://www.ncbi.nlm.nih.gov/pmc/articles/PMC1480656/pdf/canvetj00079-0049.pdf.

6. D. J. Conway, *The Mysterious Magickal Cat* (St. Paul, MN: Llewellyn, 1998).

Chapter 10

1. "How Horses Help Humans Heal—and Thrive," *Zoetis*, https://www.washingtonpost.com/creativegroup/zoetis/how-horses-help-humans-heal-and-thrive.

2. Amber Barnes, "Glossary of Horse Vocalizations and Sounds," *Open Sanctuary*, February 22, 2023, https://opensanctuary.org/glossary-of-horse-vocalizations-and-sounds.

3. Mejdell et al., "Horses Can Learn to Use Symbols to Communicate Their Preferences," *Applied Animal Behaviour Science* 184 (July 2016). https://www.researchgate.net/publication/305729336_Horses_can_learn_to_use_symbols_to_communicate_their_preferences.

4. Jiří Dynda, "Slovanská hippomancie. Koňský divinační rituál jako," DOI:10.3986/SMS.V19I0.6616, https://www.semanticscholar.org/paper/Slovansk%C3%A1-hippomancie.-Ko%C5%88sk%C3%BD-divina%C4%8Dn%C3%AD-ritu%C3%A1l-jako-Dynda/570ccc2c9f89b036fe571a443cf42feda99326b5.

5. Madame Pamita, *Baba Yaga's Book of Witchcraft: Slavic Magic from the Witch of the Woods* (Woodbury, MN: Llewellyn Worldwide, 2022).

6. Doreen Valiente, *Witchcraft for Tomorrow* (London, UK: Robert Hale, 1978).

7. Robert Means Lawrence, *The Magic of the Horse-Shoe* (Cambridge, MA: Houghton, Mifflin & Co., 1898).

Chapter 11

1. Sir Thomas Browne, *Pseudodoxia Epidemica: Or, Enquiries Into Commonly Presumed Truths* (London, UK: Benediction Books, 2009). 1672.

2. "Chinese Stories/Jade Rabbit," *WikiBooks*, last modified January 15, 2023, https://en.wikibooks.org/wiki/Chinese_Stories/Jade_Rabbit.

3. Alastair Kneale, "The Importance of the Hare in Celtic Belief and Our Duty to Protect All Wildlife," *Transceltic*, September 24, 2017, https://www.transceltic.com/pan-celtic/importance-of-hare-celtic-belief-and-our-duty-protect-all-wildlife.

4. "Notes and Queries," March 13, 1909, 11, no. 272, 208, https://archive.org/details/sim_notes-and-queries_1909-03-13_11_272/page/208/mode/2up.

5. "Why Do We Say 'Rabbit Rabbit' Each New Month?" *Dictionary.com*, https://www.dictionary.com/e/rabbit-rabbit-and-hare-hare.

Chapter 12

1. James Owen, "Bone Flute Is Oldest Instrument, Study Says," *National Geographic*, June 24, 2009, https://www.nationalgeographic.com/culture/article/bone-flute-is-oldest-instrument--study-says.

2. Ben H. Gagnon, *Church of Birds: An Eco-History of Myth and Religion* (Richmond, IN: Moon Books, 2023).

3. "The Feather Atlas: Flight Feathers of North American Birds," U.S. Fish and Wildlife Service, last modified April 17, 2023, *https*://www.fws.gov/lab/featheratlas/idtool.php.

4. Yasuhiko Sakuma, "Terms of Ornithomancy in Hittite," *Tokyo University Linguistic Papers* (TULIP), 33 (2013) 21–238.

5. Joakim Goldhahn, "Bird Divinations in the Ancient World," *Birds in the Bronze Age: A North European Perspective* (Cambridge, UK: Cambridge University Press, 2019), 53–70.

6. Michael Aislabie Denham, *A Collection of Proverbs and Popular Sayings Relating to the Seasons, the Weather, and Agricultural Pursuits; Gathered Chiefly from Oral Tradition* (London, UK: The Percy Society, 1846), adapted by Madame Pamita.

Chapter 13

1. "The Meanings Behind These (In) Famous Potion Ingredients," *Dictionary.com*, https://www.dictionary.com/e/witch-ingredients.

Chapter 14

1. Arthur Darby Nock, *Essays on Religion and the Ancient World, Volume 1* (Cambridge, MA: Harvard University Press, 1972.) https://archive.org/details/essaysonreligion0001nock/page/274/mode/2up.
2. Dr. Mark Hutchinson, "How Do Lizards Drop Their Tails?" *Australian Geographic*, May 11, 2017, https://www.australiangeographic.com.au/topics/science-environment/2017/05/how-do-lizards-drop-their-tails.
3. Judika Illes, *The Element Encyclopedia of 5000 Spells: The Ultimate Reference Book for the Magical Arts* (San Francisco, CA: HarperOne, 2009).

Chapter 15

1. Carrie Arnold, "The Surprisingly Sophisticated Mind of an Insect," *Noema*, May 5, 2022, https://www.noemamag.com/the-surprisingly-sophisticated-mind-of-an-insect.
2. Linda Alchin, *The Secret History of Nursery Rhymes* (Nielsen, 2013).
3. Ian Ropke, *Historical Dictionary of Osaka and Kyoto* (Lanham, MD: Scarecrow Press, 1999).
4. Alan R. Priest, "Chinese Cricket-Cages," *The Metropolitan Museum of Art Bulletin* 24, No. 1 (January 1929): 6–9. https://doi.org/10.2307/3255789 https://www.jstor.org/stable/3255789.
5. Colleen English, "Telling the Bees," *JSTOR Daily*, September 5, 2018, https://daily.jstor.org/telling-the-bees.
6. Saman Javed, "Royal Beekeeper Informs Buckingham Palace Bees That the Queen has Died," *Independent*, September 10, 2022, https://www.independent.co.uk/life-style/royal-family/royal-beekeeper-bees-queen-death-b2164345.html.
7. Itay Hod, "How Bee Therapy Can Help Reduce Stress, Depression," *Spectrum News*, May 10, 2022, https://ny1.com/nyc/all-boroughs/news/2022/05/10/how-bees-can-help-reduce-stress--depression.
8. Dr. Amandine Marshall, "Magical Honey: Some Unusual Uses in Ancient Egypt," *The Past*, August 8, 2023, https://the-past.com/feature/magical-honey-some-unusual-uses-in-ancient-egypt.

Chapter 16

1. Tomas Saraceno, "The Fascinating Cameroonian Art of Spider Divination is on Display at London Exhibition," *The Conversation*, July 4, 2023, https://theconversation.com/the-fascinating-cameroonian-art-of-spider-divination-is-on-display-at-london-exhibition-208987.
2. NgGam Du, https://nggamdu.org/nggam-du.
3. "Spider Divination," *Anthropological Studies of Divination: Spider Divination,* https://www.era.anthropology.ac.uk/Divination/Spider/index.html.
4. Doc Louallen, "The Myth of the Money Spider and the Power of Belief Credited for UK Woman's Lottery Win," *USA Today*, September 11, 2023, https://www.usatoday.com/story/money/2023/09/11/money-spiders-uk-superstition-national-lottery-win/70828130007.

ACKNOWLEDGMENTS

Writing a book might look like the creation of a solitary witch, but the reality is that there is a whole coven of supportive magic makers who add their talents and love to bring a book into the world. I am incredibly grateful to my book coven, who each added their special ingredients to the cauldron to make this book a reality.

Thank you to everyone at Hay House: Allison Janice for bringing me into the fold and Nicolette Salamanca Young for taking the reins so capably and kindly. I am so thankful for the capable leadership of Reid Tracy and the spirit of Louise Hay for continuing to make beauty, happiness, love, and magic in the world. My most profound admiration, wonderment, and delight to Lisa Vega, Tricia Breidenthal, and Lea Androić for creating such beauty in the design and illustration of this book.

Deep gratitude to Chris-Anne for opening the door with such generosity. Warm hugs to my resident familiar experts, Gwendolyn Pogrowsky and Marcella Kroll, who took the time to share their familiar experiences with me.

Loving appreciation to everyone at focused.space for creating a productive and supportive environment for my writing, especially Anna Fagergren and the Sunset Vampires.

A toe-bean high five to the Parlour of Wonders cat crew, Buchanan, Kelly, Bridget, and Chris, for making magic for the world while I was in my writer's cave.

Big love to my family, Manfred, Morgan, and Izzy, for always supporting my author adventures. And furry purry cuddles to my cats, Glinda and Ozma, who teach me about animal magic every day.

ABOUT THE ILLUSTRATOR

Lea Androić is a Croatia-based artist and illustrator. Using pastel colors and whimsical details, she takes inspiration from womanhood, nature, the universe, and the animal world. She loves to create art that heals.

Lea has worked on a variety of different projects, including illustrating children's books, book covers, oracle cards, and tarot decks. She is the author of *Animal Spirit Oracle* and *Feminine Wisdom Oracle*. Instagram: **@leaandroicart**

ABOUT THE AUTHOR

Madame Pamita is a Ukrainian-American witch, author, teacher, and healer with a profound connection to the natural world. With a life steeped in the practice of magic, she combines her deep reverence for animals, plants, and the energies of nature to empower and assist others on their spiritual journeys. Her love for animals is a fundamental aspect of her life and work and is reflected in her approach to magic, which emphasizes harmony, respect, and balance with the natural world.

Madame Pamita has penned several influential books that explore the realms of magic and spirituality. Her works include *Magical Tarot*, which offers new insights into the tarot as a tool for self-discovery; *The Book of Candle Magic*, a comprehensive guide to using candles as a powerful tool in spell work; and *Baba Yaga's Book of Witchcraft*, a celebration of Ukrainian folk magic practices and the legendary Slavic witch. Each of these books reflects her decades of experience and dedication to the craft, making complex magical practices accessible to both beginners and seasoned practitioners.

In addition to her writing, Madame Pamita is a sought-after teacher and speaker. She conducts workshops that delve into various aspects of folk magic, from candle magic to tarot reading, providing practical learning experiences for aspiring magic makers. Her teaching style is both engaging and empowering, encouraging participants to explore their own magical potential. She also shares her expertise through a range of social media platforms. Her popular YouTube channel serves as a vibrant resource for those interested in magic and spirituality where she offers practical advice, spells, and spiritual wisdom to a global audience.

Madame Pamita also runs an online spiritual apothecary, the Parlour of Wonders (**www.parlourofwonders.com**), where she and her small but dedicated team create witch-crafted beeswax candles, spiritual oils, and other magical essentials. Each product is crafted with intention and care, reflecting her commitment to supporting the spiritual needs of her customers. Whether through her books, workshops, YouTube channel, or the enchanting products from the Parlour of Wonders, she remains a leading figure in the world of modern witchcraft, dedicated to sharing her knowledge and fostering a deeper connection to the magic that surrounds us all.

Hay House Titles of Related Interest

YOU CAN HEAL YOUR LIFE, the movie,
starring Louise Hay & Friends
(available as an online streaming video)
www.hayhouse.com/louise-movie

THE SHIFT, the movie,
starring Dr. Wayne W. Dyer
(available as an online streaming video)
www.hayhouse.com/the-shift-movie

***

Animal Communication Made Easy: Strengthen Your Bond and Deepen Your Connection with Animals, by Pea Horsley

The Archangel Guide to the Animal World, by Diana Cooper

Intuitive Animal Communication: Co-Create a Meaningful Life and Deep Connection with Animals, by Michael Burke

Pocket Guide to Spirit Animals: Understanding Messages from Your Animal Spirit Guides, by Dr. Steven Farmer

The Ultimate Pet Health Guide: Breakthrough Nutrition and Integrative Care for Dogs and Cats, by Gary Richter, M.S., D.V.M.

All of the above are available at your local bookstore, or may be ordered by visiting:

Hay House USA: www.hayhouse.com®
Hay House Australia: www.hayhouse.com.au
Hay House UK: www.hayhouse.co.uk
Hay House India: www.hayhouse.co.in

We hope you enjoyed this Hay House book. If you'd like to receive our online catalog featuring additional information on Hay House books and products, or if you'd like to find out more about the Hay Foundation, please contact:

Hay House LLC, P.O. Box 5100, Carlsbad, CA 92018-5100
(760) 431-7695 or (800) 654-5126
www.hayhouse.com® • www.hayfoundation.org

Published in Australia by:
Hay House Australia Publishing Pty Ltd
18/36 Ralph St., Alexandria NSW 2015
Phone: +61 (02) 9669 4299
www.hayhouse.com.au

Published in the United Kingdom by:
Hay House UK Ltd
1st Floor, Crawford Corner,
91–93 Baker Street, London W1U 6QQ
Phone: +44 (0)20 3927 7290
www.hayhouse.co.uk

Published in India by:
Hay House Publishers (India) Pvt Ltd
Muskaan Complex, Plot No. 3,
B-2, Vasant Kunj, New Delhi 110 070
Phone: +91 11 41761620
www.hayhouse.co.in
